Be

By Georgia Springate

Burning Chair Limited, Trading As Burning Chair Publishing
71-75 Shelton Street, Covent Garden
London WC2H 9JQ

www.burningchairpublishing.com

By Georgia Springate
Edited by Simon Finnie and Peter Oxley
Cover by Jennie Rawlings

First published by Burning Chair Publishing, 2019

ISBN: 978-1-912946-05-1

Dedication

This book is dedicated to all those who have left this life behind; they are beyond our sight but not beyond our love.

Chapter One

Roscoe doesn't like fireworks. As soon as November 1st rolls around, Mum tries all these different things to make Bonfire Night as painless as possible, like introducing him to dog relaxation pills and music and vile incense. None of it ever works, of course, so this year she decided to go to the vets and get some knock-out meds so we could all go out and enjoy the fireworks display without worrying about him stuck at home and barking like crazy.

While everyone else from school went together in groups and had roasted marshmallows round Gee Davies' house afterwards, I had to stand with my mum and dad and 'ooh' and 'ahh' at the sky for hours on end. I really don't see the point in the stupid things anyway; they light up for about five seconds and then dissolve into darkness, as if they were never really there in the first place.

When Mum announced our Bonfire Night plans I didn't know why, after seven years of staying in with a Chinese takeaway and a barking dog, we had to change our family tradition.

But then I remembered. It's because it could be Jenna's last Bonfire Night. She's got ovarian cancer, stage 3b.

*

She told me nine weeks and three days ago at our end-of-summer BBQ.

'Alex. You know I haven't been feeling well…' She reached across the table and held out her hand. I noticed her boyfriend, Kent, out of the corner of my eye, flipping a burger and watching our conversation carefully.

'Yes,' I answered shortly, tightening my hoodie strings. I'm not good with awkward conversations. My phone vibrated in my pocket and my hand instinctively went to it.

'Alex.' Hearing Jenna saying my name like that was weird. 'The doctors figured out what's wrong with me. It's cancer.'

A message from Daisy flashed on my phone screen. I can't remember what it said now. Everything was slow, a blur.

'It's ovarian cancer,' Jenna went on, her voice catching. 'It—um—makes me tired, and makes my stomach hurt. But it's good that it's been discovered. It means I can get some treatment and... hopefully feel better soon.'

Silence, while she waited for me to say something.

'Do Mum and Dad know?' I asked.

Jenna smiled, as though this was a good question to ask. 'Yes.'

'Does Kent?'

'Yes.'

'Do your friends?'

'Yes, Alex.' She was still smiling. I hadn't seen her smile that much in ages. It was uncomfortable. Like that whole situation.

*

After that, things just haven't been the same. It's like that BBQ was the last day I felt, well, like myself. My worries now aren't about homework and girls and who's playing football at the weekend, they're about medication and appointments and statistics. It's almost like I'm not fourteen-year-old Alex Duncan anymore. Instead, I'm a robot copy: I look the same, I talk the same. But I don't feel the same. Nothing in life is the same when your sister has cancer.

'Alex! Dinner's ready!'

I close the book that I haven't been reading and head downstairs. God knows what we're eating tonight. Since the announcement, Mum's been cooping herself up in the kitchen for hours every evening preparing the weirdest, most complicated dishes she comes across. She seems to be on autopilot for housework as a whole; I've never seen the house so spotless. Sometimes I don't even want to sit down on the sofa in case I mess up the cushions.

'Ah, Alex, will you hand me a tea towel?'

I pass her the nearest one and she wafts the steam about the kitchen before producing a tray of what looks like burnt muffins. I don't know what to do. Ever since the BBQ I've felt awkward in my own skin, let alone in my own house. Yet here I am in the kitchen, watching my mum faffing around with pots and pans as if she can cook the cancer away. I think that's what she's convinced herself, anyway.

'Soufflé to start tonight!' she says cheerfully, plating things up. 'Then we've got coq au vin.' She looks at me expectantly as if I know or care what 'coq au vin' is, so I just force myself to smile at her in reply. I've learnt it's best to keep my mouth shut about these things. Most things in general, actually.

'Mmm, smells delicious, Cindy!' Dad's voice booms from the dining room with its usual forced cheer. Mum manages a smile.

'Here, love, take your dad's plate in too, will you?' She gestures to two starter plates, each containing one burnt muffin-looking thing artfully placed next to some leaves.

'Get me a beer, would you?' Dad says instead of thanking me as I slide his plate in front of him. He already smells of alcohol and tobacco.

'Beer doesn't complement the food,' Mum says with an air of annoyance as she enters the room, carrying her own plate and a bottle of sparkling water. I hate sparkling water.

'Complement the food, my ass!' Dad retorts, burping loudly.

Mum ignores him and sits in her usual seat. I slump reluctantly between them and stare down at my muffin starter. Upon closer inspection I discover it looks more like a misshapen scone.

'JENNA!' Dad bellows suddenly, making Mum jump slightly. She wrings her wrists, something she does when she's nervous. Recently I've noticed she's lost weight, especially around her face. She's always been slim but her bones seem more defined now, her cheeks almost hollow. She's never worked so she's always taken care of herself: eating healthily, going to yoga and all that. A few years ago she even got on the running hype and did a marathon, quite a big one in London. She was healthier then. She looks older now.

'Jenna's not home,' she says quietly after a moment, stabbing her fork into her starter. 'She said she'd be back for six.'

Dad theatrically checks his watch. 'Well, it's five-past.'

Mum chews slowly and swallows before deciding not to answer. Under the table, I feel Roscoe plop himself down on top of my bare feet as he always does. He weighs a bloody tonne but in situations like this his soft warm fur is reassuring and familiar. I reach down and stroke him gently.

'Don't touch the dog while we're eating,' Mum snaps, glaring at me. I freeze. Since when has that been a rule?

'What?' Dad barks, his mouth full. 'Don't give him that crap, woman. It's not like he's feeding him or anything.'

I take a bite of my food. Tastes like cheap cheese.

'I am not giving crap, George!' Mum retorts, slamming her fork down even though she's only had one bite. 'Don't speak to me like that at the dinner table.'

Dad snorts, ploughing through his food. 'My dinner table. That I paid for.'

Uh-oh. I know he's gone too far now. These stupid scraps have become worse and worse over the past few weeks, but they've never gone down this road before.

'Your dinner table?' Mum screams, scraping back her chair. It makes a horrible noise on the floor and I wince. 'Your dinner table that I cook for hours every day to lay food on? That I keep clean? That I painted?' She stands up properly now, her eyes wild. I've always thought that my mum doesn't suit being angry. Probably because I never see her mad. Even after the announcement, even after the BBQ, she's never been angry at anybody or anything. She's just been cooking. And cooking. And cooking. I sometimes sort of wish I could just coop myself up in a room all day like she does. Maybe that'd make my anger go away.

'Oh for God's sake, sit down,' Dad tells her, swallowing his last mouthful. 'Jesus. You make out like everyone wants you to slave away in that stupid kitchen for hours and come up with these weird French dinners. That's your coping mechanism, Cindy, not ours. Don't swan around on your high horse making out—'

There's a bang as the front door slams shut. Everyone freezes for a moment. Did Jenna just come in? She never has to listen to these stupid arguments like I do. When Jenna's here, everything's perfect. We're a lovely, happy family.

'Hi!' Her voice trills from the hallway. Roscoe gives a sharp bark and runs—slowly—to the door to greet her. He's a bulldog so he can't move very fast at the best of times. Mum and Dad look at each other, then me: still sat in my seat with a barely-touched dinner. Mum looks apologetic. Dad looks like he doesn't care. He never does.

'I brought Kent over for dinner, hope that's okay,' Jenna says as she enters the room, followed by a drooling Roscoe, who immediately returns to his position on my feet, and a sheepish-looking Kent. I reach down and pat Roscoe again while Mum's not looking.

'Of course, of course!' Mum beams, collecting the plates. 'Hello Kent, sweetheart, pull up a chair, there's plenty for everyone... You missed the soufflé though, I'm afraid.'

'Hi Mr and Mrs Duncan,' Kent pulls up a chair next to me. 'Squirt.' He ruffles my hair as Jenna follows Mum into the kitchen. I wish Dad would go too. His presence just seems extra-awkward now; Jenna and Kent must have heard what was going on when they came in. And although Kent's been going out with Jenna for at least a year or two, him and Dad have never really clicked. They don't hate each other, but Dad likes fishing, Kent likes cars. Dad likes beer, Kent doesn't drink. They don't really have any common ground.

'How's school?' Kent asks me.

How's school? What a complex question. I decide this is not the time or place to mention my failing grades or lack of friends, so instead go with the simple: 'Fine thanks. How's college?'

'Meh, fine.' Kent shrugs, pouring himself some water. 'Just wanna break up for Christmas already, to be honest. This is the worst part of the year, don't you think? November? Nothing-to-look-forward-to-November.'

I give an obligatory laugh but a quick glance at Dad tells me he's not amused. Luckily, in come Mum and Jenna.

'Here!' Mum sets down the chicken with a flourish while Jenna places bowls of boiled potatoes and vegetables alongside it.

'Smells amazing, Mrs D,' Kent tells her approvingly as Jenna takes her seat opposite him.

'Thank you, thank you,' Mum gushes, her and Dad acting as though five minutes ago we were just having a perfectly civil dinner without them. As she dishes up the food, I catch Jenna's eye. She looks tired, like Mum, and less put-together. She's got a couple of new spots too, but I've learnt not to comment on those. Especially since I got my first one the other day, a huge one right in the middle of my forehead, and I wanted to bury myself in bed and hide until it went away. No one warns you of these stupid things you've got to deal with once you become a teenager, like spots and feelings.

And, for some of us, sisters getting cancer.

Jenna gives me a determined smile before breaking the silence. 'So how did everyone find the fireworks yesterday?'

I glance over at Mum, who's cutting a potato extremely slowly. 'Oh, lovely!' she says. 'They were lovely. Wasn't it nice to get out this year, Al?'

Ah. So, we're not telling her that Dad and I came home early because of the angry call we received from the neighbours about Roscoe's howling. I was wondering about that. 'Yes,' I reply.

Jenna shovels some of the coq-au-whatever into her mouth. 'Great! Maybe this should become our yearly tradition, then? Venturing out?'

Everyone nods enthusiastically, telling her what a good idea it is. No one's saying what they're really thinking, though; she might not be here to 'venture out' next year. She might miss out on that particular tradition.

Chapter Two

I've started having weird dreams.

Actually, let me rephrase: I've always had weird dreams. But this week they've gotten weirder. Since Bonfire Night, they've all been fireworks-related: me flying on a firework, the Earth getting hit by a giant firework, Mum serving fireworks for dinner...

But the weirdest one was last night. It was an almost exact replay of this year's actual Bonfire Night, with me, Mum, Dad, Kent, Jenna, Daisy and Callum at the firework display. It was freezing and we'd all wrapped up warm and huddled together. Just before the last fireworks were set off, Jenna let go of Kent and gave us all a wave. Everyone waved back, like that had been the plan all along. She danced over to the bonfire and, with a huge smile on her face, jumped on it. Just jumped into the fire. As the fireworks went off, her soul flew into the sky with them. I don't know how I knew that—I couldn't physically see her ghost or anything flying—but I just knew.

I wake up crying. Not crying crying, but my eyes are watering. And my whole body just feels... weird. I lie there for a few minutes, staring at the ceiling, waiting for things to go back to normal, but they don't. My brain won't stop replaying it, like some messed-up TV show, over and over on a loop. I close my eyes and it's still there: her jumping cheerily into the fire while we all just waved at her and fireworks flashed and popped all around us.

I open my eyes and it's there again. The fire. The body. The soul. I can't bear it. I end up getting up and ready for school, despite the clock saying 6:45. I'd rather be at the gates two hours early than have to watch that ever again.

*

'Honey, are you all right?' Mum puts down her paper and breaks into my thoughts. I've been pushing my lumpy porridge round the bowl for a while now. Mum's insisted on making porridge on the hob since the announcement, even though it tastes better as a packet of oats with a splash of milk in the microwave.

'I'm fine, Mum.' I answer, shovelling a spoonful of the horrible stuff in my mouth to shut her up. Breakfasts are weird now Jenna doesn't always join us. Everything's weird. And at times like this, when the room feels so different without her, it seems so unfair. Why my family, why my sister? There's no answer. There'll never be an answer. And that just makes the whole thing even worse.

'Are you sure?' she presses, closing her paper completely. I suppress a sigh, half-feeling sorry for her. She doesn't know how to handle this any more than me, I suppose. But she's an adult. She should be more put-together. I think about saying this aloud but then a buzz from my phone tells me Daisy is outside. I'm saved.

'Daisy's here, Mum. See you later.' I leave my breakfast things on the table: she likes tidying up anyway.

'Oh. Okay.' Her voice sounds small, like she's far away. I watch her through the doorway as I pull on my shoes; she scoops the porridge into Roscoe's bowl and tosses the cutlery into the sink before folding up her paper and placing it neatly on the side. And then she just stands there, looking at the table, her eyes glazed over. Like she's not really in the kitchen, she's somewhere else.

'Finally!' Daisy rolls her eyes as I open the front door. She's got her hair in plaits today. It looks nice.

'Sorry, sorry,' I say, pulling on my coat and shutting the door. She holds out her hand for my hat as she does every morning, a faded black beanie that I've had for years. I don't mind her wearing it, but I always think she looks kind of funny wearing a hat but no coat. She says she doesn't feel the cold.

'Did you get the Science assignment done last night?' she asks, chewing her pink bubble gum loudly.

'Nah. Had other stuff to do.' I avert my eyes. Daisy's good at knowing when I'm lying. But no way am I telling her I fell asleep at eight and had some messed-up firework death dream.

'Liar.' She blows a huge pink bubble. I pop it with my finger. 'What other stuff?' she asks.

I ignore her question, waving at Yusuf and Luca across the road instead.

'Because I know,' Daisy continues, 'you weren't at Callum's. Or the park. Or the arcade.'

'What, are you stalking me?' I feel a stab of annoyance that she's already asked Callum about this. Or maybe she was at Callum's actual house, without me. Did they even ask me to go last night? I grab my phone and begin searching through my texts.

'Um, rude.' Daisy tries to knock it out of my hand.

'How was Sadie's party at the weekend, anyway?' I ask.

Daisy rabbits on about it until we get to school. Meanwhile I'm looking up at the grey sky. Do souls really go up there?

School passes by like any other day. I used to actually enjoy learning, especially Science and PE. But now nothing interests me. I don't bother with experiments, or group projects, or homework: let alone the extra credit stuff I was doing last year. I think the teachers are starting to get a bit annoyed. Maybe they believe enough weeks have passed for me to forget about Jenna's cancer and get back into schoolwork.

*

'Come on, Alex,' Mr Hobbs pleads with me after Chemistry. 'You were on track for an 'A' at the end of last year. Now this,' he holds up my mock test, 'is really disappointing. Did you revise? At all?'

No, idiot! I want to scream. Maybe if my whole life wasn't crumbling down around me then I would!

But I don't. I don't care enough about Mr Hobbs, or school in general, to fight my corner. I just nod until he shuts up.

When it gets to 3:30 pm I can't be bothered waiting for the others so I walk home with Yusuf and Luca instead. They're both super-clever and nice and don't ask me about my sister. We're discussing revision techniques for French when we run into Bruce Cleeve and his ape-like friends.

Ugh. Bruce Cleeve—also known as Duce for his lack of brain cells—one of the ugliest, stupidest and meanest guys going. He'll pick on anyone and everyone, for anything and everything, no discrimination. He even beat up Gary Nevis in Year 12 once. And Gary's apparently been to juvenile prison.

'Well, well, well.' Bruce takes a drag of his cigarette. 'Look who we have here.'

Yusuf and Luca look at each other nervously and appear to be debating whether to try and carry on walking or not.

'Go away, Duce,' I retort. Those two might be scared but I'm not. I've got bigger things to be worrying about than him.

'Oooh,' Bruce sings, taking a final drag and tossing his cigarette aside. The smell makes my eyes water. 'He speaks, does he? Haven't heard this for a while.'

I gulp, already regretting snapping at him. I'm not scared, no, but I'm not stupid. Responding to Duce never deters him, it only spurs him on. I should have known better than to even acknowledge he was there! I'm usually so good at keeping it in. Why does this have to be the one time I open my mouth? We're at the alley by the park, which is completely deserted. Bruce's friends are bigger than us. Degenerate, yes. Thick, yes. But still big.

You idiot, Al.

'Isn't he Jenna's brother?' I hear one of his Apes whisper. My breath catches.

'Yeah, yeah,' Bruce answers loudly, fiddling with his lighter. 'The one who—'

'Leave him alone, Bruce!'

I turn to face the source of the furious yell, immediately knowing who it is. Callum and Daisy are tearing up the park towards us.

'Ugh. Come on.' To my utter surprise, Bruce and his Apes leave with a scowl before Daisy and Callum even reach us.

Yusuf and Luca watch them go, their mouths gaping open. 'I was a hundred percent sure he was gonna light my hair on fire.'

Yusuf says faintly.

'He won't,' Daisy assures him, panting as she tries to catch her breath back. 'Not when I'm around.'

'Wow,' Luca says admiringly as they both gaze at her. It's not often she speaks to Yusuf and Luca, let alone save them from the school bully and his lighter.

'Good timing.' I give her a smile. I've been caught by Bruce before when Daisy wasn't around, and it wasn't a pleasant experience. We all start walking again.

'Why's he scared of you, anyway?' Luca asks. I already know what Daisy will say.

'He's got a good reason to be,' she answers firmly. 'Let's just say that.'

Callum and I look at each other. It's the answer she gives everyone, even us. Trying to find out why Bruce is scared of Daisy is like trying to draw blood from a stone.

'So,' Callum says after Yusuf and Luca wave goodbye, 'why'd you rush off after school?'

'I didn't rush off,' I retort. 'I just need to get home.'

'Why?' Daisy asks. Always so many questions with her. I just shrug, and we continue in silence for a couple of minutes.

'Something's been up all day,' Daisy says suddenly. 'I know it. What's wrong, Al? Just tell us.'

'You can tell us anything,' Callum agrees encouragingly.

I glance at them from the corner of my eye. Both striding along at the same pace as me, Daisy with her hat and plaits, Callum with his buzzcut and freckles. Two sturdy, trustworthy friends. Surely two people I can be honest with.

'I'm just having a hard time, you know. With the Jenna thing. It's all just so... She had a scan today and I just want to get home and find out how it went.' I feel my voice break slightly but carry on. 'It's difficult, you know. Everyone at home is being weird. Mum has been hoovering and cooking non-stop for months and Dad's drinking a lot again. Jenna's acting like everything's fine. It's hard to concentrate on other things when I know she's so sick. And... and I keep thinking... she'll probably die.' I sniff hard and blink away a couple of tears that I can feel brimming.

'Oh, Alex.' Daisy links her arm in mine.

'I know it's hard,' Callum says, 'and she probably won't, but…
But everyone dies. We'll all die.'

It's weird that, before this whole thing, I never really thought about death. I mean, sure, Jenna had a hamster once that had to be put down when it got old. But I was only little then. Everyone in my immediate family is fit and healthy, all the way up to my great-grandparents. Actually, my Great-Aunt June died before I was born, from a stroke I think. I've never really had to experience death. But Callum is right. Everyone dies.

'But what happens?' I wonder aloud. 'What happens when we die?'

'I think we live on,' Daisy says carefully. 'We live on in people's memories.'

Hm. It doesn't sound that bad.

'What do you think, Cal?'

'Um…' he shrugs, slowing down in pace. We're nearing his street. 'I dunno, to be honest. I'd like to think there's something…'

We all stop at the 'Sandbury Close' sign. Callum is clearly uncomfortable.

'See you later, Cal. Thanks for earlier,' I say before things can get any more awkward. He says goodbye and then me and Daisy continue on. Callum's one of my oldest—actually, the oldest— friend I have. We've been friends since we wore nappies! But I've always known this is something he's not great at: getting all deep and meaningful. When I told him about Jenna's announcement in the first place, I believe his exact words were, 'Oh. Yeah. I think about one-in-four people get that now.' He tries, though. I know he does. And some of us just don't have the right things to say in these situations. I know just how he feels.

'I've never really thought about it,' Daisy says. 'You know, dying. We're so young. It's something that doesn't really affect us. No one speaks about death at fourteen.'

I shrug. 'I suppose.'

'I mean, when my granny died,' Daisy continues, 'I was eight.

Mum and Dad told me she was sleeping forever. I think that's a nice thought: a nice, long sleep. All your memories and dreams intact.'

I shudder at the thought of my dreams lately. Now's my chance. Should I tell her? She'll think I'm weird, sure. But she must know I'm pretty weird by now anyway. Daisy moved to my school halfway through last year and we've been close ever since. Lately I've been noticing her more: the way she smells, the way little wisps of her red curls escape from her plaits. The way she doesn't feel the cold but likes wearing a hat.

'Anyway. What are your plans for tonight?'

'Nada,' I answer, snapping back to reality. 'Catch up on homework I guess. Sit in silence around the dinner table. Pretend to ignore Jenna's cancer.' Daisy laughs at this and, despite myself, I smile with her.

'I'll see you tomorrow.'

I head on, dreading getting home now. Mum will surely be in the kitchen already; probably has been since lunch time. Hopefully Dad will be at the pub, or in his man cave. I still don't understand why a forty-something-year-old deserves a bloody 'man cave' but at least it keeps him out of my way.

'Hi Mum!' I call, shutting the door behind me as I enter the hell-hole. Roscoe, as usual, doesn't arrive to greet me until I've already taken my shoes and coat off. He gives my ankle a lick and then falls to the floor for a belly-rub.

'Hi Alex.' Mum's in the hallway. Her voice is thick and she's holding a tissue.

'What's wrong?' I straighten up immediately. Roscoe nudges my foot with his head.

'Come and sit down, darling. I'll make you a cup of tea.' She shoots into the kitchen before I can ask any more questions. Half-intrigued, half-not wanting to know, I walk into the living room to find Jenna, Kent and Dad on the sofa. Great. Things must be serious if Dad's not glugging beer at 4 pm on the dot.

'What's going on?' I ask slowly, taking the chair opposite. As usual, the room looks unlived-in; Mum's cleaned it so thoroughly you wouldn't even know we had a dog. I wonder briefly where she's hidden Roscoe's toys and if he's at all happy about this new arrangement.

'You're home late,' Dad says gruffly. I ignore him and steal a glance at Jenna instead. She's staring into space, her eyes puffy. I have a sudden urge to get up and leave. I don't want to be here. I don't want any more news.

'Here you are, lovely.' Mum's come in with a cup of tea and places it down on the coffee table beside me. She swallows hard. No one says anything.

'Why does no one ever just say anything?' I think aloud, my frustration rising. Look at them, all sat there, sad and smug. Let's keep another secret from Alex. Let's all be weird and quiet and not actually let him know what's going on.

'Alex,' Kent begins as no one else speaks. 'Jenna…'

'As you well know,' Dad interrupts Kent loudly, 'your sister went for a scan today. And it seems things are… worse than we anticipated.'

My heart skips. How much worse? Mum, who had perched herself on the arm of my chair, makes a small animal-like noise and leaves the room.

'Worse?' I echo.

'Worse,' confirms Dad. I take a minute to digest. Okay, worse. Well, we already knew she has ovarian cancer, stage 3b. Does 'worse' mean moving up to 3c? Does 'worse' mean it's spread somewhere else?

'I have to have an operation. And chemo,' Jenna speaks suddenly. 'I didn't want it before. I've been putting it off. I don't want it now, still, really. It makes your hair fall out. And it can make you sick. But I have to have it now. Now is the time.'

'Now is the time?' I echo again. 'Why? Why is now the time?'

No one replies again and I feel my breath catch. Worse. Operation. Chemotherapy. The words are on a loop in my brain. I remember coming across the chemo aspect when I googled ovarian cancer. I try and remember what I'd found but I can't. My mind's drawing a blank. No one's saying anything. Are we done here? I

14

get up.

'Where are you going?' Dad asks in a voice that would normally make me sit back down.

But I don't sit down.

'Aren't we done? No one's saying anything,' I reply, matching his tone.

'Look, Alex, this is awful news,' says Kent. 'Crappy, horrible, awful news. But your sister's a fighter. And with us all by her side, she can get through anything.' He takes a deep breath, as if he's going to say more, but he doesn't. I don't think he can.

Dad's looking like he'd rather Kent shut his mouth anyway. I know what he was trying to say. I get that he wants me—everyone—to feel better about it. And he's right, we all need to be there for her. I'm going to be there for her. But…

'Being by her side won't get rid of the cancer,' I snap.

Before he can answer I leave the room and stand in the hallway, taking a moment to try and focus. I need to get out. I need to be on my own, away from these idiots. These secret-keepers, these liars. Traitors, the bloody lot of them. I clip Roscoe onto his lead and pull on my shoes, slamming the door behind me. I hope they all feel the anger in that slam. I hope they all feel bad.

It's dark, pretty much pitch black, when I get back home. I went for a long, winding walk down by the river. I forgot my coat and my hands were practically blue by the end of it.

'Where have you been?' Mum demands as soon as I slide my shoes off. Here we go.

'Just taking Roscoe out.'

'You've been gone almost an hour! And not answering your phone! You had me worried sick, Al!' She folds her arms.

Then I do something that surprises even me: I pull her in for a hug. I'm not sure why. Maybe I just need some human contact. Maybe it's my way of apologising. She hugs back, tightly.

'What's for dinner?' I change the subject, letting Mum go.

'I didn't cook tonight. We've all been… a bit preoccupied.' She chooses her words carefully. 'I thought we could order in. Jenna fancies an Indian.'

'Sounds good.' I hide the shock in my voice. Mum, not cooking? The thought of a rich balti and greasy onion bhajis make my stomach rumble.

'Great. I'll call them now.' As she gets the phone I start heading upstairs. 'Al?' she suddenly calls from the kitchen.

'Yeah?'

'I love you.'

I rub my freezing hands together and jump up the last few steps. 'Love you too.'

Chapter Three

My dream from last night has stayed with me ever since I woke up. Jenna was trying on different wigs. We were all with her in the wig shop: Mum, Dad, Roscoe, Kent and I. Though it wasn't like a nice, normal shop. It was dark and there were different mirrors everywhere, like ones you get in those Fun Houses at fairs. We were all reflected everywhere but we were bigger, smaller, longer, thinner. We didn't look like us.

'I like this one.' She decided on long, straight black hair with a fringe. It couldn't be more different to her short caramel curls. She placed the wig on her bald head and, behind her, a giant spider appeared. It was covered in fur, with a hundred eyes looking this way and that. Its eyeballs were entirely black.

'Good choice,' it said in a cracked whisper which echoed through the mirrored room. 'Here we are.' It reached behind one of the mirrors and pulled out a long, black coffin. Jenna climbed in.

'No!' I shouted. 'What are you doing?' Mum, Dad and Kent were all smiling and waving. Their reflections were too.

'Get out of there, Jenna!' I called desperately. She smiled and waved at us all and then lay down. The spider pushed the lid down and it shut with a snap.

'Al? You're quiet this morning.' Mum pats me on the head. Well, everyone's quiet this morning. Aside from being incredibly freaked out when I found a spider in the bath, Jenna's going to the hospital at eleven and we're all going with her. Mum has walked me through the day a thousand times.

'We'll get there for eleven. Have a bite to eat, a coffee maybe;

obviously Jenna's not having anything. There'll be some checks, final blood tests, et cetera. We'll stay with her until she goes in. To the…'

She always falters at that part. Basically, today is The Day. Not The Chemo Day, that would be after. The Operation Day. No one knows for sure exactly how long it'll take. But what we do know is that Jenna will be in hospital for at least three days, maybe longer. And once she comes home there's no going to college, no going to work, no going to parties. She's to stay at home and rest, rest, rest until… until she gets better?

'Is Jenna up yet?' I ask, suddenly really wanting to see her. I know we'll be together in the car and at the hospital, but that'll be with everyone else. I'd like to see her on my own.

'Go and check,' Mum suggests. I run upstairs but pause outside her room for a minute. I don't normally go in there and for a moment I'm worried. What if she doesn't want to see me? What am I even going to say to her? We've been rubbish at talking ever since the announcement. Maybe we were rubbish at talking before, too.

I dunno. I wouldn't say we've ever been particularly close siblings; she is way older than me, after all. And she can be really grumpy. And she sneaks out of the house sometimes and makes me promise not to tell Mum and Dad. And sometimes she makes me give her petrol money if she's giving me a lift.

But Jenna's also funny. She always makes me laugh. And smart: she's studying hard and she's going to University next year to do Engineering. And she's caring as well: she always gets me the best Christmas presents. As far as sisters go, I wouldn't swap her for another. She's a good person.

So why is this happening to her?

'Jenna?' I knock carefully. I hope I'm not waking her up. She won't be happy.

'Come in,' she calls.

I push open the door. She's sat on her bed, holding a mirror and plucking her eyebrows.

'Are you really plucking your eyebrows?' I ask in disbelief. 'Before you're going to hospital?'

'Sure am!' She puts the tweezers down and smiles at me. It feels like a sort of sad smile, though. 'Come sit.'

I perch on the end of the unmade bed and look around. She's changed some things since I was last in here. Some of her posters have been taken down and replaced with lots of photos. Photos of her and Kent, family photos, photos of her friends. Some of them are of places she and Kent have been on holiday. They've been to lots of places. The next one on Jenna's list is America. I wonder if they'll ever make it.

Kent went to Boston with his family last year, and Jenna begged and begged to go as well but Mum said she just couldn't afford her ticket. So a few weeks after, Kent surprised her with a trip somewhere—Germany, I think. He made me film her reaction when she opened the tickets and Mum posted the video on Facebook. Jenna literally cried with happiness. She's always happy when she's with Kent.

'You okay?' she asks me, snapping her mirror shut.

'Yeah.' I feel myself growing a little hot. What did I even come in here to say?

'I've got my bag all packed,' Jenna says, gesturing to a large suitcase on the floor. 'Pyjamas, magazines, books, iPad... Any other suggestions?'

'Roscoe?' I make a feeble attempt at a joke; although if she was to take Roscoe for real I think I'd have a meltdown.

She laughs. 'I'll miss him. But he needs you to take care of him. Not a sick, weak—'

'You're not weak,' I interrupt her. 'Not really. You're strong, Jenna. If you'd never have told me, I might not have even realised you're poorly. You act fine every day. You're really brave.'

Jenna smiles again, but her eyes are watering. Damn, now I've upset her.

'That's not to say... I mean, you've always been brave,' I rush on. 'And everything's going to be fine, isn't it?'

'Thank you, Alex.' She reaches over and squeezes my hand. She's wearing rings and it hurts a bit, but I don't mind. I wait for her to say more but she doesn't.

*

The hospital smells weird. And it's small. We're all in this little room with a huge bed waiting for Jenna to go and have her surgery. She's had to get changed into one of those nightie things. Kent said she looks like she belongs in a mental asylum. Mum didn't find that joke funny.

'Well, I'm going to get a coffee. Coming, Cindy?' Dad squeezes out of the room. Mum rolls her eyes but follows. We all know Dad is rubbish in these awkward situations. And he's probably hoping to find something stronger than a coffee.

'So how long will it take, exactly?' I ask, hoping it won't be very long. I don't like the thought of sitting in this smelly room for hours.

'Not sure,' Jenna replies. 'Depends on how much... stuff they've got to take out.'

I shudder involuntarily at the thought of some masked man taking Jenna's insides out.

'Don't worry, you don't have to stay here,' she says. 'Kent will be here when I wake up and then I'll text Mum and you guys can come and see me. If you want to, I mean. If not, I'll be here for days, so no rush.'

I consider this. She's right, she won't be alone; Kent will be here. And it means I don't have to wait in the smelly room.

'All right,' I shrug. 'If you're sure.'

'Of course.'

There's a bit of silence and I'm not sure if they want me to leave or not. I don't know where exactly Mum and Dad are, though, and the thought of wandering around on my own freaks me out.

'Right. Jenna?' A nurse has appeared in the doorway. She's holding a clipboard and she's got a pen behind her ear. 'We're going to take you down in a couple of minutes.'

'Okay. Thank you.' Kent says. I think Jenna has forgotten how to speak all of a sudden. She's staring at the wall with tears in her eyes. The nurse nods and leaves and, as she does, I feel my stomach sink all the way to the floor. This is it.

'It's all right,' Kent soothes. He's stood up and is stroking Jenna's hair. 'It's all right. It's what needs to be done.'

I know I should be trying to comfort her too, but my feet are stuck to the floor. That's my big sister; my big, brave, clever sister, crying in a hospital bed. And there's nothing I can do to help her.

'Darling, darling!' Mum and Dad are back. Mum throws her arms around Jenna and holds her tight. Dad stands in the doorway, holding his coffee.

'We'll see you very soon,' Kent assures her, planting a kiss on her forehead. 'And then you'll have your own personal maid for your every need.' He curtseys.

'You're such a brave girl!' Mum cries, tucking a strand of Jenna's hair behind her ear. 'Just a few hours and it will all be done. It will all be fine.'

The nurse is back in the doorway behind Dad, dithering awkwardly. Mum catches sight of her and takes a deep breath.

'We love you, Jenna. Okay? We love you and we'll see you very soon.'

We all shuffle awkwardly into the corridor and out of the way, watching while two nurses manoeuvre Jenna in her bed past us and through a set of double doors. She looks back and waves, a determined smile on her face.

'Love you!' calls Kent.

'Love you!' call Mum and Dad.

I wish I'd said that, too.

Chapter Four

Jenna came home yesterday. After four days in the hospital they gave her the all clear and said it was time for her to recover at home.

They were the longest four days. I felt more out of place than ever, wandering around the house without Jenna in it. It didn't even feel like my house anymore. It was just bricks and walls and awkwardness. And I thought—maybe stupidly—that that would have been the time we would all come together: Mum, Dad and me. That we'd all sit down and talk about it, finally sharing how we feel.

But that's not the way this family works. We all hide away—me in my bedroom, Mum in the kitchen, Dad in the man cave—and we keep ourselves to ourselves. Most of the time that's okay with me. But sometimes, just sometimes, I need to talk to someone, feel something.

'Do you think it will be okay for me to come over?' Daisy asks. We're walking back from school. Callum's staying late for detention so it's just the two of us today. She's wearing my hat but no coat, as usual. She really should have worn one today though, because it rained earlier.

'It'll be fine,' I shrug, hoping it will be. I haven't had any friends over in a while and I know that Jenna will probably want to sleep for most of the evening. That's all she's been doing since she's been home, really: I only really ever see her at dinner.

Apparently the op went okay: that's what I overheard Mum telling Gran on the phone, anyway. No one ever tells me anything directly. To them I'm just a stupid baby who wouldn't understand.

I've asked Jenna if she's okay, of course, if she needs anything. She said she just needs time to rest, to feel better. And I obviously respect that; Daisy and I will just stay in my room and be quiet. That's what I try and tell Mum, anyway, when we get in.

'What do you mean? Does she need dinner as well?' Mum hisses angrily. We're huddled in the kitchen while Daisy waits in the hall.

'Yes. No. I dunno! Why does it matter? She can go before dinner time if that's easier,' I whisper.

'I wish you would have asked in advance, Alex. It's not like I'm caring for your sister or anything...'

'Daisy won't care if the house isn't immaculate, Mum! And she knows Jenna's ill, we'll be super-quiet.'

Mum considers this for a moment. 'Ugh. Fine. But seriously, Alex, you should've asked first.'

I force a smile at her and shut the kitchen door. Why does she have to be so difficult? Ask first. I'm asking now! All I want, for one evening, is not to be sat feeling crap all alone in my bedroom. Is that too much to ask?

'All good!' I tell Daisy brightly. 'Let's go up.'

I feel a sudden panic as she follows me upstairs. This had felt like such a good idea earlier—some actual human contact after school—but I hadn't thought this through. I haven't tidied or anything and... My drawings! I left them on my desk this morning!

'Erm...' I whirl round as we reach the landing, my mind spinning. 'Can you... Can you wait here a sec? You could just... put your ear against Jenna's door and see if she's sleeping. Can you do that? I'll just be one second...'

I dart into my room before she can answer, though she gives me a look like I'm an absolute weirdo. Which I am, I suppose. I find the drawings where I had left them sprawled out across the desk. It's a habit I've gotten into, waking up in the morning and scribbling down stuff from my dreams. They're pretty much all still to do with Jenna. The picture I did this morning gives me the creeps. It's Jenna as some sort of demonic fairy, looking down at us from the clouds and waving her wand. I don't remember exactly what happened in the dream, but I don't want to be reminded.

'Alex?'

I shove them all in the top drawer just as Daisy enters.

'Sorry. Come in.' I quickly straighten out my duvet and sit on the bed. She comes and sits next to me, the mattress sagging slightly.

'She's sleeping, I think. It's quiet in there, anyway,' Daisy tells me, crossing her legs.

'Okay, cool. Thank you.'

Daisy nods, looking out of the window. The dim sunlight bounces off her face and I can see all her freckles. They're lovely.

'Shall we watch a movie?' she asks, her eyes meeting mine.

'Sure,' I say quickly, hoping she didn't catch me staring. 'What do you wanna watch?'

We end up with Peter Pan; it turns out Daisy likes kids' films. We slump next to each other on the bed, the TV opposite. Several times I think about holding her hand but decide against it.

'I love that film,' she says dreamily as the credits roll. 'It's so magical.'

'It's good,' I agree, leaning over to switch the TV off.

'But, kind of sad too, don't you think?'

'How come?' I ask. I thought it had a nice ending, with Wendy and the boys going back to her family and Peter going back to Neverland. It all tied in quite nicely.

'Well, you know, the Lost Boys are all dead.' Daisy says matter-of-factly. My heart sinks. What does she mean, dead? They can't be.

'And Neverland is like a heaven,' she continues. 'Don't look so shocked, it's true! I read it online once. The whole film is based on a story that used to be told to dying kids in hospitals, to stop them from being scared. You know, instead of thinking about being torn away from your families and lying cold in a grave, you think Peter Pan's going to collect you and fly you away in the night.'

'That can't be true,' I argue, thinking quickly. 'What about Wendy? How come Wendy and her brothers get to visit but still go home?'

'I dunno,' Daisy shrugs. 'Maybe they were ill but got better? All

I know is, the basis of Peter Pan is death.'

Suddenly it's not such a great film anymore. I wish we hadn't watched it. I put the DVD back in its case. The picture of Peter Pan on the front reminds me of something suddenly: my drawing earlier. Without hesitation—almost like I've forgotten that Daisy's here—I leap up and get the picture out of the drawer, holding it and the DVD case side by side.

'What are you doing?' Daisy asks. I'm too absorbed to answer, staring intently at the two pictures. There are definitely similarities. Maybe in the dream Jenna was a kind of Peter Pan, looking down at us from Neverland. But why does she look so... evil?

'What's that?' Daisy is behind me, looking over my shoulder. Weirdly, I'm not embarrassed.

'It's a drawing I did, from my dream last night,' I answer. 'The film just reminded me.'

'Oh.' Daisy is quiet for a moment, gazing at it. The picture's drawn really roughly, I have to admit. And I'm not great at drawing people. It's just... in the mornings I have the urge to document the dreams. I'm not sure why.

'Sorry.' I turn to put it away but Daisy gently places a hand on my arm. It feels like all my hairs stand on end.

'It's okay. Do you dream about it a lot? Jenna... dying?'

The abruptness of the question catches me off-guard a little, but I shouldn't be surprised. Daisy is a direct person.

'Yes. I suppose.' I know I can be honest with her. It feels silly now, me ever being scared to tell her. She'll understand. She always understands.

'Does it scare you?' she whispers. She leans in slightly closer to me and I can feel her breath. It's warm and smells of crisps.

'Yes.' I feel my eyes brimming with stupid tears. 'It really scares me, so I can't imagine how much it must scare her.'

Daisy moves closer and wraps her arms around me. I feel myself stiffen, surprised. Despite my stupid tears and my never-ending thoughts of Jenna, I become selfish for a moment and push all that aside. Because here, in this moment, a beautiful girl with curly hair and freckles is in my room, hugging me. I carefully put my arms around her as well, gently at first then squeezing a little tighter. I don't want her to let go. I never want her to let go. I sniff hard and try to suck the tears back into my eyes. Daisy opens her mouth to speak but at that moment the front door slams, Roscoe barks, and I instantly know that Dad's home and it's nearly dinner time.

'I should go.' Daisy reads my mind. 'I've got to get home for tea.'

'Sure,' I say, though I want her to stay. I walk her out, my heart still beating too fast and, instead of going to the table, I go to Jenna's room. I don't know why, but I want to speak to her. Maybe I want to tell her about Daisy, maybe I want to ask how she's feeling. Maybe I feel guilty for not checking in on her myself when we got back from school. I dunno. My head's spinning. I'm about to knock on her door when I hear a voice and I hesitate.

'I know. I'm sorry.'

It's Jenna; she must be on the phone. I turn to go but she speaks again, her voice raised.

'It's bloody hard for me too!'

I freeze. Who the hell is making her raise her voice?

'Look, you can't come over today. Not tomorrow either. I'm too weak. All I do is sleep.' There's a pause. 'No, it's not selfish, Kent. I need to get better.'

I clench my fists. So it's Kent, is it? That stupid, arrogant, know-it-all. Before I know it, I've opened the door without even knocking. The anger has overwhelmed me. Who the hell does Kent think he is, upsetting my sister? And in her condition!

'Alex! Get out!' Jenna protests feebly. Ignoring her and breathing heavily, I take the phone from her hand. It feels like every part of me is shaking, I'm so angry.

'What kind,' I say slowly down the phone, 'of lowlife idiot shouts at a recovering cancer patient?'

'Alex? Put Jenna back on.' Kent barks. I grip the phone even harder and turn away from Jenna, who's trying to grab the phone back.

'Stay away from my sister,' I instruct him, hearing the tremble in my voice. There are a thousand other things I want to yell, scream and shout at him but I can't even bring myself to listen to his pathetic reply. I click the 'End' button and toss Jenna her phone back.

'Alex,' she complains meekly. 'You shouldn't have done that. We were just arguing a little. Couples argue all the time...'

'Normal couples,' I correct her, wiping my hands on my trousers. They're really clammy.

'What do you mean, normal couples?' Jenna asks, her voice icy.

'I mean regular, healthy couples!' I raise my voice a little. 'Not—'

'Not what?' Jenna challenges, struggling to sit up straighter in bed. 'Not what, Al?'

I can hear Mum coming up the stairs. I breathe deeply, trying to calm myself down. The situation has been handled. I've handled it.

'Not DYING?' Jenna screams suddenly, making me jump. 'You mean I'm no longer normal because I'm dying?' She hurls her phone at the wall. It smashes.

'Jenna!' Mum bursts in, carrying Jenna's tray of dinner. 'Darling, what's wrong?'

'Why don't you ask your stupid son?' She bursts into tears, covering her face with her hands. I swallow hard, trying to understand how everything had happened so fast. I don't understand. Kent upset Jenna and I was trying to help her. She shouldn't be upset, ill or not, but especially in her condition. Surely any brother would help his sister? Why is she so upset?

'Darling, darling, it's all right!' Mum places the tray on the side and throws her arms around Jenna.

'What's going on up there?' Dad shouts from downstairs.

I feel my eyes filling with those stupid tears again as I take in the scene in front of me, the scene that I've caused. Jenna is so mad. Her phone is completely smashed on the floor. Dad's making his way up the stairs, I can hear him. I run into my room and lock the door, feeling like my lungs might burst. Ten minutes ago, Daisy and I had our arms around each other and it felt like nothing would ever go wrong again. Now I've annoyed Kent, upset Jenna and am sure to get a bollocking from Dad. I lie face-down on the bed; wishing, wishing, wishing that I could rewind those ten minutes and start again.

Chapter Five

I'm drawing my dream now. It's dark outside and the clock says it's 5:07 am. I knew as soon as I woke up that I had to draw this one. Even now, not even ten minutes later, part of the dream is fading away; pieces are missing, like a puzzle. I can hear myself breathing heavily and I throw my pencil down when I'm done.

There's a lot of scribbling on the page. It's Jenna, as always. She's sat on the sofa with all of us, watching TV. But she's not the same as the rest of us. She's paler and wobbly and not really there. She's a ghost.

*

It's properly morning when I wake up again. I almost forget about the drawing until I start getting my books ready for school and it's there on the desk, staring at me. It's freaky. I turn it over.

'Alex!' Mum calls. Great. Time to face the music. I take a deep breath and open the bedroom door.

'Al?' Jenna says. Her door is ajar. I can see her sitting up in bed.

'Yeah?' I push the door open a bit more but stay in the doorway. I don't want to just burst in like I did yesterday.

'I'm sorry. About last night.' Jenna sounds like she's been crying again. She's really pale. 'I shouldn't have reacted like that. I know you were trying to help me, not make me upset.'

I feel relief flood through me. Mum and Dad can shout all they want, as long as Jenna forgives me.

'Thank you. I'm really sorry.' I take a step into her room. 'I never want to upset you, Jenna. And I never want anyone else to either. So, when I heard—'

'Kent was being ridiculous,' Jenna agrees. 'I know he was. And he knows he was, now. But... his girlfriend is dying, Al. He's allowed to be ridiculous sometimes. We all are.'

I swallow the lump in my throat.

'You're not dying,' I insist. My voice squeaks a bit. Jenna smiles.

'ALEX! Come down right now!' Mum yells from downstairs.

'You'd better go,' Jenna laughs feebly. 'Love you.'

'Love you.'

Daisy seems different this morning. Shyer, maybe. Her hair looks weird as well: not as curly. We don't really talk on the way to school but it doesn't feel awkward. I feel kind of mad at her, for Peter Pan. But I also want to hug her again. I dunno. It's weird.

'Morning!' Callum calls from behind us and runs to catch up. 'You lot are a bit late.' We don't normally walk with Callum in the mornings because he is always late. So yes, we must be late if we're seeing him on the way to school.

'Oh well.' Daisy flicks her hair. 'Who wants to be early anyway?'

'I thought if you get one more black mark you have detention?' Callum asks me, grinning.

He's right. I shrug it off, though. 'I'll just say there was a thing with my sister.'

'Alex! You can't say that!' Daisy cries, half laughing, half outraged.

'Why not? There sort of was anyway. Well, there was last night.'

'Why? What happened?' Callum asks. I falter, not knowing how much to tell them.

'Just her boyfriend being an idiot. I told him to shut it.'

Callum laughs. 'Good! I never liked that Kent anyway. So, now she's single...' He raises his eyebrows.

'Shut up,' I snap. 'She's not single. Anyway, Dad got mad at me 'cos Jenna got upset. It all kicked off.'

He stops laughing. 'Is it okay now?'

'Yeah, I guess. I couldn't really sleep, though.' I check Callum's expression at this. I know Daisy was cool about the weird dream thing, but I don't know if Callum would be the same. We've been friends for longer, I suppose, but we ride our bikes and go paintballing and play football together. We don't tell each other secrets.

'How come?' Daisy asks.

I take a deep breath. 'I've been having weird dreams,' I say, more to Callum than Daisy. 'About Jenna dying. And last night I had another one. Where she died, and we all just went about our normal lives. And she was… she was a ghost. Like, she still lived in our house and watched TV with us and stuff, but she never spoke. She was just a pale, shadowy ghost.'

We've almost reached the school gates now.

'Messed-up, man,' Callum mutters. 'That must be… weird.'

'Do you think…' I trail off, unsure if I want to know the answer. 'Do you think that's what happens? And ghosts are real?'

'Nah. You hear loads of stuff about bad ghosts,' Daisy says. 'Evil spirits and stuff. You never really hear about good ghosts.'

'Hurry up!' Mr Cooper calls from the gates. 'You're seven minutes late!' He waves his clipboard.

'Shall we all go with the Jenna thing?' I ask as we hurry down towards him.

'You are awful!' Daisy laughs. I give her a wink and I think she blushes.

*

'Alex. You've really got to do some homework.'

I'm watching TV. Mum's popped her head around the door and gives me a cross look.

'No, Mum, I don't have any,' I lie absent-mindedly.

'Yes you do.' She waves my Homework Planner at me. Damn it. After a long, boring day at school and a very awkward dinner with Mum and Dad, all I want to do is relax. But one look at Mum's face tells me that's not going to happen.

Roscoe follows me into the dining room, where there are 'no distractions'. I lay out my Science textbooks, wondering where to begin. I've got a two-week long project that was due three days ago.

Mr Hobbs gave me an extension until Friday and I know that if it's not done by then, that's game-over.

'Mum!' I call. 'I need the laptop!'

Mum's old-fashioned in that she doesn't think everyone needs individual computers. We have a family laptop, Jenna has an iPad and everyone else just has their phone. It's very annoying when we're all trying to use the internet at once.

'Here you are, honey.' She brings it in to me along with a cup of tea. I'd thank her, but I think she's just done it to stay in the kitchen a bit longer. While the laptop starts up—which takes forever—I check the ink and paper in the printer and flick open my textbooks to the right pages. I feel a sudden rush of motivation and interest like I used to with Science. I'm good at this. I can do this. And it'll take my mind off everything else in the real world for a bit.

It takes me a good hour-and-a-half to put together my project. I print off articles, draw pictures and even use some old plasticine to make some organ models. Putting it all carefully in a shoe box, I feel pretty pleased with myself; the first homework I've done since the announcement that I actually feel proud of. I didn't do it for the teacher, I didn't do it for the stupid school—I did it for myself. And I think that makes a difference.

Under the table, Roscoe rolls off my feet and onto the carpet with a loud snort. He's been sleeping for ages. I climb under the table and sit with him for a minute. His little fat body is rising and falling slowly, his snores loud and grumbling. I lay down next to him, pulling him in like I used to when I was younger. Roscoe has always calmed me down, made me feel safe. The satisfaction I felt a moment ago on completing my work has faded. I'm back to sad, nervous, angry and distracted: like I've constantly felt since the announcement.

I stroke Roscoe gently, trying to form a solid thought about school, Daisy, anything. Sometimes my mind does this: it just goes blank. It's like I get trapped in a bubble, a Jenna-shaped bubble, and I can't get out. I can't think or feel anything but the dull ache of worry that's always inside me. I wonder when that will stop. I think it will when Jenna gets better.

If she gets better.

Chapter Six

We're back at the hospital and I hate it hate it hate it.

At least I don't have to go into an actual smelly room today. We're sat, Dad and I, in the waiting area with the comfy chairs and the little wooden tables and the coffee machine. Mum and Jenna were taken into one of the officey rooms by Doctor Something-Or-Other, for the meeting or whatever the hell we're here for, at least twenty minutes ago.

I wonder what they're talking about. I mean, really, what is there to say? 'Jenna has cancer. She has had an operation. She will have chemotherapy now.' Oh yes, and the important part: if she's getting better or not. I presume that's what's being said, anyway. It's been a couple of weeks since Jenna's op and I figure it's about time for some tests and results and stuff.

But that's just me using my brain: no one's actually told me anything. As bloody usual. Yesterday, Mum just asked if I want to come to the hospital with them for Jenna's appointment. I said yes. I got to miss double English.

Dad coughs and it sounds like he's about to clear his throat and finally say something, but he doesn't. We haven't really spoken since that whole thing over Jenna's phone call with Kent. We never really spoke before that anyway, so it makes no difference to me.

It feels more like we're two separate people living in the same house rather than father and son most of the time. I don't care about his day-to-day life, he doesn't care about mine. Well, I'm guessing he doesn't anyway: he never asks how school was, or if I need a lift anywhere, or if I want to go to the golf course with him. Maybe that's just not what dads do. What is a normal father-son relationship anyway? Is it when your dad takes you to football practice on Sunday mornings and cheers you on from the sidelines? Is it when you make him birthday cards and he opens them with a smile on his face and puts them on the mantlepiece? Is it when you go fishing, or go-karting, or watch films together? If so, my dad and I are far from normal. But I've got a feeling that sort of 'normal' only exists in the movies.

'Is this seat taken?'

An old man is hovering over the spare seat next to Dad.

'Go ahead.' Dad shuffles to the side slightly and the old man slowly sits down, breathing heavily. I watch him for a moment. He's barely got any hair and his glasses make his eyes look cartoon-like. His skin is all papery and wrinkly and looks uncomfortable, like he needs to shed it. He must be seventy or eighty or maybe even older.

My mind wanders. Does he have a wife? Family? You hear all about elderly people being lonely and sad, with no friends and never getting to see any family they do have. If Jenna goes, I think I'll be one of those old people.

I feel bad for this man, a skeleton of a person, alone in the hospital waiting room. What is he here for? Results, like Jenna? It wouldn't surprise me if he was ill. Even if he isn't, I can tell life is eating away at him; the days and weeks and years scraping at the layers of skin and muscle, chewing them up and spitting them out. Soon there'll be nothing left. It'll happen to everyone, I guess. The thought of it makes my skin crawl.

Jenna and Mum finally resurface. They both look like they've been crying.

'Jenna?' Dad leaps up and hugs her tightly. I feel a little twang in my chest. Dad and Jenna's father-daughter relationship seems pretty movie-like.

'It's not great news.' Mum sniffs hard and puts her arm around me. Dad and Jenna break apart and Jenna's got tears running down her face. My heart is no longer twanging, it's sinking. Right through my body and down to the floor. Not more bad news. Please, no more bad news.

'What is it?' Dad asks, breathing heavily.

Mum's face crumples. 'It's not gone. The cancer's not gone.'

My heart's back in my chest, thumping away. It's like it's going one hundred miles-an-hour. It's no better than the sinking feeling. This can't be happening.

'But the operation was meant to take it away!' I can't help but shout. 'Why is it still here?' I know I'm probably making a scene, embarrassing everyone, but I don't care. What the hell has this all been for, then? The days in the hospital, when she was all alone? The coming home and sleeping, all day and night, no one allowed to make a noise? What was the point?

'Shh, shh. It's all right.' Mum hugs me tightly. I grip her back so hard I could be hurting her but I need to hold something. I feel like I might fall over.

'What's the plan, then?' Dad demands, patting Jenna on the head as the tears continue to spill silently down her face. 'What's the next move?'

Mum lets go of me and I wish she wouldn't. I feel too weak to stand on my own. I grip the back of the chair instead. I look at the old man, still sitting on the next chair. He's reading a magazine, either deaf or pretending to be oblivious to what's going on right next to him.

'Chemotherapy, as planned.' Mum struggles to keep her voice steady. 'That will... prolong things.'

'Prolong?' I echo. 'What does that mean?'

Jenna places her hand over mine, still gripped to the chair. With her other hand, she wipes her tears and gives me a smile. The same empty smile she's worn since the announcement. It suddenly strikes me that I might not see her real smile ever again.

'It means the cancer's here to stay, Al,' she says softly. 'But the doctors have plans. Chemo and medicine and all sorts. Maybe even another operation down the line.' She ruffles my hair and that's that.

We make our way out of the hospital in silence, Mum holding Jenna's hand, Dad and I following. I concentrate on putting one foot in front of the other, on making it to the car park without collapsing. I feel as though I haven't eaten in about a week. It's like this second big announcement—possibly even worse than the first—has drained the rest of what life I had left in me. I'm back to my empty, numb feeling; it's just too much effort to even think and feel. Right now, all I can do is move my legs and get to the car. The car that will take our family home, ripped apart now more than ever before.

*

The sky has turned black. I'm not sure when that happened. I remember seeing it light blue, pink and orange, navy. But I don't remember seeing it turn black.

I must've fallen asleep. I've been in bed for hours, pretty much since getting home from the hospital. It was mutually decided without being discussed that I wasn't going back to school today. We just got home and did what we always do after these big announcements: go our separate ways. Mum went into the kitchen. Dad went to the pub. Jenna and I went to our bedrooms. And that's where I've been ever since.

My mouth feels dry and my stomach hurts; I can't remember eating since breakfast. I check the time, thinking it must be late, but it's only 9 pm. My head hurts like it always does when I have a nap in the evening, and I swing my legs out of bed. I need water. And food. My stomach grumbles as I think of peanut butter on toast. I'm not sure who's awake or asleep. Mum and Dad's lights are off, but Jenna's is on. I linger outside her door for a moment; then I hear her soft voice.

'It's just overwhelming, you know?'

I know, Jenna. It's overwhelming for me, too. I lean against the wall next to the door.

'I know sweetheart.' Kent's voice replies. He must have come over when I was asleep. 'It's a lot to take in.'

Jenna's voice mumbles something and I take a step closer to the closed door, almost pressing my ear against it. I know I shouldn't be eavesdropping, but something keeps me rooted there. Maybe it's the fear that Kent will say something to upset her again. Maybe I just need to hear her voice.

'You can't know the answer to that, Jen.' Kent replies gently. I envision him stroking her hair like he normally does when they're cuddled together on the sofa.

'I just... I hate the not knowing.' Jenna's voice breaks slightly and I know she's crying. I feel a lump rise in my own throat and quietly back away from the door and head downstairs.

She hates not knowing. Not knowing what? Why it's happening? When it's going to happen? What's going to happen after? I don't know those answers either, Jenna. Why are there no bloody answers to all of this? My head's spinning as I switch on the kitchen light and grip the counter for something to hold.

It happens before I can even try and hold it back in the slightest: the heavy, loud tears. They echo through the kitchen, maybe through the whole house, but no one comes to comfort me. No one but Roscoe. I smile through my tears despite myself and bend down, expecting him to roll over for a belly-rub like he always does. He doesn't this time, though, and instead looks at me intently, eye-to-eye, as if he knows something's up but he doesn't know quite what.

'Jenna's sick,' I whisper to him thickly. He stares at me, his droopy eyes unblinking. I wipe my face with the back of my hand and sniff hard. Pull yourself together, Alex. Roscoe leans in and licks my face, as though he's helping to get rid of the tears.

'Thanks, buddy.' I straighten up and get myself some water and toast and then sit on the floor with Roscoe, feeding him the crusts. He comforts me somewhat, but my brain is still replaying Jenna's words: the not knowing. The not knowing bothers me, too. It has for a while, through my dreams, but now the need for an answer is overpowering, overwhelming, and as I crunch through my toast every fibre of my being needs to know: what's going to happen to Jenna? What's going to happen to the man in the waiting room? To me? Strangers across the world right now are taking their last breath from old age, illness, accidents. They're leaving this life and going... Going where? Somewhere beyond this life. Where that is,

what that is, I don't know.
But I think I need to find out.

Chapter Seven

Today is Jenna's first round of chemotherapy. I asked if I could miss school and come along again, but Mum said it would be boring and not very nice. Jenna also didn't want me to see her attached to all the tubes and things. I said I didn't mind tubes, but Mum said Jenna does mind. That was that. So Mum went with her this morning, and Dad went to work, and I went to school. Just like every other day. As if this is all normal now.

'Alex, can you stay behind a moment, please?'

Mrs Lee has just taken the morning register and everyone's going off to the first class. She beckons to me from behind her desk and I force myself up to the front. She waits until the rest of the kids have filed out of the room before she speaks.

'Alex, I know you're having a difficult time. At home.' She pushes her glasses right up to the bridge of her nose and gestures to a chair opposite. 'Your mother phoned yesterday, to update us on the… situation.' I sit down. 'And I just wanted you to know that we—all of us at school—are here for you.' She pauses as if waiting for me to speak. I have nothing to say. 'You know you can always speak to me or any other member of staff about anything worrying you, or any issues you may be having. In fact, I think it would be an excellent idea to refer you to the pastoral worker, Mrs Moss.'

I don't care.

'Okay.'

'Lovely. Right. I'll speak to her today and get you booked in for some sessions, then.' She glances down at a piece of paper in front of her; I think she's made notes on what she wants to say. 'And I've spoken to a few teachers who have had problems with homework and decided you're going to be put on a reduced homework timetable for a while. So you'll just get the core subjects—English, Maths and Science—to do every week. Do you think that's helpful?'

No.

'Yes.'

She sighs and leans across the desk slightly. 'Alex. You're an incredibly bright, lovely young man with a great future ahead. I know things are tough at the moment but, here at school, we want to support you. Please let me know if there's anything else we can do.'

There's nothing you can do, stupid woman.

'Yes. Thank you, Miss.'

I leave the classroom, that same stupid, numb feeling pulsing through me. I feel like a zombie: like a brainless, idiot zombie. But the one thought on my mind isn't blood: it's my dying sister.

I walk home alone today. My class is late out and when I get to the gates Daisy and Callum are nowhere to be seen. I don't care, anyway. Some days its nicer to be alone. I put my headphones on and play Nirvana and try to ignore the idiots sat on the hill, yelling stuff.

It's Bruce Cleeve and his Apes, smoking and eating, a gaggle of girls next to them laughing and tossing their hair. How the hell those Neanderthals have attracted females to sit with them, I have no idea. I suppose a couple of Duce's friends could be classed as eye candy—I know Daisy always says so—but Duce himself is repulsive. His face is like a 'before' advert for spot cream and his nose hooks over at the end like a bird beak; it's like the ugliness inside him just oozes out.

Duce catches sight of me and begins pointing, his friends joining in. Crap. He'd better not come after me. I know I'm an easy target on my own: classed as a 'nerd' thanks to being caught in the library several times. And I guess I look a bit weedy. But come on. Give a guy a break.

'Alex!'

I'm sure someone called my name. I turn my music down slightly but carry on walking. I don't want to look back. I don't want to see Duce's ugly face again.

'Alex!'

It's not Duce, it's Luca and Yusuf. I stop my music and dither on the corner for a minute. I'm far enough away from Duce and his cronies to wait safely but Yusuf and Luca are rushing past them now, heads down, speeding towards me.

'You late for something?' Duce calls out at them. Luca goes a bit red.

'Aw, look at them,' one of the girls jeers loudly. 'Running away from big bad Bruce.' The others laugh exaggeratedly. Duce slides down the hill towards them.

'Hold up, boys. Hold up.'

Yusuf slows down, unsure of what to do; if Duce tells you to stop, you stop. Equally he knows that, if he did stop, there's a high possibility that Duce would beat the crap out of him. Luca, however, slightly more street smart, breaks into a run and tears past me, into the alley and out of sight. He doesn't even look at me as he goes past. His survival instinct must've kicked in.

'I said: hold up!' Duce thunders. Yusuf stops completely, blinking rapidly as if the sun is in his eyes. He's a rabbit caught in the headlights. I stand, frozen on the corner, torn: to stay or to go? I'm safe here. But my friend's not.

'Good boy.' Duce gets right up to Yusuf's face. He says something, too quietly for me to hear, but Yusuf's face drops and Duce's friends laugh again. I can hear my heart in my ears, pounding with fear and fury. Whatever he's saying, it's not nice. This won't end well for Yusuf. But is it going to end well for me? I can't just stand here and watch them beat him up, can I? Or can I?

'Alex!' Yusuf calls out, his voice shaking. Duce has put him in a headlock. Yusuf's glasses fall to the floor.

'Oooh, Alex!' Duce parrots in a high voice, tightening his grip and smiling at me. 'Come and play, Alex.'

I stare at his hideous face, my mind ticking. Yusuf is slowly turning a darker shade of red. He looks like he's about to cry. Am I about to cry?

'Alex!' Duce shouts tauntingly. 'Come and get your little

boyfriend, Alex.'

No, I'm not going to cry. I'm going to go and get Yusuf. Taking a deep breath, I start towards them, walking at first and then running. Duce is laughing.

'Whoops!' He leads Yusuf straight into my path; I stop just in time. I'm panting even though I didn't run very far, my heart going a million miles-an-hour. Duce gets up in my face, grinning, Yusuf still under his arm. Up close his spots are crusty and hideous and his teeth are wonky. I don't think I've ever been this close to Duce. I don't think I ever want to be this close again.

'Let Yusuf go.' I try to sound stern but I hear my voice crack slightly. Damn it. It's not because I'm scared, that's just been happening lately. And maybe I am a tiny bit scared. I've seen Duce take countless kids' lunch money, or steal their things, or give them a black eye or bruises. Once I even walked around the corner to see him and his friends giving a boy cigarette burns. I didn't tell anyone, though; no one tells on Bruce Cleeve. Life is better if you just keep quiet and deal with it. And usually, if you're lucky and you avoid him enough, he doesn't take much notice of you. I've always been pretty successful with that, though it seems like the news about Jenna lately has brought me back onto his radar. Another great side-effect of her cancer.

'I'll let him go when I feel like it, dork.' Duce laughs, squeezing Yusuf tighter. I bend down to try and get Yusuf's glasses before Duce can, but he does something worse than putting his greasy hands on them. Crack. He breaks them under his massive foot in one swift stomp. The frame snaps completely, the glass scattering into tiny shards on the floor. I freeze. Yusuf's told me before how much they cost and they're not cheap.

'Hey!' Yusuf squeals. 'My glasses!'

'My glasses!' Duce echoes him in a stupid voice. His Ape-friends point and laugh from the hill and one girl, Patty, runs down towards us giggling. She's quite pretty actually; her freckles are a bit like Daisy's. Anyway. Focus, Alex. Yusuf's head is still under Duce's arm, but he's given up squirming. He's just staring down at the floor, probably wondering what the hell he's going to do about his glasses. And Duce is grinning at me, like he's silently saying, 'Come on, then. What're you gonna do about it?'

'Let him go, Bruce,' I say again, my mind whirring. Come on, Al. Okay, okay, options…

Option 1: make Duce angry enough to swing a punch at me, therefore letting Yusuf go. I'm faster than he is, I can outrun him.

Option 2: kick him in the nuts so he lets Yusuf go and, again, make a run for it.

Option 3: shout for help; we're not far from school, there must still be other kids around, or adults. Even as this idea enters my mind, I push it away. I know it's ridiculous. No one helps save you from Bruce Cleeve.

'Go on, make me,' Duce sneers.

I'm considering the initial two options when suddenly Patty puts her arm on Duce's shoulder and starts winding her hair around her finger. His eyes fly off me and stare at her like he's under a trance as she starts twirling a new strand. She stares back at him, half smiling. Gross. But he seems to be slowly forgetting about Yusuf, his grip loosening. I try and catch Yusuf's eye, bending down slightly and gesturing with my head. 'Come on, Yusuf. This is our chance.'

'Come on,' Patty says after a moment. 'Let's get out of here.'

I hold my breath. Duce looks down at Yusuf, then looks at Patty again. Without a word, he lets Yusuf go and takes Patty by the hand. Yusuf scrambles away, coughing.

'Are you all right?' I ask him, patting him on the back. He looks like he's choking slightly. 'Sorry about your glasses.'

'It's okay,' Yusuf wheezes. 'Not your fault. I needed new ones anyway.' He straightens up and we both watch in disbelief as Duce and Patty walk back up the hill. Patty turns around, and I swear she smiles at us.

'What the hell…?' Yusuf grabs his inhaler from his bag and takes a long drag. 'I really thought he was gonna knock me out.'

'Well. I'm glad he didn't,' I say truthfully. We begin walking home, Yusuf limping slightly—although I'm sure Duce never touched his leg—not talking, not addressing the fact that I very nearly left him for dead meat. But I think the important thing is that in the end, I didn't. I went back for him. To his rescue. Though actually, after all that, I think it was Patty that rescued us both.

Chapter Eight

'So, Alex. What would you like to discuss today?' Mrs Moss adjusts her notepad and pen and looks at me expectantly. The 'talking to someone' arrangement happened much quicker than I'd anticipated; it has been less than a week from speaking to Mrs Lee and I'm sat in Mrs Moss' office, at the end of the corridor in the West Wing.

'I'd like to talk about my sister. I suppose.' I shift awkwardly in my seat, not sure whether that's the right answer. Anyway, I bet she's one of those teachers that doesn't think there's a right or wrong answer. Mrs Moss is quite young, with a neatly-cut fringe and pretty eyes. She seems kind and patient, the type of person I could talk to. If I wanted to talk. Which I'm not sure I do.

'Okay. Your sister, Jenna. She's...' She briefly flicks through her notepad. 'Older than you?'

'Yes.'

'And what does she do?'

I sigh, the feeling of numbness returning, spreading through my veins like ice. What does she do? She sits at home, feeling sick. She goes to the hospital for tests and appointments and soon she's going back for her next round of chemo. She cries when she finds hair on her pillow in the morning. She watches daytime TV quiz shows and sometimes I play along with her when I get back from school. She goes for drives with Kent, and sometimes to the movies. She takes different drugs every morning with a swig of water and assures Mum that she's fine, she's not going to chuck them back up.

I'm not going to go through all of this with Mrs Moss, of course.

I know her question was stupid, but she probably doesn't know it was stupid and I don't want to offend her and ruin this whole counselling thing already. Not after Mum was so happy about it.

'It'll be really beneficial, Alex,' she'd told me the evening Mrs Lee had called her to confirm. 'Such a good idea. It will really help you open up and deal with things.'

'I dunno,' I'd told her, focusing on scooping up the last of the rice in some complicated, spicy curry she'd made. After the second big announcement she was back to cooping herself up in the kitchen. And Dad was still being his annoying self every evening, when he wasn't down the pub. So no change there, then.

'I want you to give it a go,' Mum had said sternly. 'Honestly, Alex, it's like a little weight off your shoulders. I had a really good session with my counsellor today.'

'What?' Dad had bellowed, slamming down his fork. 'You don't have a bloody counsellor, Cindy!'

'Yes, I do,' Mum had said impatiently. 'And maybe you should see him too. He's really very good, very professional.'

The conversation was left at that, with Dad mumbling that he didn't need some shrink to tell him that his daughter is ill and he feels crap about it.

'Alex?' Mrs Moss makes a note in her book. 'How are you finding school?'

I think back to my reduced homework timetable and my rubbish grades and my encounters with Duce.

'All right,' I answer. 'I get to see my friends. But I find it hard to concentrate.'

'Yes,' Mrs Moss nods, pleased to have finally got a proper answer out of me. Maybe I was judging too soon: maybe Mrs Moss does think there are right or wrong answers. 'I can imagine. What do you find yourself thinking of in class?'

I shrug. 'My sister. How she's doing.' The numb feeling seems to be slowly easing out of me. I feel—actually feel—emotions right now.

Annoyed, that the clock is ticking too loud. Tired, because I didn't sleep well last night. Upset. Upset over everything.

'I think of Jenna,' I carry on with a sudden urge to speak about it. 'And if Jenna's feeling sick or if any more of her hair has fallen out or if she's with Kent or Mum today or if she's alone. If she's sleeping okay or if she struggles like I do. I think about what's going to happen in a week or two or three: more chemo. And I think, is she going to be bald for Christmas? That's soon, you know. And then I think about after Christmas: how long will she be here after Christmas? Years, I hope. But maybe months? We don't know. I don't know. And I hate not knowing.' I catch my breath, my heart beating fast. I know I've been rambling on a whim and probably not making sense, but it was honest rambling. I think Mrs Moss knows this is a Right Answer. She makes a note.

'I understand,' she says softly. 'Do you often think of the what-ifs? And the future?'

'Yes,' I nod, my heart still thudding away. It's the first time I'm opening up in what feels like forever. It's weird.

'But nothing is certain,' Mrs Moss says, clicking her pen. 'You know that, don't you Alex?'

'One thing is certain,' I tell her. 'Death. Death is certain.'

I study her face as I say this, expecting her to be outraged or upset or confused or something. But she smiles instead, a sympathetic kind of smile.

'Yes,' she agrees. 'It is certain. We will all die.'

I'm glad she didn't lie or try and skate around it. It's almost a relief to hear her say it: a grown-up, finally admitting that all our lives come to an end. That Jenna's life will come to an end. It feels like all the other adults in my life zip their mouths shut when it comes to this. I think Mum and Dad think that if they don't talk about it, it won't happen. I know they're wrong.

'I've been having these dreams,' I say, 'about Jenna dying. In all sorts of ways. And then things happen to her after: she floats away, or she becomes a ghost or something. I dunno. It's weird. I draw what happens in them. And then I can never really get back to sleep.'

'Do you have any drawings with you?' Mrs Moss asks. 'I'd be interested in having a look, if you wouldn't mind.'

'No. They're at home,' I say truthfully. I would never bring them to school. That'd be the day that Duce steals my bag or something; next thing I'd be the laughing stock of the school.

'That's okay,' Mrs Moss says, making another note. 'And are these dreams scary at all? Unsettling?'

'Some.'

'And they're all about Jenna after she dies?'

'Yes.'

Mrs Moss scribbles something down on her notepad. 'Have you spoken to your mum about your issues with sleeping? You really should get that sorted, Alex. Lack of sleep at your age can have a detrimental effect on—'

'I'm not here to talk about that,' I interrupt her. 'Sorry, Miss. But I'm not.'

'Okay. I understand.' She pauses, looking over her notes. 'Are you of a certain religion, Alex?'

'No.'

'You don't have a specific belief or idea about what happens after death?'

'No.'

'Well.' Mrs Moss closes her notepad and looks me dead in the eye. 'I believe, Alex, that you're an incredibly brave, strong boy. You're coping well, considering the circumstances. And, understandably, you're very concerned for your sister: not only in her wellbeing in life but after life, too. And your uncertainty in what will happen to her—and indeed, as you said, what will happen to everybody—is disturbing you. So much, it almost torments you.'

I stare back at her. The clock is still ticking. She's right. She's given me a Right Answer.

'Alex, I wish I had a simple answer for you,' she goes on. 'But there are so many different beliefs and theories and ideologies out there about what happens when we die, I can't just thrust one of those on you. That would be wrong. It's up to you to come to a conclusion. I believe that when you do, you will feel a lot more comforted.'

I open my mouth and then close it again.

Then it clicks. The not knowing. The not knowing upsets Jenna. And the not knowing upsets me. It must upset everyone, in fact. Every single person, surely, must wonder, at some point, what happens when their lives end. So that's it: the answer to Jenna's happiness and my peace of mind and actually everyone in the whole world's peace of mind, is to just find an answer. That's what I've got to do.

'Thank you, Mrs Moss.' I spring up out my chair and grab my bag. I've got work to do.

'Our time isn't up yet, Alex...' she protests, standing as well. The sun hits her face and I can see faint freckles dotted across her nose. It makes me think of Daisy.

'It's okay. I'm done now.'

'Well, okay. We made a good start.' She follows me to the door. 'Same time next week?'

'Sure!' I call from the corridor. And I mean it; today was helpful. Mrs Moss led me to the most obvious solution to my numbness, my dreams, my worry for my sister. All I need to do is discover what will happen to her.

All I need to do is find out what lies beyond.

Chapter Nine

It's the last day of school before breaking up for the Christmas holidays. Finally. The last week -and-a-half dragged massively and even with a 'reduced' homework timetable, my studies have been piling up and taking up hours in the evenings.

Daisy came over last night, for the first time since we watched Peter Pan, and we worked on Maths together. We sat at the dining room table, with Roscoe laying on my bare feet and Mum bringing in tea and biscuits. For an hour or so, even though I was doing algebra, I actually enjoyed myself. After completing each equation I would treat myself to a glance across the table at my homework partner: her red hair frizzed from the rain that had poured down on our way home, her shirt crumpled and stained with pasta from lunch. She had worn mascara that day and some had smudged under her eyes. She looked beautiful.

And she'd come on a great day; a day of Jenna staying at Kent's for dinner, a day of Dad being nowhere to be seen and Mum dancing around the house dusting, her mood better than I'd seen it in a while. I found out later it was because she'd finished the Christmas wrapping that day. Mum loves Christmas.

'What are you looking at?'

I snap out of my daydream with Daisy and remember I'm actually in the canteen with Callum, who's way less pretty to look at.

'Sorry.'

'It's cool.' Callum slurps up the remainder of his apple juice and chucks the carton into the bin behind him. One of Callum's many skills: the ability to land things exactly where he wants them without looking. He used to be on the basketball team. Mr Brown is constantly begging him to return; he was the best shooter they had.

'Where's Daisy?' I ask nonchalantly. We normally meet at the corner table for lunch every Thursday. We'd walked to school together, as usual, this morning; Daisy hadn't said anything about going somewhere else for lunch. Sometimes she hangs out with some girls in our year, Kelly and Gee, but she always drops a text to let me know where she is. Not that I worry about her or anything.

'Probably got a detention' Callum answers, scrolling through his messages. 'Heard she had a meltdown in French earlier.'

'What? Why?' That's weird. Daisy doesn't have meltdowns. She's not stroppy; she's rarely unhappy at all.

'Dunno. Steve said Duce walked past the door and said something or gestured to her and she just went mental.'

Ah. The giant scab that is Duce Cleeve.

'Gestured?' Okay, Duce's fat fingers in any form are not nice to look at. But the middle finger's never made Daisy cry before, so what was different this time? In fact, Duce never fazes Daisy, fingers or not. If anything, she fazes him.

'But Duce is scared of Daisy, right?' I press, confused. 'He's never bothered her. Why would he suddenly…'

I trail off, realising Callum's not listening. He's watching Gee Davies swan over to a table full of girls, neatly balancing her lunch tray in her hands and walking with a sort of wiggle. Gee Davies seems to have grown very pretty this school year. Before, I never massively took notice of her. Not that I take notice of her now; I don't think about girls at all apart from my sister and Daisy. But she's definitely caught Callum's eye, and quite a few other boys' too. I notice her skirt gets very short and tight as she bends to sit down and look away quickly. Callum's practically dribbling.

'Cal!' I hiss as one of Gee Davies' friends points at our table. 'Stop staring!'

'Sorry,' Callum turns away. 'I mean, come on, though. What do you reckon?' He nods at Gee's table.

I roll my eyes and go back to our conversation. 'Why was Daisy so mad at Duce?'

'Well, I dunno. I reckon it's because she heard all about what happened with you, Duce and Yusuf the other week,' Callum says, opening his yoghurt. 'You know. The thing you never told us about.'

I wait to see if he's angry or not but he just raises his eyebrows. I deliberately didn't tell anyone. I knew for a fact it wasn't a huge deal: Duce bullies people all the time, it's hardly news. I didn't want to bore Callum and Daisy with the details of the ordeal.

Plus, even more so, a tiny part of me didn't want Daisy to think I was... well, a wimp. I can stand up for myself: I did stand up for myself, and Yusuf. In the end.

'Why would she be so mad about that, though?' I wonder aloud. The worst thing that happened was Yusuf's glasses breaking, but I didn't think Daisy was a good enough friend of Yusuf's to be mad about that.

'Not sure.' Callum scrapes up the last of his yoghurt. 'She never tells us anything. About Duce, I mean. The whole thing's weird.'

'I wouldn't say weird,' I insist. 'Pretty good, if anything. It means he leaves us alone.' Most of the time, anyway.

'I reckon she's got some kind of deal with him.' Callum leans in towards me and lowers his voice. 'Like, she does something for him, he does something for her. I mean, think about when she first came here. She's never had trouble with him, ever. Why? How? No one's ever been immune to Duce before.'

My stomach twists at Callum's implication. What would Daisy do for Duce?

'There's nothing Daisy would exchange for that,' I hiss, feeling insulted on her behalf.

'Dunno,' Callum shrugs. 'Think about it, Al. We haven't known Daisy that long. Have we ever met her mum? Been to her house? How much do we really know about her?'

I don't like where this is going. He's right, though; we've been outside Daisy's bungalow, but never inside. I've seen her mother quickly once or twice but we've never spoken. But so what? So what if I've never been formally introduced to Daisy's mum? That's nothing dodgy. Is it?

'We know Daisy,' I insist. 'She hates Duce. She'd never make some sort of weird deal with him. He's just scared of her.'

Callum raises his eyebrows. 'I dunno, Al. It's like she's hiding something just as much as he is. Okay, it's weird that he tiptoes around her. But it's even weirder that she won't tell us why.'

'She just likes being mysterious.'

'Yeah, right,' he snorts. 'There's being mysterious and then there's hiding a whole other part of your life from your best friends.'

Okay, that's going too far. 'She's not hiding anything! You're overthinking this, idiot. Do you take everyone you've ever said hi to on a grand tour of your house and then write them a list of all your secrets? What've you got against her all of a sudden?'

He holds up his hands. 'Nothing, mate! You know I dig Daisy. Not as much as you do, though.' He winks.

I roll my eyes. This is going nowhere. And as much as I really wanna get to the bottom of this whole thing, I can't be analysing every single thing Daisy's ever done right now. She's upset, she's probably all alone, and whether her and Duce are secretly best friends or have some kind of weird truce, I need to go and make sure she's okay. I need to shut this conversation down and worry about it later.

'Daisy's cool,' I say. 'And if she keeps Duce away from us, she's even cooler. I bet she beat him up when she first came here or something, and that's why he runs away whenever she's within ten feet.'

Callum laughs and we both know it could be true. Duce would be no match for her. Still, I need to go find her. Alone it seems, as Callum slides over to join the table right next to Gee's.

'You sure you don't wanna come?' I ask again hopefully, hovering at the table. Callum smooths his hair down and barely tears his eyes away from Gee to answer.

'Nah, nah. You go. I'll see you later.'

*

I find her eventually: sat outside Mrs Moss' office, knees tucked into her chest, head hanging down. She doesn't look up but she must hear my footsteps coming closer. I don't know if she wants to talk to me. But I want to try.

'Hi.' I sit on the plastic chair next to hers. She sniffs hard and doesn't look up.

'Go away.' She sounds like she's been crying. Her long hair is covering her face, but I imagine tears staining her freckled cheeks and my heart sinks. It's kinda weird, actually: how sad I feel, just looking at her like this. I wish more than anything that I could take those tears from her and make it all go away. Or at least hug her, for God's sake. Instead, being my awkward self, I shuffle a bit closer to her and say, 'Whatever Duce did, he's an idiot. The stupidest, ugliest idiot I've ever seen. Don't let him upset you.'

Daisy doesn't answer.

'Are you free tomorrow?' I change tactics. 'We could go to the cinema? There's that new horror movie out that looks good. We can invite Cal too if you want.'

Still no answer. I try to think desperately of anything else to say but my tiny brain has run out of ideas. Even Duce would be better than me in this situation. All I want to do is comfort her, make her laugh, make her realise that Duce Cleeve is the grossest human on the planet Earth and she is the most beautiful. But I'm tired, like always. And I'm rubbish at helping, like always.

Maybe I could go to the root of the problem and confront Duce? I snort out loud at the thought. What would I even say to him? 'Hey, Duce, I heard you may or may not have upset my best friend / dream girlfriend, Daisy! Come here so I can try and hit you!' Ridiculous. I remember last time I tried to intervene, with Jenna and Kent, and how upset everyone got. Maybe I should just leave it. I wish we were back to yesterday evening, homework partners at my dining room table.

'Well, you know where I am. Text me.' I place my hand on the edge of her chair to push myself up. As I do, without moving her head at all, Daisy places her hand gently on mine. Relief and happiness and electricity floods through me all at once. Her hand is soft and warm. I never want it to leave mine.

Chapter Ten

I haven't heard from Daisy yet.

It's Christmas Eve today, and it's been a whirlwind of a holiday so far. Yesterday, Jenna was rushed to hospital.

It all started when we were watching some black-and-white Christmas film that Jenna insisted on having on. Dad was asleep, snoring in his armchair, empty beer cans scattered around his feet, as usual. Mum was in the kitchen, cleaning and faffing, as usual. Jenna and I were sat together on the two-seater: me on my phone, Jenna engrossed in the TV.

Her hair is patchy now, after two rounds of chemotherapy. After the first time only a few strands would fall out at a time, mainly when she brushed it or in the shower. It used to really upset her. Now, she tucks her fallen strands under different hats and makes Roscoe wear them, takes photos of him and uploads them to social media. She and Mum think it's hilarious; I'm not sure how Roscoe feels.

But anyway, a funny part happened in the film. At least I thought it was supposed to be funny; the people on the screen laughed and Jenna laughed, and it sounded like for a minute she carried on laughing. It turned out she wasn't. She was making noises, weird retching noises.

'Jenna?' I put my phone down to see my sister bent over in pain. Her nose was bleeding heavily. And suddenly she was sick all over the carpet. Really, really sick.

'Mum!' I shouted. I'd never seen anything so horrible; I didn't know what to do, I didn't know what to say. I just patted Jenna on the back, making shushing noises like you see in the movies. Mum ran in, tea towel in hand.

'Oh my God!' she screamed. At first, I thought she was upset about the carpet but then she shook Dad awake vigorously, tears streaming down her face. 'George! Ring the ambulance!'

She ran over and crouched next to Jenna, who was still vomiting, while Dad dialled 999, practically shouting down the phone over Jenna's sick noises and Mum's cries. I felt frozen. It was the first time I'd really seen something to signify my sister being so sick. I mean, I've seen her tired and weak. And balding. But she's always been in a good mood: happy and joking and curled up on the sofa with Roscoe when I get home from school. I'd heard her throw up once or twice, but it had never sounded particularly painful. Not like that. Never like that.

And while I watched Mum rock my limp, bleeding sister, a sudden realisation hit me: this is how it's gonna be from now on. There's no going back. There's no getting better. There'll only be more blood, more sick. And less of Jenna's smiles, her jokes, her advice. Less of her.

The ambulance finally arrived after what felt like far too long. By this point Dad had packed a bag for Jenna (Mum wouldn't leave her side) and Kent and Gran had been called. Jenna finally finished throwing up but it didn't seem to make her feel any better. Mum got to ride in the ambulance with her and the paramedics while Dad and Kent followed in the car.

And where was I? At home. In the stupid house with Gran. Apparently, it would 'Only upset Jenna', for me to see her that way. As if I hadn't just watched her vomit all over the carpet already. And anyway, did they give a toss if I was upset? No. Of course they didn't. They never bloody do.

I was still waiting on the stairs like a little kid when they got home. Gran made me to go bed at about eleven, after she'd scrubbed the carpet clean, and the door opened not long after.

'Oh, thank God.' I peered over the banister to see Gran pull Mum into a hug. 'What happened? Is she okay?'

'She's staying the night,' Dad said heavily.

Staying the night? I felt sick.

'Oh, Lord. Come on, I'll put the kettle on.' Mum followed Gran into the kitchen and I snuck down two more stairs.

'I'll be...' Dad slid off, presumably to his whiskey and his man cave. I felt the anger boil inside of me; he didn't even care enough to sit and explain to Gran what had happened! So how come he was allowed to go to the hospital while I had to sit at home not knowing what the hell was going on?! It wasn't fair. None of it was bloody fair.

'Thanks, Mum.' I strained to hear them over the kettle boiling. 'God, what a night.'

'I know, love. I know. It's okay.'

What is it with adults saying it's going to be okay? It's clearly not going to be okay. Jenna's staying overnight, all alone in the hospital! That's far from okay, in my opinion.

'So, did they say what caused the sickness?'

I crept down another two steps.

Mum sighed; the fridge opened and shut. 'Fluid in the abdomen. Apparently it's very common.'

'Sounds uncomfortable.' The chairs scraped across the floor.

'Yeah. Nausea is a common symptom, but the doctors said they rarely get people projectile vomiting like Jenna did. It's... It's not...' Mum's voice broke.

'Shh now, it's okay,' Gran soothed her. 'She's in good hands.'

Mum sniffed. 'I know she is. I know. It's just the hardest thing in the world, seeing your baby like that. All tied up to tubes and bags and...' She broke off again.

'I know, love. But it's just one night. Just one.' I couldn't see them, but I imagined Gran reaching forward and stroking Mum's hair, like she always does. 'I presume they're draining the fluid?'

'Yeah.' I think Mum blew her nose. 'It'll only take a few hours, then she can rest. But it could come back... it can even spread...'

I'd heard enough. I couldn't listen to Mum's what-if's; I've got enough of those on my own. No. I had to remember that, like Gran said, she was in the best place she could be. It was now a waiting game.

It took a while but I finally managed to get some sleep. I woke up with my mind still whirring over Mum and Gran's conversation last night. I could hear every sniff, every chair scrape over and over, amplified by a hundred. The louder the sounds, the worse I felt; they melted together like an angry buzz, filling my head with pain. I had to get out, spend some time with the one family member who couldn't possibly make things any harder. Roscoe.

The fresh air did help and as we come home I feel a little better; ready to do something productive. I go straight to my desk and straight to my scrapbook. It's something I've been working on since my talk with Mrs Moss. It's called the 'Scrapbook of Beyond' and it's the start of the huge quest I'm on: to discover what's going to happen to my sister, and myself, and everyone when we leave the Earth.

So far it doesn't have much in it. What with school work and end of term and Daisy and Duce and everything else going on, I haven't had much time to invest in it. Though the dreams are a reminder, almost every night, that Jenna's going to leave one day. And that I need to know where she's going.

So far I've done a big mind map with 'Beyond' written in the middle and my initial ideas:

Heaven.

Hell.

Ghosts.

Spirits.

Reincarnation.

Some ideas I'd picked up from school trips to church, some from films.

I think back to Peter Pan and add 'Neverland' to the mind map.

I stare down at the initial list, my writing quick and untidy in blue biro. It looks messy. I have half a mind to tear it out. Plus it's all too general. I need a solid starting point. I need an order to explore and research things.

Since the rush to get Jenna to hospital it's all I've been thinking about. Well, that and how selfish and stupid I've been, letting Jenna even momentarily slip to the back of my mind. What kind of brother lets red-headed girls and fat bullies and homework get in the way of what really matters? Me, that's who. It's like before all this Duce and Daisy drama, Jenna and her illness were all I could think about. But for the past couple of weeks it's hardly crossed my mind. I clench the pen in my hand, a surge of anger and guilt running through my body.

'Alex?' There's a soft knock on the door before Mum pushes it open gently. I quickly shove the scrapbook under my 'GCSE Biology' book and turn to face her. She looks exhausted but at least she's finally showered; she's still wearing the towel on her head. I smile at the sight of it. Mum's always said that when I was little I would cry at the sight of her wearing it after washing her hair.

'Don't get upset,' she jokes feebly and sits on the end of my bed.

'You okay?' I ask, trying to fill the silence.

Mum sighs. 'I suppose. Rough night last night.'

'Yeah.' I don't know what she wants me to say.

'You did the right thing though, Al.' Mum holds my gaze, her eyes tired. 'Calling me straight away. And Dad says you even remembered to walk Roscoe this morning.'

I shrug, deciding against telling her that the real reason I took Roscoe for a walk was to get away from the house for ten minutes. To get away from my family.

'Your sister was so brave yesterday,' Mum continues, her voice trembling. 'And I know the doctors said everything will be fine for the time being, but I just want to warn you. Christmas probably won't be the same this year, Al.'

I stare at her. Does she think I own even half a brain cell? I know Christmas isn't going to be the same. How could it?

'I'm still going to cook and everything of course,' Mum hurries on, mistaking my confused pause for sadness. 'Presents, movies, the lot. But we probably won't be up early. Or staying up particularly late. Jenna will be tired. Even more so from yesterday. She might even need a daytime nap. If she does, we need to respect that.'

'I know, Mum,' I answer, struggling to keep the annoyance out of my voice. 'I know all this.'

'All right, all right!' Mum snaps, the gentle tone to her voice vanishing.

'Seriously!' I hiss, my voice matching hers. 'I'm not a baby, no matter how much you guys treat me like one. I can understand what's going on here. I'm not an idiot, either. Jenna's sick. She's going to die. So this Christmas won't be as nice. I know that!' I don't know if it's my lack of sleep creeping up on me or if it's everything else, every single thing in the world. Nothing's okay. And to make matters even more not okay, Mum's treating me like a four-year-old.

'Alex!' Mum gasps. 'Don't speak to me like that!'

'I'm not speaking to you like anything,' I retort. 'It's the truth.'

'Well, maybe you should hold your tongue if you've got nothing nice to say!'

I snort. There's nothing anyone could say about all this that'd be nice. 'That's all I ever do.'

A silence stretches out between us. She stares at me, looking old and frail and defeated; not how she normally looks on Christmas Eve. On Christmas Eve, she's usually happy and bouncy and annoyingly loud. She plays Christmas music on the radio while she prepares food and does last-minute decorating and wrapping. But this is far from a normal Christmas. I want to look away from her but I also don't want to be the first one to break eye contact. I don't want to look guilty; I have nothing to feel guilty about, anyway.

'I think,' she says eventually, 'that you need to have a long, hard think about how you just spoke to me, Alex Duncan. Because that was not acceptable.'

I know I should leave it. Tomorrow's Christmas. But as she gets up to leave, I can't help but whisper, 'You're not acceptable.'

She whirls round so fast her towel nearly falls off her head. 'What did you say?'

'Nothing,' I lie, turning back to my desk.

'That was not nothing!' she raises her voice. 'What did you say, young man?'

I can't help it then. It all just comes pouring out of me. 'I said you're not acceptable, Mum! You and Dad, neither of you are! Dad just drinks and shouts and isn't helping anyone in any way. And all you do is cook and clean and hide from us all! This is the first time you've come into my room for weeks! And were you even coming to check if I was okay, or was it your plan all along to sit and patronise me about my own sister? No one's helping, Mum! I'm all alone! I'm months behind at school and failing classes. Did you know I've been put on a reduced homework timetable, like an idiot? Daisy's not talking to me. Callum only cares about girls. Duce Cleeve won't leave me the hell alone. I don't think I've had a full night's sleep since the bloody BBQ. And where have you been through all this? NOWHERE! So don't come skulking in here, on Christmas Eve and try and start a conversation like you care all of a sudden. Don't.'

Somewhere in all that I'd turned back round to face her and stood up so quick I knocked the chair over. I quickly straighten it up and sit back down. Mum's towel has properly fallen off her head and she holds it in her hand now, her hair hanging down, damp on her back. Tears start falling from her eyes. For God's sake. Now I've upset her. I take a few deep breaths, calming down. I've said everything I needed to say; maybe a bit too harshly.

'Mum…'

'Don't.' Her voice is shaky and quiet. 'Don't you dare say anything else. You've said enough, you horrible, selfish boy.' She leaves, closing the door behind her.

Great. So voicing my feelings apparently makes me selfish. On top of that, I made my own mum cry. Could this Christmas be any worse?

A voice in the back in my mind argues, Yes. Something worse could've happened to Jenna yesterday. Don't forget that

*

As instructed, I don't wake up early on Christmas morning. The usual childish feeling of excitement just isn't here this year, anyway. Usually, Jenna (being the big baby she is) comes and wakes us all up before 7 am. This year, I wake naturally at half-past eight. The house is silent. I lie in bed for a while, going over the events of the last couple of days. I check my phone, but still no text from Daisy. One from Callum though, wishing me a Merry Christmas and asking if I want to go for a kick-around tomorrow. Some people don't like leaving their family on Boxing Day, but this is what Callum and I do pretty much every year. A couple of times we've had snowball fights instead, but no such luck this year. I send a sleepy reply, 'Merry Xmas. Yes mate. Meet u at park at 11 tomoz' and pull the duvet back over my head.

*

The doorbell rings and Roscoe barks loudly.

'Go and get the door, Alex. That'll be your gran and grandad,' Mum instructs me frostily.

I do as I'm told, glad to be out of the room. We've been sat on the living room floor, like every usual Christmas morning, opening presents. The mood, as expected, is far from jolly. Dad is hungover: though to be fair he is actually making a slight effort and has a Santa hat on, cracking jokes. Jenna's not feeling great and, although she's thanked everyone for her gifts, you could tell by the sad smile on her face that what she got wasn't what she really wanted. Or maybe they were what she wanted, but she knew she wouldn't really be going anywhere fancy enough to show off the new handbag or studying enough to use the leather-bound notebook and posh pens. And then, to top it all off, it seems Mum hasn't forgiven me for my rampage yesterday. Maybe I haven't forgiven her, either.

'Happy Christmas darling!' Gran throws her arms around me and hugs me tightly when I open the door. I squeeze her back, pleased she's here.

'Merry Christmas!' Grandad follows her in, staggering under the weight of some huge presents.

'Do you want a hand, Grandad?' I take two boxes off the top and stand aside to let them in. Roscoe jumps up and down, slobbering excitedly. He loves Gran and Grandad, too.

'Hi, Mum.' Mum appears behind me and takes some bags from Gran. 'Merry Christmas.'

'Yes, yes, hello lovely,' Gran says breathlessly, sliding her shoes off and making her way into the living room.

'How are you?' Grandad asks, planting a kiss on Mum's cheek.

'You mean since yesterday?' Mum says through gritted teeth, shooting me a glance. I ignore her and carry the presents into the living room.

Gran and Grandad are a great ice-breaker. Gran chats about anything and everything, and, although Grandad is quieter, he cracks brilliantly awful jokes at random points in conversations and lightens the mood. They're the best at present-buying too; I got new PlayStation games, trainers, face wash and a football. I didn't even give them a list this year, what with everything going on.

Jenna did well, too, and got loads of make-up and clothes and DVDs and books. She even cried at one present: Gran got her a zoo experience day for her and Kent. It's one of those vouchers that you can book in for whenever, Gran says, so that Jenna can go on a day when she's feeling up for it.

It's evening now, and Gran and Grandad have just left. There's a Disney film on the television and Dad, Jenna and Kent are falling asleep on the sofa. Kent came over a couple of hours ago for some turkey sandwiches. As soon as he walked through the door Jenna's face lit up and she's been stuck to him ever since. Her head's resting on his shoulder now, her arms wrapped around him so tightly it looks like she'll never let go. It's nice that she's got someone to cling like that to. I wish Daisy and I were on the sofa as well.

'Alex?' Mum calls from the kitchen. 'Come and help me wash up.'

Great, she's still punishing me. I grab the tea towel and we come to the silent agreement of her washing, me drying. It's awkward for a couple of minutes.

'Did you have a nice day?' she asks eventually, handing me a plate.

'Yes, thank you. Did you?'

'Yes. It was lovely. All things considered.' She pauses, looking down into the soapy water. 'I think Jenna did well. We all did well.'

I say nothing and put the dry plate away.

'Including you,' Mum continues. 'You did well, Alex. You always do. Which is why, I suppose, you've been sort of... slipping my mind recently. You're always so independent and strong-willed. You've always just got on. I didn't realise you were finding things so difficult.'

'My sister gets diagnosed with cancer and you thought I would just... get on?' I ask, struggling to keep my voice level.

'It sounds stupid, I know.' Mum lets the plug out of the sink and hands me the last plate. 'I'm so sorry. I truly am. I dropped the ball. I've been so entirely focused on one child, I've forgotten to check in with my other one.' She smiles wryly. 'And sharing your feelings doesn't for one second make you selfish. Please forget I ever said that. It was just... You're just such a brave, mature boy, Alex. I wish I was as brave as you. And your sister.'

My anger diminishes as Mum draws up a chair and holds her head in her hands. I can tell she's sorry. I finish drying the last plate and sit down next to her.

'I'm sorry, too, Mum. I didn't mean to shout. It just all... came out. It does that sometimes.'

'I know, darling. I'm sorry.' She hugs me tightly and we sit in silence for I don't know how long, Roscoe at my feet, the sound of the TV drifting in from the living room, and I find myself thinking: this has been a pretty good Christmas after all.

Chapter Eleven

'Heads!'

The ball comes flying towards me from the other side of the pitch. I judge its speed and angle perfectly and head it to Joe.

'Go on, Joe!' Callum shouts from beside me as Joe dribbles it up the other end of the pitch.

'Watch out!' I call as two defenders corner him. Joe neatly nutmegs one of them, shoots... and scores! We all jump up and down wildly as Marco, the goalie, rips his gloves off in anger.

'Yes! Well done mate!' Callum claps Joe on the back as he runs over to us.

'Thanks,' Joe grins, giving me a high five. As a team, we jog over to the sidelines for water and snacks, never standing still as we slurp and crunch. It's way too cold to be stationary. Other than that and the light frost on the grass, though, the conditions are pretty much perfect for a game.

We're doing six-a-side: a pretty good turn out this year. There've been boxing days when it's literally only been Callum and I doing penalties for hours and hours. Callum has branched out a bit in terms of his friends since when we first started playing: he doesn't just hang out with me and Daisy anymore, that's for sure. I eye up the opposition (the blue team) as I chug down some Lucozade. I recognise them all, and could name most, but none are my friends. Same with our team (the reds). Some I know from the odd class, most I've seen at lunch and around town, but I doubt some of them know who I am. They're all Callum's pals.

I consider this as the other guys break into conversation about tactics and positions. I've never been completely hated or unpopular or anything but I've always just had Callum and, in the past year, Daisy. Now, as we're getting older it seems like just one or two friends aren't enough for Callum. No, I'm being too harsh: most people have more than one friend or two. It's normal. I should have more and be normal too.

'Damn it. Look!' Callum nudges me sharply and points to the far side of the park. Even from a distance, I know who it is; I can tell by the monkey-like walk. Duce Cleeve and his cronies, here to ruin our Boxing Day.

'Ugh, can't stand that bloke,' Joe mutters as our whole team stares at them approaching. Damn it. What the hell is he doing here? Why does he have to ruin everything?

'What does he want?' I hiss to Callum.

'He'll want to play, of course,' Joe says loudly, putting his water bottle down. 'Looks like he's got enough for a team. I say we take him on.' I sigh, my breath fogging like smoke in front of my eyes. The last thing I want is to play a game with that moron. Especially after the way he's treated Daisy.

A couple of boys from the other team go over and greet Duce and the Apes as if they're actually welcome here. Duce looks possibly smugger than I've ever seen him, dressed in the new Arsenal kit. He's also gelled his hair, which makes him look like he's suffering from a receding hairline. I point this out to Callum who laughs too loudly. Duce glares at us.

'Seriously,' I whisper to Callum, pulling him aside, 'I don't think we should play with Duce. He's a freak of nature. He'll cheat and probably break my legs. And what if Daisy finds out?'

Callum laughs. 'He won't break your legs, dummy. You're quicker than him, anyway. And what do you mean about Daisy?'

'You know,' I say quickly as Duce approaches, 'the last day of school? She was upset, remember, about Duce.'

'It's not like we're his friends,' Callum shrugs. 'We'll beat him and then him and his Apes can do one.'

'Well, well.' Duce folds his fat arms and smiles at Callum and I. His teeth look very yellow today. 'Surprised to see you here.' He gestures to me.

'Why?'

'Well, isn't this your sister's last Christmas?' He snorts. 'Shouldn't you be crying by her bedside?' He mimics a girls' cry and a couple of his friends join in. I feel myself flush, my hands tremble. How dare that fat, ugly...

'Oi! That's out of line.' Joe interrupts them and stands by my side. 'What the hell's wrong with you?'

'You're messed-up,' Callum agrees. Duce narrows his eyes.

'Yeah, seriously, Bruce. Why the hell would you even joke about his sister?' A boy from the blue team who was originally speaking to Duce—Eric, I think his name is—stands to the left of me as well, his arms folded. A couple other boys pipe up too, agreeing. I can slowly feel myself returning to my normal temperature.

'Whatever,' Duce growls, turning red. 'Shut up about it. Let's just play.'

'No.'

The boys' heads all turn to look at me in unison, gobsmacked. I think I'm a little gobsmacked myself.

'What did you say?' Duce takes a step towards me.

I swallow hard. There's still time to escape this... No. No there's not. I am not playing football with this man-ape and I am not going to be a wimp about it.

'I said, no, Duce. Are you deaf?' My voice is steady. A couple of the boys laugh. Duce steps towards me again.

'Who the hell,' he says slowly, 'do you think you are?'

I don't miss a beat. 'I'm the kid with the dying sister. And the friend you upset on the last day of school. And the other friend whose glasses you broke a couple of weeks ago.' I puff out my chest, stand up straight and look him in the eye. 'And I say you're not playing.'

A couple of the lads make 'oooh'ing sounds. One of Duce's friends makes a fist and waves it at me.

'Well. Guess what?' Duce straightens up too. 'I am playing.'

No one speaks. No one looks away. Duce and I are still an inch away from each other, stood tall and straight, breathing heavily. At this point I don't care if I get punched. I don't care if he calls me names. I've made up my mind and I'm not playing with him.

'You're not playing, Bruce.'

Duce turns to face Joe, who has spoken suddenly, loudly and with a slight quiver to his voice. I don't think he's ever felt Duce's true wrath, but he's got friends who have. He's heard the stories: everyone has. So the fact he's just chimed up and put himself in danger to defend me... well. Maybe some of these boys are my friends after all.

'Yeah. Get lost, Duce. You're not playing.' Callum sticks his finger up, and Joe, Eric and the other boys laugh.

'Go away, Bruce.'

'Yeah, on your bike mate.'

'See ya.'

Duce raises his fist and puts it under my chin. He hovers it there. Every instinct in my body is telling me to run, make a break for it; never mind the boys, the football, the dignity. But I stay. And I hold Duce's gaze for as long as I can: not moving, not even flinching.

'Leave, Bruce!'

As the final boy speaks, Duce's arm falls limp. He takes a step backwards, away from me and his friends look at each other, not sure what to do. They've never been turned away from anything before. They've definitely never been turned away from a younger group's football game before.

'This is embarrassing. C'mon,' I hear one say and off they go: two of them running, the other two walking, glancing over their shoulders to see what their King Ape is going to do. He's still here, now looking past me to the alley; whatever he sees makes his face drop even further. Without a word, he turns and runs after his cronies. The lads around me break into laughter, slapping each other on the back and waving goodbye to Duce.

'We'll pay for that, I'm sure,' Joe says as the figures disappear behind the hill. 'Back at school.'

'Oh well,' Callum shrugs. 'Worth it.'

'Thanks, everyone,' I say, eventually finding my voice. 'Thank you.'

'No worries, mate.' Eric pats me on the back. 'He was weird. What a messed-up thing to say about your sister.'

'Yeah,' Joe nods. 'Not funny at all. What a jerk.' They all break into a discussion about it. I say nothing more, but feel... Well, how do I feel? Not even angry anymore at what Duce said, I don't think. More relieved that he's gone, happy he didn't punch me and surprised, completely surprised, at all the other boys sticking up for me. They knew the risk of being beaten to a pulp and they still defended me and Jenna.

They start sorting out another game, some still making fun of Duce's face, and as I turn to make my way onto the pitch I see a figure making her way back down the alley behind us. An unmistakable figure with ripped jeans and red hair. Daisy.

'Wait!'

It takes me ages to catch up with her. She had a huge head-start, anyway, but after I called out to her she broke into a full-on run. She's quick but I'm quick too and as soon as I'm close enough I grab her arm.

'Ow!'

'Daisy!' I slow down and she slows down with me, trying to wriggle her arm free.

'Get off!'

'Sorry.' I let go. She's still got her back to me but has finally stopped running. We stand in the middle of the street, panting.

'Why are you running away from me?' I take a step round to her side and she turns her back to me again. 'Daisy? Talk to me. I've been worried about you.'

She sniffs; I think she's trying to hold back tears. Even from behind she's beautiful, in old jeans and a knitted jumper. Her hair is in huge, frizzy bunches. I reach forward and stroke one before I can stop myself.

'Stop!' She flinches away, folding her arms.

'Sorry.' I take a step to her left again and this time she doesn't turn away. Her face is pale and she's got bags under her eyes. 'Why are you running from me?'

She sighs and turns to face me properly. I notice it straight away. What I thought was tiredness from a side-angle is actually a huge, purple bruise around her right eye.

'Oh my God.' I can't tear my eyes away from it. Deep purple on the socket, fading to green round the edges, it spreads above her eyebrow and down almost to her cheekbone. The eye itself is squinty and red, like she's been crying and hasn't slept in a week.

'I know. I'm hideous!' Daisy kicks a stone and shoves her hands in her pockets.

'You're not hideous!' I exclaim. 'Far from it! It's just… It's huge, Daisy. What happened? Who…' I lower my voice. 'Who did this to you?'

Daisy walks over to the kerb and sits down, resting her chin on her hands. She looks defeated.

'No one.' She replies eventually, her tone flat. 'I fell down the stairs.'

I take a seat on the kerb next to her and wait for her to tell me the truth, but she doesn't. She doesn't speak, she just sits, silently, kicking the odd stone and sighing the odd sigh, until at least five whole minutes have passed.

'Daisy.' She jumps at the sound of my voice breaking the silence. 'Sorry. Please tell me what really happened. You didn't fall down the stairs, did you?' I place a hand on her knee. She says nothing, but edges slightly closer to me so that our arms touch.

That same familiar feeling of electricity sparks through me, though not as strong as usual. It's overshadowed by my confusion, my anger. Who has done this? Why have they done this? And why is Daisy not telling me what really happened? I think about someone hitting Daisy—my Daisy—in her freckled, pale face and I feel like I might throw up. I take my hand back from her knee and put it over my mouth, actually scared for a moment that my breakfast might make a reappearance. Daisy jumps again at my sudden movement and springs up off the kerb, her face crumpled.

'Sorry.' I feel like I've apologised a thousand times now.

Her face relaxes slightly until she glances behind me and her eyes widen. I turn quickly to see Callum running towards us.

'Don't tell him!' Daisy hisses. And then she goes, running faster than I've ever seen her go before, around the corner and out of sight before Callum gets to me.

'That was Daisy, right?' He pants, doubled over. 'Ah! I've got a stitch! What was she doing?'

I hesitate, weighing up my options. Should I tell Callum the truth? I'm ninety-nine percent sure I need to tell someone what I saw. I think Daisy needs help and she needs it now. But is Callum the one to tell?

'Nothing,' I answer eventually.

'Oh. Well, come on, we're about to kick-off.' Callum gestures back to the park, surprisingly not too bothered about Daisy running off.

Well, I'm bothered.

'I've got to go, actually,' I tell him, starting to jog away.

'What? Why?' Callum yells after me.

'I've got to go home!' I shout back. 'I'll text you!'

I break into a run to the pitch, grab my things and go. I don't know what I'm going to do exactly, but I know where I'm going to go. And it's not home. It's Daisy's house.

*

I wait for a few minutes at the door, catching my breath. Should I really be doing this? Barging into Daisy's home, uninvited? I picture her face, bruised and scared. Yes, I should be doing this. Someone needs to look out for her.

Taking a deep breath, I knock twice. My mind whirls with possible openings when she opens the door: 'Come on! We're going to the police.' 'Can I come in?' 'Daisy let me help you.'

But I don't get a chance to say any of these things. No one opens the door. I can't even hear anything stir inside, either. I knock again, twice, louder than before. It hurts my knuckles a little. Still nothing. I peer into the living room window—I know I shouldn't, but I'm desperate—and see her, curled up on the armchair.

'Daisy!' I rap my knuckles on the window. 'Hey!'

She rushes to the window and opens it a crack. 'You've got to go.' Her voice is low and urgent. 'Seriously, go away Alex. They'll be back soon.'

'Who? Your Mum?' I try and reach for her hand through the gap. 'Please, are you okay?'

Daisy looks away. 'I'm fine. Go home. I'll text you.' She closes the window and pulls down the blinds.

I wait a moment, catching my breath. What the hell is going on? She's never acted like this before. I mean, I've always thought her mum might be a bit strange since we've never met her... Did her mum hit her? And if not her, then who? And why? My head's buzzing with questions, each one more confusing than the last. I can only form one straight thought and it's a worrying one; she's in trouble.

Daisy's in trouble.

Chapter Twelve

I don't see Daisy again until we're back at school.

After the promised text never happened, I tried phoning, texting and knocking on her door several more times over the days following Boxing Day. She never opened the door, never picked up the phone, but I did receive a text one night, saying, 'Stop'.

I thought long and hard about telling someone, of course I did. The evening it all happened, after I'd sat on Daisy's front step for a few hours, I went home, rehearsing in my head what I was going to tell Mum. But when I got in I took one look at her asleep on the sofa, cuddling Jenna, and realised I couldn't. Like she said at Christmas, if her own son slips her mind then how could Daisy stand a chance staying in there? Jenna needs all of her attention at the moment, and that's the way it is: I'm just an afterthought. And if I'm an afterthought, then Daisy would... Well, she'd only stay in Mum's brain for about five seconds.

I thought of calling the police myself and even dialled the number that night before realising how stupid I was going to sound when I spoke to someone. It's not illegal to have a black eye. And it's definitely not illegal to fall down the stairs. If that's what Daisy was going to tell them, then there'd be nothing they could do. Nothing anyone could do.

The doorbell rings. Roscoe barks and I finish my cereal and answer it. It's Daisy.

'Morning!' she beams, all sunshine and smiles. I stare at her, like she isn't real. The bruise has completely gone.

'Alex!' Mum calls from the kitchen. 'Who is it?'

I just stare and stare at the smiling girl in the doorway, not knowing whether to laugh or cry.

'It's me, Mrs Duncan!' Daisy calls back as Mum emerges from behind me in the hallway.

'Oh, good morning! I thought you said Daisy wasn't walking with you to school this morning, Alex?'

'I didn't think she was,' I mutter, finally finding my voice and grabbing my rucksack and coat.

'Did you have a nice Christmas, Daisy?' Mum asks, scooping up a dribbling Roscoe who had been slowly making his way towards the open door.

'Yes, thank you,' Daisy replies without missing a beat. 'How was yours?'

'Lovely, thank you. Oh, Alex!' Mum hands me my hat from the hook as I step outside. 'Don't forget this.'

'Thanks, Mum. 'Bye.' I slam the door behind me.

'What?' Daisy asks.

'You know what!'

Daisy pulls my hat onto her head and pops a piece of bubble gum in her mouth. She turns around and makes sure no one's behind us.

'Where has your…' I gesture to my eye. 'Your bruise gone?'

'Shh!' she hisses, pulling the hat further over her head. 'It's faded away. Bruises do that.'

I stare at her; she can't be serious.

'Stop looking at me!'

'How can I not look at you, Daisy?' I snap. 'I haven't seen you in over a week! You haven't been answering my texts or calls. And when we did last see each other…' I double-check behind me before lowering my voice, 'you had a massive black eye!'

Daisy sighs and blows a large bubble. 'You mean the tiny bruise I had?'

I can't believe it. Is she really gonna down-play this? Pretend it never happened? This must mean—my stomach drops at the thought—that she definitely didn't fall down the stairs. She's hiding something. Someone hurt her.

'Daisy.' I struggle to keep my voice level to hide the fear and anger bubbling inside of me. 'We both know it wasn't a tiny bruise.'

'You're overreacting!' she laughs, handing me a piece of bubble gum. 'Here. Let's see who can blow the biggest bubble.'

I take it from her silently. The last thing I want to do is let this go and pretend nothing happened. The second-to-last thing I want to do is shout at her and make her run away again.

'Did you see that one? It was huge!' Daisy scrapes the gum off her face, grinning. I manage a small smile back at her, my mind ticking over. I need advice. From a grown-up, but not Mum or Dad. Gran? No, she's got enough on her plate.

'Good morning!' A teacher is stood in the distance by the school gates, greeting the pupils loudly and waving at parents. It's Mrs Moss. Mrs Moss will help me.

'Come on, your turn,' Daisy says impatiently. I chew the gum for a moment then blow a bubble, tiny in comparison to Daisy's.

'Pathetic!' she snorts. 'Watch this.'

I watch her, my anger melting away at the sight of her frizzy hair and freckles. Okay, I'll pretend nothing happened. For now. But I will help you, Daisy. I promise.

*

3:03 am. That's the time right now. I've been awake since 2 am after a very realistic Jenna nightmare. It was maybe the scariest one yet, and not in a creepy-monster way.

She was lying on her hospital bed, taking her last breaths. When the machine went 'beeeeeep' and she died, nothing happened. Her spirit didn't leave her body, she didn't become a ghost, she wasn't carried up to Heaven by angels. She just stayed there, no longer thinking or feeling, waiting to be buried in the cold, dark earth all by herself. She wasn't a person anymore. She was just a body, just the shell of my sister, silent and still, not at peace but not awake. Just... dead. And there was nothing anyone could do, except cry. We all cried.

I even woke up crying. Surely there can't be nothing after death? There must be something after life, something beyond all this. There has to be.

Since waking up I've been sat at my desk, scrapbook open, working on lists. Lists and lists and lists of places to go and people to speak to and research to do to find an answer.

Mrs Moss was right: I won't be at peace until I know what's going to happen to Jenna. I don't think Jenna will be at peace either. It needs to happen sooner rather than later, this whole investigation and, once I've counted all the places I need to go and people I need to see, I realise I can't do this alone. I just can't.

I carefully write 'Daisy and Cal??' at the bottom of one of the lists. I think if I ask them, I won't feel as alone in this. I can get it done much quicker. I can get second opinions when I need it. It might help Daisy take her mind off things.

I think about Daisy now and how she acted yesterday, so carefree and confident. It's like when we met back on Boxing Day she was a completely different person.

When I tried to tell Mrs Moss about the situation at school yesterday, she wasn't very helpful.

'I understand it must be difficult, Alex, to see your friend upset,' she'd said after I told her I knew someone in trouble. 'Teenagers do go through phases when life can seem very difficult. If you'd just tell me a little more, I might be able to—'

'No, no.' I shook my head. 'That's all I can say. She's in trouble, I just know it.'

'In trouble how?' Mrs Moss persisted. 'With a boyfriend? At school?'

I don't bloody know.

'How do you know that she's in trouble? Has she told you?'

Not exactly.

'Is she a student here, Alex? Because we have a fantastic pastoral team who—'

'It doesn't matter!' I snapped. God, why were people so nosy? All I needed was a simple answer, some plain advice. Not that much to ask, was it?

Mrs Moss sighed. 'Look, I can't force you to tell me anything, Alex. But if you're not willing to tell me more about your friend, how can I support her?'

I shrugged. 'I just wanted some help.'

She made a note in her little book. 'You know I'm always here to help you. And your friend, too, if she'd like. Why don't you tell her that she can come to my office anytime, hmm? Just say I'm free for drop-ins. You can mention it casually, so she wouldn't suspect a thing.'

So I did. I told Daisy that Mrs Moss had 'casually mentioned' that her door was always open. She didn't really say anything, but she did smile. And I think, more than anything, she was happy I was trying to help. That's all I want to do, Daisy. Help you.

I place my pen down, thinking. I have so damn much to think about that sometimes it all becomes a blur. One thing's for sure though: now I've told a grown-up about Daisy, I've done what I can do. Until she tells me more about what really happened, my hands are tied. If she does need anything else, she knows I'm here: and Callum, too, I guess.

But right now, the main thing on my mind is Jenna, and how I need to find her an answer to the biggest question ever. So that means starting this quest properly as soon as I can. There's no more time to waste.

Chapter Thirteen

'What do you mean, find out what's beyond?' Daisy asks.
'I mean, what's after life. What happens when you die,'
I explain. 'Look, I need to know. I need to. And I know Jenna
needs to know too—'

'How do you know Jenna wants an answer?' Daisy interrupts
me. 'Have you spoken to her about it?'

'Look, I know she does,' I insist. 'I just do. I need to do this one
thing for her. I need to find out where she's going to go.'

'Mate,' Callum says uncomfortably. 'How on Earth are we
gonna do this? We're only kids. How are we gonna find the answer
to life's biggest mystery?'

'We're not kids!' I snap. 'I'm fifteen soon. And anyway, we're
gonna look where people haven't looked before. We're gonna do
loads of research. We'll find the answer.'

We walk through the school gates slowly together. My heart's
pounding in my chest. I knew as soon as I woke up this morning
that today was the day to ask them. Who knows how much time
we have left?

'Please,' I touch Daisy's arm. 'I need you two to help me.'

Callum rolls his eyes, but Daisy looks deep in thought. 'You
know, he's right,' she tells Callum. 'There has to be an explanation,
an answer. I think we should help Alex find it.'

'But…' Callum sighs deeply. 'Okay. Yes, Al, I'll help you.'

'Me too,' Daisy says firmly. I feel a weight lift off my shoulders.
The ball is finally rolling.

*

'Hey, Al.' Jenna's waiting by the door when I get in, shoes and coat on, ready to go.

'Hi. You going out?'

'We're going out. I'm dying for a McDonald's Coke.' She reaches across me and grabs her car keys. 'Come on.'

As we ride in the car, Jenna tells me about her day—TV dramas and homemade hot chocolates and phone calls with Kent—barely pausing for breath.

'All sounds… I mean, I'd better get one of those hot chocolates.'

She raises her eyebrows, pulling into the drive through. 'Were you even listening?'

'Sure I was!' I was. Well, I was trying to. It's sort of hard to think of anything other than my conversation with Daisy and Callum right now. But I can't tell Jenna that, obviously. She can't know about any of this unless—until—we get a proper answer. She orders us two Cokes and we pull into a parking space.

'You're so brave, Jenna.' Ugh, I hate the sound of my own voice when it comes to this stuff. I'm crap at it. I'm crap at everything, really. But I need to say it. After hearing all that about her whole day and she didn't even mention once how sick she's feeling… 'I wouldn't even know you were ill, the way you're smiling and laughing all the time. But you don't need to pretend, not to me. You can talk about how bad you're feeling… If you are feeling bad, obviously… I mean, I hope you're not… You know what I mean. Like you said, we can all have down days. And you can tell me about it, if you are.'

Well, you made a huge mess of that. Well done, Al. Next time just keep your bloody mouth shut.

Jenna smiles, though. 'Thank you, I know I can. And you can tell me anything, too.' She sips her drink. 'When did you get so wise, little bro?'

I shrug. 'I've always been the one with the brains.'

'Ha!' She punches my arm. 'Anyway, you're the one who's meant to be having up and down days, you teenage brat. How're things going with Daisy?'

I feel myself go a bit red. 'What do you mean?'

'You know what I mean!' She rolls her eyes. 'Fine, don't tell me. You'll come crawling back for girl advice sooner or later. I was your age once you know. I know just how teenage boys' minds work!'

'Yeah, yeah.'

'I do! Ah, I remember my first boyfriend, Johnny. Do you remember him? What a stud.'

'Nope. Gross.' I finish my Coke. 'And boys' minds work different to girls' anyway, you know-it-all.'

'Nope.' She shakes her head. 'Trust me. Love in your teenage years works both ways.'

We'll see about that. My mind's not on romance right now, anyway. Like I said, it's on the quest my friends have just agreed to join me on. And where exactly we're going to start.

*

'So what do Christians really believe in, anyway?'

Callum, Daisy and I are walking to church. It's almost eleven so we're a little behind schedule—Daisy was ten minutes late—but that's okay. It's not like I called ahead to make an appointment with a Priest or anything: if that's even possible. Anyway, after going over my lists last night, I decided the most logical place to start would be with religion: more specifically, Christianity. So here we are, walking down to our local church, armed with notepads and a voice recorder and lunch money, finally taking the first step on our mission. And it feels right. It feels kinda exciting.

'Callum, we learn about this every year in school,' Daisy rolls her eyes. 'They believe in one God. And that Jesus died on the cross for our sins. And—'

'I know, I know,' Callum interrupts. 'I mean what do they think happens when... when we die?'

'Well that's what we're going to find out,' I say firmly. I feel confident. The awkwardness and anger I felt towards Daisy a couple days ago has vanished; Mrs Moss has spoken to her, and I think she's getting the help that she needs. She'll tell me what really happened when she's ready. In the meantime she knows I'm here for her. She looks lovely today, with her hair in tight plaits. She's skipping ahead of Callum and I now, one earphone in, probably listening to some random Indie band or something. My heart skips along with her.

'When are you gonna ask her out?' Callum whispers, jabbing me with his elbow.

'What?' I laugh uneasily.

Callum rolls his eyes. 'You two are practically together anyway. You should ask her to be your girlfriend!'

'Why would you say that?' I laugh again awkwardly. Dammit. I thought I'd been subtle, never staring too long or texting too much. Obviously not.

'Come on, mate. I'm your best friend! I know these things,' Callum winks. 'Plus you can never take your eyes off her.'

Daisy trips slightly and laughs to herself before kicking the kerb with her huge black boot.

'She's crazy if you ask me,' Callum mutters.

She's wonderful.

'We're here!' Daisy sings. We stand by the churchyard, gazing up at the building. I'd forgotten how huge it is, with its spire touching the clouds. The churchyard itself is eerily quiet and so well-kept it looks like all the blades of grass are exactly the same length.

'Looks like my mum does the gardening here,' I joke to fill the silence. 'Come on.'

We traipse through the gates—two boys in hoodies, one girl in dungarees—and follow the path to the church door. It's closed.

'Shall we open it?' Callum whispers. Before I can answer, Daisy pushes the door; it opens with a slow groan.

'Daisy!' Callum hisses. We all hesitate for a moment.

'Do you think we're even allowed in?' I ask quietly.

'Why are we all whispering?' Daisy asks, her voice sounding too loud as it echoes round the big space inside. 'It's a church. They're always open, right?' She steps inside slowly and Callum and I follow.

Inside the church is just how I remember it from school

services when we used to come here, years ago. We have photos on our landing of Jenna and I doing an Easter service, carrying those massive candles around and wearing funny robes. It feels so different inside from how I remember it being back then: there are no kids hymns, no teachers shepherding us to our seats, no warmth from the flames. It's empty and cold and somehow unwelcoming. I know that's probably disrespectful to say, but it's true. I feel somehow like we've disturbed a sleeping beast, one that lies still and quiet until it's filled up with people. Not until it's poked by three nosey teenagers.

'Where is everyone?' Daisy wanders further inside and Callum and I follow her, our footsteps echoing through the building.

'Wow.' She stops to gaze at the mosaic windows. 'They're beautiful.'

Like you, I want to reply, but I don't of course. I never do. I smile at her instead, taking in the wonder in her eyes as she comments on the colours and the detail of the stained glass, her head tilted upwards, the light hitting her face.

'Can I help you?'

We all jump at the sound of the deep voice from behind us. Whirling round, I see it's the priest—well, I assume it's the priest from what he's wearing. He doesn't seem angry at us for letting ourselves in; he's actually smiling as though we're a pleasant surprise. Suddenly, I don't feel as much like we're trespassers.

'Hello. We just came to see if we could maybe ask you some questions?' I walk toward him, Daisy and Callum following.

'Of course.' The priest shakes his sleeve to check his watch. 'The morning service starts in half-an-hour.' He gestures to the nearest pew and takes a seat. I slide awkwardly in next to him, followed by Daisy while Callum dithers at the end. 'How can I help you?'

'Well…' I scramble around in my rucksack for my notebook and pen, and Daisy immediately begins doing the same for her voice recorder. 'I'd just like to know, really, what you think… What you think happens after death.'

The priest looks slightly taken aback. Daisy presses the Record button and holds it out towards him eagerly.

'What's that?'

'A voice recorder,' Daisy explains. 'We're hoping to document our findings.'

'Findings for what?' he asks hesitantly.

Daisy glances at me and I sigh. I suppose I should have known a group of teenagers can't just waltz in and demand to know about life-after-death without giving an explanation. Especially when they're recording the conversations. No doubt the poor man probably thinks he'll end up in a YouTube video or something.

'My sister has cancer.' I flip open my notebook and rest it on my lap. 'She's going to die. I'm trying to figure out what... where she's going to go. When it happens.' My voice sounds as matter-of-fact as I feel about the whole thing today. Like I said, sometimes the numbness takes over. And I'm grateful for it right now; it means I can stay professional. We are here to do a job, after all.

His face softens. 'I'm very sorry to hear about your sister,' the priest says gravely. 'Very sorry indeed. What an awful predicament.'

'Thank you,' I say without really meaning it. I always say thank you when people say sorry about Jenna. It's what you're supposed to say, right? Thank you for apologising on behalf of this hideous illness that's slowly taking my sister away and ruining her family and friends' lives.

'We just want to know,' Daisy presses on, 'what you think will happen to her.'

'Well.' The priest shifts in the pew, looking a little uncomfortable. 'I believe that, when your sister passes on, her spirit will leave her body and go to Heaven. Where she will be at peace with God.'

I make a note of this.

'How will we know, Mr Priest, that her spirit has left her body?' Daisy asks, holding the voice recorder under her own mouth then putting it back under the priest's like a microphone. Callum turns away to hide his sniggering. Usually I'd be laughing along with him but now's not the time. Now's the time to ask, listen and learn.

'Please, call me Father David,' the priest smiles. 'And, unfortunately, there is no clear physical indication to the outside world of when her spirit leaves. It happens undetected.'

'So there's no evidence to back this up?' Daisy clarifies. Callum makes another noise and strolls back over to the windows, pretending to admire them. It suddenly starts to feel awkward between Daisy and the priest, between all of us. Daisy, though I know she's just trying to be thorough, doesn't sound like she believes Father David one bit.

'Anyway,' I interrupt before he can answer, 'what is there in Heaven, Father David?'

He seems just as uncomfortable with my question. 'There really is no straightforward answer to that, I'm afraid. I'd like to believe it is a place in which you can have no more suffering; a place to be united with God.'

I consider this, jotting down the words, 'Heaven united with God.' Our family's never really been religious. Jenna and I did church services with school. We go to christenings and weddings and funerals in churches and join in with the hymns and prayers. But it's not like I sit and pray on my own to God. I don't think Jenna does either.

'We don't go to church,' I tell him. 'No offence. But, do you think that matters? Do you think Jenna will still get to go to Heaven?'

Father David smiles and nods. 'It's never too late to commit yourself to God. And if you haven't been as devoted recently, He shall forgive. Jesus died on the Cross so we shall be forgiven for our sins.'

I make a note of this, too, but I'm not sure about that. If I was God, and someone never spoke to or even believed in me, I don't think I'd let them into my Heaven.

'So how long does a spirit stay in Heaven?' Daisy asks.

'For eternity,' Father David answers simply.

'And how do you know that?'

I shoot Daisy a warning look but she ignores me, holding the voice recorder by Father David's mouth again.

Luckily, he doesn't seem annoyed. 'I believe in the all-knowing, all-loving power of our Lord. He cares for us all unconditionally and wants us all to be happy and safe, both in this life and the next.

If you've been a good person and lived a good life, you shall return to be with God. You shall be at peace.' He turns to me. 'Again, I'm deeply sorry to hear of your sister. Please do let us know if there's anything the Church can do to help.'

Our cue to leave. 'Thank you, Father David.' We all stand and he shakes my hand.

'If you'll excuse me, I have to prepare for the service now. You're welcome to stay and join us, of course?'

'We've got to get back. Thanks though,' Daisy answers for me. Father David nods and makes his way to a door at the back of the church.

'Well. That wasn't massively helpful.' Again, Daisy speaks too loudly as he disappears out of sight.

'Daisy!' I hiss. 'Shh! And you were pretty rude to him!'

'Was I?' she asks in a tone of voice that clearly states she doesn't care if she was or not. A tiny part of me feels a little miffed with how she behaved, but I know she wasn't deliberately trying to be annoying. She was just trying to get to the bottom of it all.

'Come on,' Callum waves at us from the doorway and we follow him back out into the churchyard. Daisy carefully shuts the door behind us.

'So, what do you think?' Callum asks as we begin back down the pathway to the gate.

'I dunno,' I say. 'I mean, like Daisy—rudely—said,' I raise my eyebrow at her, 'it wasn't a huge amount to go on.'

'And there's no evidence,' Daisy points out, leaning on a nearby gravestone. 'It's not like the spirits come back down to Earth and tell everyone all about Heaven.'

'Daisy!' I hiss. 'Get off that!'

'I don't think that's the point,' Callum laughs as Daisy pats the gravestone. 'There's no evidence as such for any of these religious beliefs, is there? It's just what people believe in. From the Bible and stuff.'

'But does that make it any less real?' I wonder aloud. 'I mean, does everything have to be backed up? Look around us; all these people chose to rest right here, outside the church. To be with

God, do you think?' We all take a moment to look around. There are rows and rows of gravestones, all different shapes and sizes, sort of like sets of mismatched teeth. It makes me shudder a little, the thought of all of the people under the ground we're standing on. Well, their bodies are under the ground. Their souls are... somewhere else?

'Well c'mon,' Callum says after a moment. 'This place is giving me the creeps. And going back to your question, Al, I think you should be telling us the answer to that. You're the clever one!'

I know what science tells us. And I know it's not to believe anything without real tests and real evidence. But can science itself ever be wrong?

'If there's a Heaven then there's got to be a Hell,' Daisy says solemnly. 'I wonder what that's like.'

'You better not be implying that Jenna's going to Hell,' I joke warningly, nudging her. She nudges me back and I catch Callum's eye—he winks at me.

'Of course I'm not implying that, dummy!' Daisy squeals. Her stomach rumbles loudly. 'Hmm. Time to eat I think. Shall we lunch, boys?'

'I've got...' Callum slows down and scrapes the change out of his pocket. 'Three quid. Decent, if the sandwiches have been reduced.'

'I could murder some sushi,' Daisy whines, holding her stomach. 'To town! Race you!' She breaks off into a sprint, her plaits flying behind her.

'Why does she still act like she's about five, half the time?' Callum growls, half smiling. I shrug. That's just part of who she is. The excitement, the dramatics, the rollercoaster of happiness and sadness and immaturity that is Daisy.

'You think it was worth the trip today?' Callum asks as we follow her down the street.

'It was a good starting point,' I say truthfully. I sort of agree with Daisy; the information Father David gave us wasn't massively detailed or backed up with real stories. But I like the concept of Jenna being safe and peaceful, with someone who will care for her and forgive her. 'We'll have to look into the whole Heaven thing a bit more.'

'Sure,' Callum agrees. 'Like, no offence to the priest, but when he was talking, I just thought, what a load of nothing. But then, when I was looking at those crazy windows Daisy loves so much, I thought about how many people actually believe in it. In God, and Heaven and Jesus and everything. And then I thought, how can that many people be wrong?'

Chapter Fourteen

Our visit with Father David proved more useful than originally thought. When I got home that afternoon, I went straight on the laptop and, after a couple hours, had pages and pages of notes on what I'd discovered.

Turns out there is some sort of evidence, after all. In magazine interviews and YouTube videos and blogs there are hundreds, maybe thousands, of people claiming they went to Heaven, or had visits from their dead loved ones' spirits. Okay, some are clearly crazy; there was an eight-page-long post written by a man who was sure the spirit of his chihuahua was opening his Bible every night. But there was some realistic stuff too, by people who seemed in a pretty sound mental state.

I've compiled a few of the most interesting, real-looking videos and burned them onto a blank DVD. I'm sitting now, hours later, at my desk, surrounded by the day's work and deciding where to go next.

I shuffle my papers so the general 'Religion' page is at the top. Underneath is a list of all the different religions to explore: Christianity, Hinduism, Buddhism... I stare at the words so long they start to not even look like words anymore. Is there any point looking into all of these different religions? They all probably have very similar ideas about what happens when we die—they all believe in a God, right? So they must all think we go to Heaven, like Father David and the Christians?

Maybe I shouldn't be too quick to jump to those sorts of conclusions. Don't be narrowminded, Alex. Still, maybe I should do some computer research into them before dragging Callum and

Daisy around to all the different places of worship. I might save us a trip or two. Having formed some sort of structured(ish) plan for tomorrow, I slide all the loose pages back into the scrapbook, switch off the light and jump onto the bed, suddenly exhausted. All this researching and interviewing and discovering is tiring.

I'm just closing my eyes and envisioning Daisy's face when the front door slams loudly and Roscoe barks. It's almost 1 am.

'Shhhh, shhhhh,' someone's hissing downstairs.

An intruder? My heart thumping, I climb out of bed and open my bedroom door a crack. Mum and Dad's door is shut, as is Jenna's. How they're sleeping through this racket, I'll never know. Whoever's downstairs is now clanking around the kitchen while Roscoe snorts excitedly.

Who the hell is in our house? Someone with a key, as there was no sound of a breaking window or anything. Someone who's been here before, because otherwise Roscoe would still be barking. Kent? Daisy? I grab the baseball bat from where it was leaning against my wall and slowly make my way downstairs, not sure who I'm going to see but certain that I have to go and find out. Controlling my breath, I tiptoe towards the kitchen and slowly push open the door.

And there she is. Jenna. Grating—without much success—a block of cheese while sitting on the kitchen counter.

'Jenna! What the hell?' I drop the bat. Roscoe ambles over and I pick him up, stroking him to calm him down. He's obviously just as surprised as I am.

'Good morning, little brother,' Jenna drawls loudly, hopping down from the counter. She looks as far from the real Jenna as possible. She's wearing a wig, one I haven't seen before; blonde and waist-length, like Barbie. Her clothes are... Well, Dad wouldn't let her out in that outfit let's just say that. She's heavily made-up too; her eyelashes look like they've multiplied by a million. Toast springs out of the toaster with a sudden noise, making her jump. She laughs.

'Toastie, toastie.' She scoops up handfuls of the grated cheese and presses it onto the toast.

'Careful!' I put Roscoe down and walk over to the counter to help her. I can't help laughing at the sight of the burnt bread covered in squashed, grated cheddar.

'What?' Jenna sniggers, pouring the last handful of cheese directly into her mouth. 'I'm making cheese-on-toast.'

'I don't think this is how Mum usually makes it,' I tell her, trying to stop laughing. She takes the two slices and totters over to the breakfast bench.

'Are you… drunk?'

Jenna laughs loudly.

'Shh! You'll wake Mum and Dad.' I sweep the remainder of the cheese and crumbs off the counter and put them in the bin.

'Yes. Yes Alex, I have had a slight drink.' She speaks with her mouth full, looking pleased with herself. I've seen her like this a few times before, when she used to sneak in late at night still dressed in those sorts of clothes, mumbling to herself and fixing toast and water before crawling up to bed. Right now sort of reminds me of that. Of a time when she was happier and healthier and just a normal girl her age: going out to clubs and pubs and parties. In that way, weirdly, it's kind of nice to see her swaying on the stool now, cramming the last of the toast into her mouth and giggling. Roscoe sits beneath her, catching the scraps.

'Where'd you go?' I ask, taking a seat next to her. She swings round to look at me, swallowing her last mouthful and wiping her mouth on the back of her hand.

'Just to town. With some friends.' She stares at me for a moment and then burps.

'Jenna!' I stifle a laugh. 'Stop being so loud. You'll wake Mum and Dad.'

'Pardon me,' she says formally, patting her stomach. 'That was just my belly saying how delicious that snack was.'

'Good. Did you have a nice time out?'

She leaps up. 'Yeah, man! I had a dance. I can still dance, Al! Look!' I really don't want to look, but I do anyway. And, God, it's awful. Jenna's never had great rhythm—something I think we both got from Dad—but it's safe to say now's the worst I've ever seen it. She looks like she's trying to move her body like a worm while her arms do the Robot. Oh, and head-banging as if the best rock song ever is on.

'Well done.'

'Wait, there's more...' She switches to ballet-style, tiptoeing about Roscoe in a circle. In what I'm sure is an escape attempt, he tries to shuffle over to his bed but Jenna swoops down and lifts him up, clinging him close to her chest and swaying.

'Okay, okay.' I prise Roscoe off her before she smears her make-up all over him.

'See?' She flops back down, slightly out of breath. 'I can still dance. I can still do everything.'

I know I should say something. Something encouraging, like, 'I know you can. You're still my sister. You're still you.' But I don't. I don't because that's not entirely true. And the only thing worse than not saying anything would be saying a lie. So we sit in silence for a moment, Jenna slumped in her seat, her eyes fluttering weirdly. I'm not sure whether I should suggest she goes to bed or not.

'Water.' She states suddenly, sitting upright. 'Some H2O.'

'Right.' I slip off the stool and pour her a big glass from the bottle in the fridge. She gulps it down in one.

'More please.'

I pour her another glass, watching as she downs half of it messily before slamming it down.

'Jenna! You've got to be quiet,' I beg, putting the bottle back in the fridge. 'Mum and Dad will be so mad if they wake up. Do they know where you've been?'

'No,' Jenna shrugs defensively, itching her head. 'They think I was at Kent's. Ugh this wig is so bloody itchy!' She pulls it off and throws it on the floor. Roscoe pads over to it, sniffing excitedly.

'You've... it's all gone,' I comment feebly. I hadn't realised she'd shaved the last patches of her hair completely off. She's properly bald now.

'Yes.' She runs her hand over her head. 'It's smooth. Wanna feel?'

'No thanks,' I say awkwardly. I can't think of anything worse than stroking Jenna's bald, drunk head right now.

'Oh my God!' she shrieks suddenly, pointing to the floor. I look past her to see Roscoe cocking his leg and weeing on Jenna's wig.

'Roscoe! No!' I step towards him and he scuttles away but it's too late; the wig is quite clearly sat in a pile of dog urine. I look at Jenna, unsure of what to say. Even though her shoulders are shaking, she's not sad. She's laughing. Laughing like she's just seen the funniest thing ever. Her mouth open wide, the kitchen light bouncing off her bald head, she's sat, shaking with laughter. I haven't seen her laugh this way in months. I know I should shush her again and be the sensible one but I can't help it. I start laughing too.

*

Monday. A new day. A new week. A week I'm actually feeling pretty good about.

Instead of researching all day like I'd planned to yesterday, I spent the day with Jenna. She eventually crawled out of her room at about midday and we took a drive to McDonald's and ate Happy Meals in the car, music turned right up, not talking but just singing along and munching away. Even though she was wearing sunglasses and kept chugging back water and making the occasional retching noise, it was the happiest I've seen her in ages.

We'd decided not to go home straight away—Mum and Dad would only be their usual annoying selves—so we took a drive to the bowling alley. We played two games and I won both. Jenna said it was because she was weak, and that I was mean not to let a cancer victim win, but she was only joking. I think.

'Happy Monday!' Daisy sings as I swing open the door. 'So what did you get?'

'What?'

'What did you get? You know, on the research,' she whispers, bending down to pat Roscoe who has ambled over to her even slower than usual.

'Shh!' I check behind me for my snooping Mum but, luckily,

she's washing-up in the kitchen. 'Come on.' I hand her my hat and push her outside before she does any real damage.

'Okay, okay,' she laughs, pulling the hat on her head. 'Someone's grumpy this morning.'

'Nope,' I insist. 'Genuinely. I've had a great weekend.'

'Oh.' Daisy sounds taken back. Probably because it's the first time I've told her I'd had a good weekend since the announcement. 'What did you get up to?'

'Not much. I had fun hanging out with you and Callum on Saturday. And then me and Jenna spent the day together yesterday.' I feel myself growing hot at the memory of Daisy running ahead of me from the church, her plaits flying behind her, and kick a stone for something to do.

'Aw, that's cool.' She doesn't mention my red face and instead unwraps some bubble gum. 'Want some?'

'Sure.' I hold out my hand, but she pops it straight in my mouth instead. Okay. I'm definitely red now.

'We're going to a party this weekend,' she announces after a moment, tossing her hair back and readjusting her—my—hat. 'Stacey's. She told me to invite you and Cal.'

'Oh.' Now it's my turn to be taken back. Party? Me? Stacey? I run the name through my brain, but I don't think I know who she is. 'Stacey who?'

'Stacey Willis, silly!' Daisy laughs. 'Don't look so scared! It'll be fun. Your first grown-up party.'

'What do you mean, grown-up party?' I ask suspiciously.

'I mean a party with alcohol,' Daisy says, a wicked little smile on her face.

My stomach flips at this. The only time I've ever tried any form of alcohol was last New Year's Eve when I was allowed one small blue WKD. But I've seen the effect it has on Jenna and my Dad. I'm not sure I want any more.

'Well, I thought we were going to do some more research next weekend,' I say quickly. 'We can't if we're hungover!'

'Sure we can,' Daisy insists, blowing a huge bubble. 'Did you see that? Ha-ha!'

She carries on chatting about outfits and timings and drinks but I'm barely listening. I can't really go to this party, can I? Would Mum let me? Even if she did, would I want to go?

*

'Alex.'

I've zoned out again. In my mind I was on a dancefloor with my arms around Daisy. The world had seemed a lot slower.

'Are you all right?'

No.

'Yes,' I lie to Mrs Moss. I don't want to talk about Daisy today.

'Good. Now where were we... Your research. How is that going?' She leans forward in her chair.

I shrug and avoid eye contact.

'You can be honest with me, Alex,' she says gently. 'This is a safe space, you know that. Have you made any worthwhile findings yet?'

The phrase 'safe space' sort of makes me want to be sick in my mouth. Nowhere's safe from Jenna's cancer. But Mrs Moss is trying; she's one of the few that still does, I suppose.

'Not really,' I tell her honestly. 'It's difficult, you know? We're looking into religion at the moment.'

Mrs Moss nods eagerly and makes a note. 'Great place to start, Alex. Which religious beliefs have you explored so far?'

I cast my mind back to my internet findings.

'Sort of all of them, generally. Most of them believe there's some sort of Heaven where you go when you die, if you've been good.'

'Yes, that's right,' she nods encouragingly. 'A safe space where they can be at peace.'

'Yes.'

There's silence for a moment. A million thoughts are rushing through my mind, like they did when we spoke to Father David. Heaven. Hell. Good and bad. There are so many factors to the theories, so many unanswered questions. Like, what is Heaven? Where is Heaven? Maybe Mrs Moss will have an idea.

'The priest we spoke to,' I say carefully, 'Wasn't too specific about things. I just... Well, what do you think, Mrs Moss, about Heaven?'

She sighs a little.

'I mean, if it exists,' I hurry on, 'and you believe in it. But if not... I mean, all these people believe in a Heaven and a Hell. But where are they? Why has no one ever found them? And why don't people visit us from Heaven?'

Mrs Moss takes a deep breath. 'Well, Alex... To be completely honest, I think my personal beliefs in this situation don't matter in the slightest. And as for your questions, I don't know the answers. Like we said before, you'll come across a lot of questions on this voyage that people won't be able to answer for you. They're questions that maybe don't have answers, and that's something you'll need to accept.'

I know what she's trying to say. It's what they all try and say: that I'll never find the answer. I feel like the bubble of stress inside of me is about to pop and explode all over Mrs Moss. Like an actual bubble, one you can blow with a tube of gunk in the garden on a hot sunny day with your big sister, who has a full head of hair and a huge smile, while your mum and dad sit and laugh on the deckchairs, not drinking alcohol, just lemonade—

'Alex.'

'It's the least I can do.'

'I'm sorry?' Mrs Moss leans in. My voice came out as a whisper; I clear my throat.

'I said it's the least I can do. You know, find out where Jenna's going. It's the least I can do.'

'Oh, Alex.' She turns away from me and grabs a tissue from the packet on the side. 'That's... I mean...' She trails off, her voice cracking. I don't think she wants to talk any more so I end the session there. Sometimes I think speaking to her doesn't help anyone, least of all Mrs Moss. She just ends up sad or confused.

Chapter Fifteen

It's here. Party night.

I look at myself in the mirror, readjusting my hair for the hundredth time. Skinny jeans, trainers, River Island T-shirt. I don't know if I look dressed up enough. Or casual enough. Maybe I should gel my hair some more? I slowly reach for the gel pot, not taking my eyes off the mirror. No: enough gel. Behind me, I can see my litre bottle of blue WKD, staring at me. When Mum brought it home I was so shocked I asked if it was supposed to last me a few parties.

'No, silly!' she'd laughed. 'But of course, don't feel like you have to drink it all.'

She'd been surprisingly easy to convince, both to let me attend the party and to buy me alcohol. She seemed even a little excited about it, offering to give Daisy, Callum and I a lift to Stacey's house. Jenna said she'd pick us up at the end of the night; she said if it was Mum doing it, she'd be outside by ten-thirty, waving at everyone and generally being embarrassing.

'Alex?' Mum pushes the door open gently. I leap back from the mirror and pick up a can of deodorant for something to hold. 'Aww. Don't you look handsome!' she smiles, reaching forward and straightening my shirt. 'Shall we take a picture?'

'No, Mum!' I back away from her shaking my head. I can already picture it: her latest online post. 'My beautiful baby boy off to his first real party! Xxx'. Comments from Aunty May and her work friends: 'Aw how sweet!' and 'Isn't he handsome.'

Yuck. I think not.

'Oh, okay. Well, we'd better get going.' Mum picks up the

WKD.

'Mum! It's only seven.' We're supposed to be picking Daisy and Callum up at half-past.

'Well, there might be traffic,' Mum insists, heading downstairs and giving me no choice but to follow. I text Daisy and Callum quickly, warning we might be early, before I'm herded into the living room so that Dad and Jenna can laugh at me.

'Got enough gel in there?' Dad chuckles, gesturing with his beer bottle at my head. Damn it. I knew one of them would say something to make me feel self-conscious. Is it really too much? I touch my head lightly, wondering if it's too late to re-wash it and start again.

'Ignore him, sweetheart. You look lovely,' Mum coos, shooting Dad a look.

Jenna's curled up on the armchair with Kent, a blanket draped over her. She's in her pyjamas still; she's been in them all day. This weekend couldn't be more different from last. Today she's been tired and quiet, napping on and off all day in front of the TV. When I'd asked her for advice on what to wear earlier she'd ignored me, waving for me to go away with her skinny little hand. She sits up a bit straighter now, though, and gestures for me to come closer. I perch on the arm of the chair warily. I don't want any more comments about my hair.

'You look great, Al,' she whispers.

'Thank you,' I whisper back. Why are we whispering? She pats my arm weakly. Her hand is freezing.

'Sorry,' she breathes, curling back under her blanket.

'You're so cold.' I tuck her in. 'Do you need anything?'

'No. Just for you to go and have a great time tonight.' She smiles, a smile that doesn't quite look real, and curls up into an even tighter ball. She looks tiny.

'You look sharp, Al,' Kent nods. 'You'll have your pick of the ladies.'

'Erm, thanks.' I turn back to Jenna. 'Are you sure you still want to pick us up?' I'm a bit worried she won't be able to stay up; Daisy said I shouldn't expect the party to finish any earlier than twelve.

As in midnight.

'I'll do it if you want, Jen?' Kent offers.

'Don't be silly!' She jerks her head towards the door. 'I can pick my own brother up from his first party! Just call me when. Now go. Be safe.'

'Come on, Alex!' Mum calls from the hallway.

I wait for a moment, not sure whether to try and give Jenna a hug. But she's curled up too tightly and I'm too awkward, so up I get and off I go.

'So. Are you excited?' Mum asks as we climb into the car after a five-minute argument about firstly whether or not I should be taking a jacket and secondly if I should be taking a scarf.

'I dunno. Sort of,' I say, gripping the WKD bottle. 'I'm nervous.'

'Oh, sweetheart! Don't be. You'll have a lovely time,' Mum gushes. I'm not sure why my mum thinks that a group of young teenagers drinking alcohol in a crowded living room until midnight—or maybe later—is having a lovely time, but I don't object.

We pull up outside Daisy's bungalow first. As she swings open the front door and runs out, I'm taken back to Boxing Day. The day I waited and waited for an explanation. An explanation I am still yet to receive.

'Hi Mrs Duncan! Hi Alex!' She climbs into the backseat.

'Hello Daisy my love, how are you?' Mum asks.

'Fine, thank you. How are you?' Daisy's rustling around behind me. I turn to see her produce a small bottle of vodka from a Tesco bag. Vodka! Daisy laughs at my expression and puts a finger on her lips. I shake my head and, as she puts it away, I get a proper look at her. Beautiful as ever. Her eyes and cheeks look sparkly and her lips are pinker than normal. Her hair is extra curly and wild; my favourite style. I can't overly tell what she's wearing but it's silver and glittery and every bit as out-there as I'd expect.

'What number is Cal's, now?' Mum asks as we turn down his street.

'Fourteen. Just pull up here.' I point to the left-hand kerb in front of his house and we wait, in a sort of happy silence, for

Callum to appear. I'm not sure what this night has in store but I'm definitely feeling more positive about it since seeing Daisy in her sparkly dress.

We were too early. I knew we would be. There were only four other kids here when we arrived; two of them being Yusuf and Luca, who no doubt arrived at least an hour before the designated start time. There was music playing loudly, and a little disco light. On a long table sat plates of crisps and sweets with paper cups and litre bottles of cola and lemonade.

While Daisy danced with Stacey (who was in a very tight pink dress), Callum and I perched next to Yusuf and Luca and watched the girls. Callum talked about how nice Stacey's bum looked and Yusuf and Luca cracked up. Then I think we spoke about which other girls would be here tonight, and if they'd be in tight dresses too…

I dunno. I can't really remember now. I've finished my WKD and we've been here for at least two hours. A lot more people have arrived and the room's full of people. So many people. Some dancing, some by the snack table eating, some sat on sofas, some sat on the floor.

'Alex!' It's Daisy, right up in my face, smiling. 'Come on! Do you need a drink?' She's shouting because the music is so loud.

I'm not sure if I need a drink. I've finished my WKD already and I'm not thirsty. But I've heard lots of people asking other people that question here and they always say yes and then go and get one so I think that, yes, I do need a drink. She pulls me up off the sofa to the snack table, rummaging around underneath it for her vodka bottle.

'Why is it down there?' I ask.

'What?'

'Why is the vodka down there?' I repeat, raising my voice. I feel like whenever I try and talk the music gets turned up.

'I hid it,' she yells back. 'Otherwise people will drink it. Here.' She pours a small amount in both of the cups. 'It's a shot. You have to down it in one. Ready?'

No, I'm not sure that I am ready. But Daisy is, so I have to be.

I pick the cup up.

'One...' Daisy picks hers up too. 'Two... three!'

I pour the vodka down my throat. Oh my God. The worst burning sensation I've ever felt is scalding my throat. I feel as though my eyes are watering.

'Yuck!' Daisy pulls a face and pours two more.

'No, no, no,' I mumble, the taste of the last 'shot' still with me. Absolutely not.

'Come on, Alex! Just one more. It'll make you drunk. It's fun!' Daisy thrusts the cup into my hand.

I feel sick. I feel sick. But Daisy wants me to drink it. Daisy wants me to. So I do. Down in one, just like last time. It's even worse than the first one, if possible. Daisy laughs and tosses hers back too.

'Yay! And just one more...' She snatches the cup off me and starts pouring the poison in again. No, no, no. Not again.

'No,' I manage to say again and back away from the table.

'Aw, come on!' She holds it out to me, smiling. The Daisy smile. So pretty. But...

'I can't,' I shake my head. As much as I want to do anything that'll please her, I can't. I'll be sick. Possibly on her face. 'Sorry.'

Daisy stares at me for a moment, one hand on her hip, one holding the paper cup.

'Fine!' she shouts. Turning her head wildly, she then pulls John Groves, a boy in our class, by the sleeve and gestures to my cup still sat on the table. They start talking, but I can't hear what about. Daisy's laughing now, tossing her curly hair. They touch their paper cups together and drink the vodka. The sick feeling is one-hundred times worse now. I turn and push people out of the way to get to the toilet. Quickly, Alex, quickly. Don't be sick on the carpet. Don't ruin the party.

*

'Alex?'

Someone is saying my name.

'Alex!'

Someone is pounding on the door.

Slowly—I feel like I'm moving so slowly—I manage to move my arm and unlock it. There's Callum.

'What are you doing?' He's laughing.

I'm not sure what I'm doing so I'm not sure what to answer. I am lying on the bathroom floor, it seems.

'I am lying on the bathroom floor, it seems.' I tell him. This makes him laugh even more.

'Is that Alex Duncan?' A girl behind Callum peers over his shoulder.

'Hello there,' I say, in hopefully a smooth voice.

She joins in laughing with Callum. They're both acting like I'm the funniest thing they've ever seen. Now what I need to do is get off the bathroom floor. But how? I'm not sure my limbs work.

'I'm not sure my limbs work.' I announce. It's like everything I think just comes out of my mouth straight away.

'Come on mate, you're fine,' Callum pulls me up and leads me away from the bathroom, through the living room and outside into the back garden. 'There we go. Nice bit of cold, fresh air.'

Yes. Very cold. Not so fresh. There are people smoking. Callum and I stand in silence—well, I'm not sure if I'm standing; it feels like I'm swaying—watching them. I think they're the same school year as us, if not maybe only one year older. My skin crawls at the thought of putting a cigarette in my own mouth and inhaling all that disease.

'They rot your lungs, you know,' I point out loudly. They ignore me.

'Shut up!' Callum hisses, jabbing me with his skinny elbow. 'You'll get us into a fight.'

I sit down on the patio because I suddenly want to. Callum joins me. The cold on my bum and legs is strangely satisfying. I feel more alert now.

'So. Are you enjoying yourself?'

I consider the question. Am I enjoying myself? Is enjoying yourself not fully appreciating where you are and who's surrounding you? Is enjoying yourself being unsure of how long you were lying on Stacey Willis' bathroom floor? Is enjoying yourself feeling as though you may or not be sick at any given moment?

'No,' I reply eventually. 'I don't think so. Are you?'

'It's all right.' Callum offers me his beer bottle.

'No thank you.'

He laughs. 'Finished your WKD already?'

'I believe so.' I want to expand on this but I'm suddenly tired and talking feels like such a colossal effort. I want to close my eyes, just for a minute…

'Hey!' Callum snaps his fingers in front of my face. 'Wake up. No more napping.'

'Sorry.' I force myself to sit up straighter and widen my eyes.

'You not normally up past eleven?'

'It's not that. I think it's that vodka Daisy gave me.' The thought of the burning liquid makes me shudder.

'You had some? No way! She never let me have any!' Callum complains.

'Trust me. You don't want any.' Talking feels a bit easier now. I feel cold, very cold, almost too cold. 'She's handing it round to all the other boys, anyway.'

'Huh?'

Okay, maybe that was a slight exaggeration. 'She gave some to John.'

Callum grins suddenly and pokes me sharply in the rib. 'Are you jealous?'

'Ow! I'm not jealous!' I shuffle away from him slightly.

Callum clearly doesn't believe me and gives me another poke.

'Stop it!' I try and stand up. Mistake. Sitting back down.

'You okay?' Callum guides me by my arm back down to the patio. 'I was kidding, Alex. And anyway, you know Daisy. That's just how she is.'

I do know Daisy. Sort of.

'There's something you don't know about Daisy,' I say suddenly before I can even think about it properly. 'Something that happened on Boxing Day.'

*

My phone is ringing. I can feel it. Somewhere. Not back jeans pocket. Not front jeans pocket. Ah—jacket pocket. Hello.

'Hello.'

'Alex? Are you all right?' It's Jenna.

'Yes, thank you, how are you?' I shout over the music. I can't really hear her, but I presume she's asking about picking us up. 'Yes. You can pick us up now.' I can't hear if she answers or not, so I just repeat myself then hang up. The music's too loud.

Right. Must round up friends. I can't remember how much time has passed since I was in the garden with Callum; maybe minutes, maybe hours. I start back towards the garden, anyway. I spot Callum straight away, talking to Joe and some other football boys by the door.

'Jenna's on her way,' I call to him. He puts his thumb up and points to the door. 'Where's Daisy?'

'I don't know!' he shouts back. 'I'll meet you at the door in five.'

Searching for a red-headed girl in a sparkly dress would be much, much easier in a room less dark and crowded. Even the little disco light that was on earlier has been switched off; it's pretty much pitch-black. I don't know why Stacey wants everyone to look like faceless shadows at her party. I call Daisy's name over and over again and tap random people who averagely look like her from the back until I find her.

'Daisy,' I say for the hundredth time, and there she is, sat on the sofa, on another boy's lap; Larry someone-or-other.

'Hi, Alex!' She leaps up and throws her arms around me as if we haven't seen each other in years.

'It's time to go,' I say in her ear. 'Jenna's here now.'

'Oh, really! But it's only…' She checks her phone. 'Eleven-fifty-eight!'

I'm not sure why eleven-fifty-eight is not a reasonable time to leave so I just look at her. The sparkles have smudged off her eyes.

'Well. Jenna's here now,' I repeat after a minute. She stares at me for so long I don't think she's going to answer but eventually turns and says goodbye to Larry someone-or-other and the rest of the people squished up on the sofa and gets her things from underneath the snacks table. Thank God. I could never leave her alone here. And I don't want to be here a minute longer, I've decided. I don't feel dizzy or swaying anymore. I just feel thirsty and tired. And confused. Did I have a good time or not tonight? I can't work it out. I'm not sure if I ever will. I'll just add 'parties' to the list of things that don't make sense in my life right now.

Chapter Sixteen

I don't really know where today went, but it's 4 pm and I'm only just getting dressed. I woke up this morning—I think—and the day didn't feel real. I felt weird, like I was a cartoon or something. So I went back to sleep.

Mum knocked on my door at lunchtime with a sandwich and a drink for me, but I can't have eaten it because it's still on the side now. I just remember my head feeling fuzzy, like the TV when it's not connected to a channel and it's all static. And my stomach felt all knotted: like I needed to throw up, but I also needed a hamburger. God, it was horrible.

Anyway. Eventually Jenna woke me up and forced me to down the water Mum brought in and have a shower. I feel more alive now, but I'm not sure if the fuzzy headache will ever go away.

'Knock, knock!'

Jenna pushes open the door and sighs dramatically. 'Come on, lazy!'

'Why?' I pull the zip up on my hoodie.

'We're going for a Maccies, silly.' She looks me up and down for a minute. 'You look much better. Alive again! Mum will be so pleased.'

I follow her downstairs. 'Why? Was she worried?'

'Where are you two off to?' Mum appears in the hallway, arms folded. 'I'm not sure it's such a good idea for you to be going out, Alex.'

'He's fine!' Jenna insists before I can answer. 'He's showered so he doesn't stink now. As much.'

I flick her ear instinctively.

'Ow!' Jenna laughs, grabbing her keys.

'Really, Alex darling, are you feeling better?' Mum feels my forehead with the back of her hand. 'You've been in bed all day. I didn't realise one bottle of WKD would have that much of an effect...'

Jenna shoots me a look that plainly says, 'Do NOT tell her what else you had to drink,' so I just shrug and put my hands in my pockets. Luckily, at that moment Roscoe decides to emerge. He attempts to jump up at me but slides down right away and settles on licking my shoe.

'Hey buddy!' I bend down to give him a belly-rub.

'He's been wondering where you've been!' Mum says crossly. 'Honestly, Alex, we should probably have a chat about how to behave...'

'Oh, leave him alone!' Jenna rolls her eyes. 'He went to a party and had fun, Mum. Isn't that what you and Dad did, back in the day? It's nice that he just went out and forgot about all the crap here for a while, isn't it?'

Mum stiffens. I carry on stroking Roscoe.

'Don't use that language, Jenna. What are you referring to?'

Jenna sighs and opens the front door. 'Nothing, Mum. We're going to McDonald's; do you want anything?'

Mum checks her watch. 'Well, it's not too long until dinner! I've put a casserole in the slow cooker.'

Jenna makes a face at me. I disguise my laugh in a cough and Roscoe makes a sort of whimpering noise, giving me his big droopy puppy-dog eyes.

'He's been waiting for you to take him for a walk,' Mum says coolly.

I look at Jenna, not sure what to say. Mum's probably right—poor Roscoe has been stuck in the living room with Dad all day.

'Well bring him with us,' Jenna says decisively, stepping outside. 'Come on, Alex.'

Avoiding Mum's gaze, I bend down and pick Roscoe up.

''Bye, Mum!' Jenna calls. I follow her to the car and turn just in time to see Mum half-smile while shutting the door.

*

'You feeling okay today?' I ask the obligatory question, though I know Jenna hates it. She gets asked it all day, every day.

She rolls her eyes. 'I'm as good as any other day, Al: you know that. Even better, actually, now I've got this.' She holds up her chips. 'Anyway. You were very chatty last night.'

We're sat in the McDonald's car park, in the furthest space from everyone else. Jenna has a Big Mac, I've got a McChicken Sandwich and Roscoe's got four nuggets, which I think he's very pleased with.

'What do you mean, very chatty?' I ask, swallowing a mouthful of chips. I try and cast my mind back to even speaking to Jenna at all after the party, but I can't remember anything.

Jenna takes a long slurp of cola before replying. 'I mean, you wanted to tell me everything about last night. All the details.' She raises her eyebrows. I feel myself get a bit sweaty. Details? Of what? How much have I embarrassed myself this time?

'Don't look so scared!' She laughs. 'Nothing too bad. You just told me all about a certain girl you like the look of...'

Oh, excellent. I've embarrassed myself quite a bit then. I shove some more chips in my mouth to avoid answering.

'It's fine, Alex,' Jenna says after a moment. 'It was nothing too gross. Just that you really like Daisy. And you were very mysterious in saying that you betrayed her in some way last night—a bit melodramatic if you ask me but, now you're awake and sober, I've been dying to know how?'

Betrayed Daisy?

'What?'

Jenna hits me on the arm softly. 'What did you do last night to upset her? You can tell me. Did you kiss another girl?'

'No!' I snap. But even as I say it I grow even hotter. Did I? No, surely not. Surely, I'd remember something like that! Then how and why have I betrayed... Something on my face must have changed as the awful realisation washes over me.

Jenna gasps. 'You remember! What is it, then? What did you do?'

I can't tell her. If I told her, I'd have to also tell her all the background info, including how Daisy got her black eye in the first place. Which I don't even know the answer to. Damn it. It's flooding back to me now, being in the garden with Callum. Telling him—

'Alex!' Jenna cries, stealing one of my chips. 'Tell me!'

'Oh…' I trail off. Think, Alex. Think, think, think. 'I just… I drank some of her vodka without her knowing. That must've been what I was talking about.'

'Oh.' Jenna rolls her eyes, clearly disappointed with my lie. 'Well, don't feel bad about it, I'm sure she wouldn't have minded. Everyone shares drinks at parties. Sharing is caring.'

I nod as if I knew that already and slurp up the rest of my drink. I avoid Jenna's gaze and instead watch Roscoe inhale the last of his nuggets in the back seat.

'I knew you couldn't just have had the drink Mum gave you,' Jenna carries on matter-of-factly. 'I mean, I know you're a lightweight but even you wouldn't get that drunk off one WKD.'

I force a laugh. Normally, being in Jenna's car and eating McDonald's is one of my happiest places to be. Right now, happiness is the last thing I can feel. I can't concentrate on anything but the memory of last night. Why the hell did I think telling Callum would be a good idea? I need to talk to him. Now.

'I'm just gonna make a phone call,' I tell Jenna and climb out the car.

'Very business-like,' she snorts.

I walk a few paces away from the car, pull out my phone and dial Callum's number. It seems to ring for ages.

'Hello?'

Finally.

'Hi Cal. You okay?'

'Yeah, mate. You?'

'I'm fine. Um…' I feel suddenly scared to talk about it. What if I didn't actually tell him? What if my weird drunk mind just manufactured that memory into my brain?

'How funny was last night?' Callum interrupts. 'Daisy getting her dress caught in the car door, you falling over in the bathroom... Oh my God, hilarious. You were in the toilet for ages! I think Stacey has a video...'

'Yeah, look, did I... er... tell you anything last night?' I interrupt him, my heart thumping. 'Anything in the garden?'

'Oh!' Callum lowers his voice. 'You mean about Daisy?'

I clench the phone. So I did tell him.

'Yeah, that's pretty messed-up, man,' he continues. 'I mean... hitting your own kid? That's...'

'Wait, what?'

'It's crazy. That family must have some serious issues.'

I rack my brains, trying to piece together what the hell I told him last night. I'm drawing a blank. 'Callum.' I take a deep breath. 'What exactly did I tell you?'

I can hear Callum chewing and swallowing something. 'Well, you said someone hit Daisy. And you said your theory is that it was her mum.'

Her mum? Where would I have got that from? Something Daisy did? Said? I think back to Boxing Day when she slammed the window: she said they'll be back. They. As in her mum and...

'Not much we can do though, I suppose,' Callum continues in my ear. 'I wish you'd have told me sooner, so that—'

'Okay, thanks Cal. I've got to go. See you at school.' I hang up and shove the phone back in my pocket. I don't want to hear anything else he's got to say. I know it's not his fault, but I feel angry at him. And Daisy. But mostly angry at myself. I told her I wouldn't tell anyone but I've broken that promise and she'll never trust me again. Not only that, I've told Callum that her own mum is behind the bruising!

I mean, it's not out of the question, though. She was definitely scared of her mum and someone else coming home and finding me there on Boxing Day. But who is the someone else? I think of Daisy last night, in her sparkles, and my heart feels like it's going to break into a million pieces.

Okay, be rational, Alex: think. Daisy doesn't need to know that Callum knows, does she?

A sharp BEEP breaks into my thoughts. Jenna's sounding the horn.

'Hurry up, your food's getting cold!' she yells out of the window.

I hold up a finger to her and redial Callum's number before I can change my mind.

'What now?' Callum answers warily. I can hear the PlayStation in the background.

'Sorry. I just wanted to ask you something.'

He sighs on the line.

'Could you... keep it to yourself? What I told you last night?'

'What? About Daisy?'

'Yes about Daisy!' I can barely keep the frustration out my voice. 'And her mum. I don't even know if... Yeah, just don't say anything.'

'All right, all right,' Callum hisses. 'Calm down. I won't tell her.'

'Or anyone?'

'Or anyone,' he echoes after a moment. I can tell there's a hint of annoyance in his voice but right now I'm too relived to care.

'Thanks, Cal. Thank you.'

He grunts and hangs up. I know I should still feel guilty, but Callum promising to keep his mouth shut has definitely lifted a weight off my shoulders. I shouldn't have told him, sure, but what's done is done, and as long at Daisy doesn't find out... God, I don't even wanna think about what would happen if she did find out. Not only did I tell Callum her biggest secret (a super-serious secret, too), I called her own mum the culprit. I mean, I'm not completely convinced Daisy's mum is innocent. But if she is and I've just thrown her under the bus...

'Come on!' Jenna beeps the horn again and I jog back over to the car. She asks again what the 'mysterious' phone call was about but I don't tell her. I can't tell anyone. And definitely not Daisy.

Chapter Seventeen

It's Monday morning and the party seems weeks ago already. So does my betrayal of Daisy.

I tell myself it's no biggie: Callum says he won't tell. I'm sure I only told him for some advice or something, anyway; I wouldn't just spill a friend's secret over nothing. Would I? I stare down at my glass of orange juice, the kitchen light so bright I can sort of see my face reflected in it.

Who am I, really? Who was I before I became the kid with the dying sister? I was happier. I was less stressed. I slept better, that's for sure. And I feel like I was definitely a better friend. But can I really blame Jenna's cancer for that?

'Hurry up, Daisy will be here in a minute.' Mum starts tidying the dishes.

'Yeah. Sorry.' I gulp down the bright liquid, wincing at the lumps of orange sliding down my throat. Mum's been buying this juice for three weeks now, but I can't bring myself to tell her I don't like it. Picking the family orange juice is the last of her worries right now. I move a groaning Roscoe off my feet and hand her my empty bowl and glass; she barely looks at me when taking them. I dunno: I thought things would've improved since Christmas. I guess not.

'Morning!' The front door opens and a familiar voice rings through the house. She's here.

'Morning, Daisy,' Mum calls back. 'Come on then!' She ushers me out of the kitchen to the sight of Daisy crouched in the hallway, stroking Roscoe's belly.

'Hey.' Daisy straightens up.

Hey? That sounds a bit blunt. Why? Does she know? My heart's beating so loud I'm sure Daisy can hear it.

'What? Is there something on my face?' She rubs her nose with her jumper sleeve. 'Pen or something?' She looks at me expectantly.

Come on Alex, you idiot. Talk!

'No, no,' I say quickly, clearing my throat. 'Sorry.'

Don't apologise! Now that sounds suspicious.

'You're very starey,' she laughs. I feel my cheeks flush; she's onto me.

'Sorry,' I repeat, pulling my coat on and handing her my hat. 'I'm tired.'

'Must be 'cos I look extra pretty today,' she continues, pulling the hat over her curls. 'I did get a new mascara.'

My heart feels though it's slowing slightly. She's laughing, joking. She's not mad. She can't know.

'Yes,' I agree quickly. 'Your eyes look... lovely.'

She smiles again, shyly now, and I feel a stab of guilt. I'm normally too embarrassed to give Daisy compliments so obviously like this, and now the first one I give her comes from fear and guilt. Damn it. I follow her out the front door, watching her carefully.

Though she always does have lovely eyes, so it wasn't really a lie.

'So, why are you tired?' she asks after a moment, popping some bubble gum into her mouth. 'Have you been having those... dreams again?'

I shrug. 'On-and-off. I did have a bit of a weird one last night.' My heart rate finally feels back to normal and my skin has cooled in the cold air. There's nothing to be on edge about. Daisy doesn't know.

'What happened?'

I shudder involuntarily, remembering the unfamiliar smile on the new Jenna's face. 'Jenna died and came back as someone else. Someone I didn't know.'

'Far-out.' Daisy blows a bubble half the size of her face. It pops loudly all over her lips and cheeks. 'Like... what's that thing... reincarnation?'

'Yeah, I guess.' An urge shoots through me to reach across and peel the gum off her face. I shove my hands in my pockets instead.

'That's something we should look into, you know,' Daisy says, oblivious to my twitching hands. 'Reincarnation. I think the idea is that if you're good in life, you'll come back as someone cool. But if you're bad and kill people or whatever you come back as, like… a beetle. A dung beetle.'

'A dung beetle?'

She laughs. 'You know! Those freaky bugs that love poo.'

'I know what a dung beetle is, Daisy.'

'Shut up!' She gives me a gentle push. 'I'm sure I read it somewhere.'

I consider it. 'I just dunno… Like, think of how many people are living on the Earth. There's so many, compared to hundreds of years ago. So…'

'Yeah. But not everyone has lived already,' Daisy interrupts, blowing and popping another bubble. 'Some people are new.'

She could be right. At the very least, it's worth looking into. Last night's dream replays in my head again: my sister in a stranger's body sat in her place at the table. Sleeping in her bed. Driving her car. And the stranger was so sinister, with her thin face and bony figure. Like something from a horror movie. Why did she have to come back so creepy?

'Do you think we get to choose?' I ask Daisy. 'Choose who we want to be?'

'Hope so!' Daisy throws her gum on the floor. 'I'll be a Queen. Or a celebrity.'

I'm about to laugh when I see him. He's leaning against the school gate, half-eaten breakfast bar in one hand, phone in the other. I feel a bit sick.

'Hi, Cal!' Daisy starts waving and quickens her pace. I hang back, my stomach doing flips.

Come on, Alex. What did I think, that I'd never be with both of them in the same room ever again? Idiot. With a deep breath I push away the fear, the guilt, the anger, and plaster a smile on my face.

'You are going to be so pleased with me!' Daisy's got a huge grin on her face. She sets her lunch tray down opposite mine with a triumphant bang, her plate shaking with the force of the impact.

'Why?' I ask cautiously.

'I'm making a contribution to your... our... expedition.'

'Yeah?' I'm still cautious. Sometimes Daisy doesn't follow through with promises. And when she does, sometimes her contributions are... minimal, to say the least. I remember when we worked on an English project last year: Of Mice and Men, I think it was on. We had to make a time capsule that one of the characters would have made, full of diary entries and knick-knacks and stuff, and then present our 'findings' in front of the class. I thought it was a pretty cool assignment of Mr Hook's; I really enjoyed staining paper with tea to make it look old, covering stuff in dirt, ripping old fabric to be strips of a dress. Daisy said she'd be in charge of one thing: the time capsule itself. She kept putting off showing me, saying it was fine, it was done, stop worrying! The day of the presentation she showed up with a plastic carrier bag. It ruined the whole thing.

'Anyway, hurry up and eat!' Daisy commands, shovelling pasta into her mouth. 'We've got a date with destiny.'

I know she's quoting something but I can't work out what, so I just smile at her and finish my lunch. Daisy quotes all sorts of movies and books and TV shows; sometimes when she makes me guess where they're from, I get them wrong and never hear the end of it. So it's best just to smile with my mouth shut.

She drags me to the field when we've finished lunch. Right to the back, under the big oak trees, where no one ever sits because it's close to the bins and the grass is too long. No one sits on the field, anyway, because it's supposed to be off-limits. Too cold. Too wet. But someone is on the field—other than me and Daisy—sat directly beneath the biggest tree, hunched over, a hood pulled over his head... fear flits through me. What has Daisy gotten us into? Who is this weirdo?

'Who is that!?' I hiss as we approach the figure. 'Daisy, I mean it, if this is some weird…'

'Shut up, Al!' She laughs so loud it rings around the air, and the figure looks up slightly. Daisy runs ahead of me, her long hair flying behind her. My hat flies off with a sudden breeze onto the damp grass, but Daisy doesn't stop or even look back. For God's sake. I break into a run too, swooping down to pick my hat up on the way. She's a nutter sometimes. But the way the winter sun hits her… I dunno. It still makes my breathing weird.

'Ta-dah!' Daisy cries, pulling the hood back off the mysterious figure's head. Thank God. It's not some dodgy man at all. What is wrong with me today?

'Hi, Alex,' Julie Matthews smiles shyly. Julie Matthews. A tiny, dark-haired girl in the year above me at school. Julie Matthews, who's always scuttling around with armfuls of books and extra bags as though she's going to camp in the library for a week. I can't believe I was momentarily scared of Julie Matthews.

'Hi, Julie Matthews.' I say her last name automatically, short of breath as I flop down next to her and Daisy.

'Julie's agreed to have a little chat with us,' Daisy says, rummaging around in her bag.

'Er, okay…' Was Julie Matthews at the party? Did she overhear me and Callum? There's no getting out of this one. Oh crap. My heart's going again, a thousand beats-per-second. This is it, the confrontation…

'Ah, here we go.' Daisy pulls out a notebook and chewed biro and hands them to me expectantly. 'Julie's going to tell us all about reincarnation.'

'Oh!' I can't help laughing slightly in relief. Idiot. Not everyone's out to get you, Alex. Daisy shoots me a 'calm down' look and crosses her legs. 'So. What religion are you, Julie?'

'I'm a Buddhist,' Julie answers. Her voice is just as squeaky as her appearance. She's like a little mouse.

'Cool. And what do you think happens when people die?'

'Well,' Julie pauses to cough delicately, 'we believe people are born again.'

Daisy catches my eye. 'Alex. Make some notes!'

Right, yes. Notes. I write 'Reincarnation' and underline it.

'Basically,' Julie continues, 'everyone's in a cycle. The cycle is painful; no one wants to live forever, right? So, when—and if—you've lived a pure life, and created enough good karma, the cycle will stop.'

'Stop?'

'Yes,' Julie nods. 'Ends, completely.'

'And you'll… die?' I frown. This doesn't sound right. 'Your rewarding for being good is… actual, permanent death?'

Julie nods. I'm not sure if I want her to go on. The idea of Jenna leaving forever is making my hairs stand on end. What kinda messed-up idea is this, anyway? You work hard all your life to be the best person you can be, and for what? To be torn away from everyone you love forever? That just doesn't seem right to me. And even if Jenna doesn't qualify for the top prize, what if she's been here before? As in, she's lived loads of good lives already and this is her last one?

'That's so interesting,' Daisy says, staring at Julie in fascination. 'So, what happens when they really die?'

'I'm not one hundred percent sure,' Julie admits. 'Me and my parents don't really discuss it. I think you just become a God.'

'Wow,' Daisy whispers, her eyes shining. I'm sure she's picturing herself sat on a cloud, dressed in white with a crown on her head.

'But you have to have so much good karma for that,' Julie shrugs. 'In the meantime, you come back as an animal or a human or whatever.'

'What do you mean by "karma"?' I ask.

'It's how you live your life. Right, Julie?' Daisy starts plucking blades of grass from the ground and winding them into plaits. She always likes to be doing something.

'Sort of,' Julie agrees. 'It's the actions you do, the choices you make: they all impact on what you'll come back as in the next life. For example, if you're a good, generous person, you'll get good karma and come back in a human form or better for your next life. But if you're selfish and greedy, you won't get any good karma and you'll have to come back as an animal.'

This sort of links back to what the priest said, about living a good life. If you live a good life, you'll have a good afterlife. That seems to be the theme so far.

'I'd be a crocodile,' Daisy says, making the shape of its mouth with her hands. Julie looks at her like she's a weirdo.

'My sister isn't greedy,' I say. 'But she probably hasn't been here long enough to get enough good karma to be a God.' I make a note—God?—in the notebook. Jenna's kind and funny and helpful. But she also drinks alcohol at parties and wears short skirts and swears. Sometimes, when we were younger, we'd fight and she would pinch or bite me really hard. Is that all bad karma?

'I don't know what she'd come back as.' Julie looks like she wishes she did know. 'I'm sorry. But don't worry; whatever happens to her will be based on the life she has chosen to lead. Like all of us.'

There's silence for a moment. The cold and wet have started to seep through my trousers; I want to get up and leave, but I also don't. I'm too busy thinking. Worst-case scenario, Jenna has been so good that she leaves the Earth forever. But she'd be happy and in a great place: she'd be a God. Best-case scenario, she comes back as a human again and we can spend way more time together. She'd be younger than me, which would be weird. I'd be her older brother!

'Alex.' Julie is looking at me sadly. 'If—when—Jenna comes back, we don't know what form she'll be in.'

It's as if she read my mind. I stare back at her. 'What are you trying to say?'

'Well, she could be anyone, anywhere... Over the other side of the world...' She trails off uncomfortably. It hits me then, like a tonne of bricks. If Jenna comes back, she's not going to be Jenna. Not really. She'll be someone completely different. And even if she wasn't, even if parts of her were the same, how would I find her? How would I know where she is? I swallow the lump in my throat, sensing the awkwardness between the three of us now. Daisy's even stopped plaiting and is staring at me.

'What?' I ask, sounding snappier than I meant to. It's not her

I'm angry at. It's the universe and its bloody unfairness. It's like Heaven all over again. It sounds great in theory but, once you get down to the nitty-gritty, it wouldn't work. It wouldn't guarantee Jenna's happiness.

'Nothing.' Daisy looks back down at the ground, going a bit red. I know she doesn't mean to make things worse. But still, sometimes she really, really does.

'Look,' Julie picks up her bag. 'I'm sorry this isn't the answer you were looking for, Alex. I know it's... unpleasant... to think that when Jenna comes back, she won't be who she was before. But surely her having another chance at life is better than nothing at all?' She smiles at me encouragingly and stands up. I stand up too.

'Where's the evidence for this, Julie?'

'What?' She looks a bit taken aback.

'The evidence,' I repeat. 'You know, proof.'

She raises her eyebrows. 'This is my religion, Alex. My way of life. And I don't need science to back that up.'

'Well, you should.'

I know I'm being mean. I know this poor girl doesn't deserve me ripping her beliefs apart and analysing them with a magnifying glass. But I don't care about being mean right now. Life is mean.

'Okay, well, thanks Julie.' Daisy is standing now as well, sort of between us as if she can sense that a tiny part of me wants to scream right in Julie Matthews' face.

'Okay. 'Bye then.' Julie scuttles off awkwardly. The sight of her receding figure calms me slightly. At least that's over. I sink back onto the grass.

'Well. That was interesting.' Daisy sits down next to me, so close our knees touch. 'Bless her. She's so... mousey.'

'She'll probably come back as one,' I mutter.

Daisy stares at me in shock. 'Alex!' She breaks into laughter. 'Meanie. You're probably right, though.' She's quiet for a moment, pulling at the grass again.

I watch her, trying to block everything else out, trying to stop the numbness creeping back. Just watch her, Alex. Just watch the beautiful girl in front of you. But I can't. Jenna's there, like she

120

always is, frail and weak, begging me to find an answer. I can't just keep pushing her away, shutting her in a box that I open and close whenever I feel like it. She needs me. But then, so does Daisy. She's just as fragile, just in different ways.

'Why are you staring?' She narrows her eyes.

Damn. Caught in the act. 'Sorry.'

'Don't say sorry,' she laughs. 'You're going red now! Have you farted?'

'Shut up!' Okay, now I'm really going red.

Daisy holds her nose. 'With that smell, you're definitely coming back as a dung beetle!' I shake my head, meaning to look mature and above her nonsense, but I can't help but laugh. It's hard to feel numb when Daisy's around.

Chapter Eighteen

'I'm home!' I don't always announce my arrival. But today, after what happened, I'm in a weirdly good mood. It's like sitting on wet grass and picturing Julie Matthews as an actual mouse has melted some of the stress away. It had been piling on my shoulders like shovels of snow, getting heavier and heavier, colder and colder, slowly freezing me. And then, finally, Daisy came over and slowly poured warm water over me. Reviving me.

'We're in the living room!'

Kent and Jenna are curled up under a blanket, watching The Chase. Mum and Dad are on the other sofa, mugs of tea on the tables, an open packet of Ginger Nuts on Dad's lap. I hover in the doorway a moment, taking it all in. I can't remember how long it's been since I've seen them all sat together, watching TV. And Dad actually has a normal, non-alcoholic drink. I want to pinch myself. Is this another weird dream? Is Jenna suddenly going to float up into the ceiling, never to be seen again?

'Hey, Al,' she croaks, her pale face peeking out from the blanket. 'Come sit down.' She shuffles over a little.

'Don't worry,' I say quickly, flopping down on the armchair.

'How was your day, love?' Mum asks, pausing the TV.

Pausing the TV. Can't she just leave it on in the background? Would it matter that much if she missed thirty seconds of her crappy show? Well. This stupid re-run is clearly more important than anything I have to say. A flit of anger runs through me. She'd never do that with Jenna.

'Fine.' I want to add, 'Don't let me keep you from the telly,' but I don't. I take a breath. The stress is melting, remember?

'Good. We're having stew for dinner.'

'Okay.'

Mum waits a moment before pressing Play again. I sit in the armchair feeling... How do I feel? Awkward. Awkward in my own chair, in my own living room, with my own family. This is messed-up. I can't get over the sight of it; Dad has his arm around Mum, Kent's yelling out answers at the TV, Jenna's laughing. This isn't normal. This isn't right. I stand up. I'm not watching this a minute longer.

'I'm taking Roscoe for a walk.'

Mum barely looks at me. 'Okay, love. Don't be too long.'

Like you care how long I am. They don't need me there, stiff in the corner, to complete their afternoon. They've got their tea, their biscuits, their dying daughter. They don't need me. And if that's how they're going to be, I don't need them right now either.

*

Roscoe and I sit on the bench by the canal, where we always sit to talk.

'I'm sorry we haven't been here in a while.'

Roscoe looks at me.

'No, I am. Things have just been... busy. With my project, you know?' I pat him on the head and he nestles into my coat, the feel of his warmth melting the snow a little more. I tuck my arm around him, my hand on his chest, feeling his little heart thudding away. It's always been soothing. I open my mouth to speak again but a couple walk past. Two women, holding hands, chatting away. I doubt they'd even hear if I spoke to Roscoe but I wait anyway. The last thing I need is for someone to spot me talking to my dog.

'Do you think I'm being stupid? Be honest.'

Roscoe looks up at me with his droopy brown eyes. I know he's saying: 'Yes.'

'I knew it.' I look away from his soft face and across the water. On the other side of the canal there are houses, neatly lined up like toy soldiers, their gardens small and tidy. I wonder if Roscoe would like to live by the canal. He definitely likes to come on walks here; he always waggles his tiny tail when we round the corner towards it. And he always hesitates slightly by our bench, as if he's waiting for me to lift him onto it and sit next to him like we've done so many times before. Like today.

'I suppose… it's just weird, isn't it? It's weird when Mum's always faffing and cooking and cleaning, and Dad's always drinking, and Jenna's always sleeping. But it's weird them all together, too, acting like a bloody normal family. Because we're not. A normal family.' I feel my eyes welling up. Roscoe climbs onto my lap as if agreeing. But what can he say, if he even could say anything? Nothing. Because there's nothing anyone can say, nothing anyone can do. And whether Mum lives and breathes housework, or sits on the sofa and drinks tea, nothing can take Jenna's cancer away.

'Well, well, well.'

Oh great.

'What are you doing here, dweeb?' Bruce flicks his cigarette onto the floor and stamps on it like he wishes it was me he was squishing.

'Nothing…' I lower Roscoe onto the ground and stand up, blinking harder than I ever have before. Go away stupid tears.

'Having a cuddle with your little doggy? Precious.' He laughs loudly at his own joke. Well, I suppose someone has to. I take a deep breath, leaving the emotion of the moment behind me. No way is Duce Cleeve making things worse. Especially when he doesn't have his cronies to back him up.

'What are you doing on your own?' I peer past him to double-check. 'No friends?'

He folds his arms. 'Just been at a girl's house, actually, dweeb. Doubt you'd know much about it.'

I wind Roscoe's lead round my hand. I've got to be ready to go after this. 'Funny, I was just at your mum's house last night and she had no complaints.'

'Oi!'

Okay Al: go, go, go! I race away from him, own the alley, scooping Roscoe up as I go.

'Hold up!' Bruce calls. I am not holding up. I quicken my pace, walking as fast as I can without running. On a different day, I might stand my ground a bit longer—I mean, sure, I can rip him to shreds with words. I think even a four-year-old could. No, it's his fists I'm worried about. I can't be dealing with a bloody nose tonight on top of everything else.

'Wait, I said!' he thunders. Okay, time to run now. I can hear the footsteps behind me, Duce's croaky laughter. Roscoe licks my face encouragingly.

'Almost there, buddy,' I tell him through gasps. My ribs hurt. It's that sort of running. We shoot through the alley and take an immediate right behind some houses. Catching my breath, I crouch behind the bins, pulling Roscoe in close beside me.

'Where is he?' Duce's footsteps grind to a halt. 'Damn.' I peer around the bin; he's by the alley entrance, doubled over. He's surprisingly fast for someone his size, I'll give him that. Though this does look like the most exercise he's possibly done all year. I hardly dare to breathe behind the bin. One sound, one move, and he'll spot me. It feels like I'm there for an eternity. I peer round once more and hear the familiar click of his lighter. Duce takes a drag of his cigarette, peering about with his beady eyes. I grip Roscoe so tight I feel like he might have pinch-marks later.

'Sorry, buddy,' I breathe. I just can't risk him squirming, not now. Not when Duce is so close to leaving. Roscoe grunts and I duck my head back behind the bin, measuring my breathing carefully. Go, Duce. Just get lost!

Eventually I hear footsteps fade back into the alley. Roscoe wriggles out of my arms, bored of hide-and-seek. He looks at me, unimpressed, as I straighten up and tiptoe out from behind the bins. I can't help but laugh out loud at the whole situation. Maybe I was being stupid earlier, literally crying over a paused TV. It's like that encounter was surprisingly just what I needed. And it really couldn't have gone any better. Ha! Alex: one, Duce: nil. Let's hope it stays that way.

Chapter Nineteen

It's been a week since I ran away from Duce and I've been avoiding him at school ever since. But I've got bigger problems than him and his Apes; Callum, Daisy and I have decided it's time to explore more avenues on our quest to discover what lies beyond. So after school we're going to the hospital.

'Are you excited?' Daisy asks, biting into her apple. The juice dribbles down her chin.

'About what?'

'Speaking to the doctor!' she exclaims.

'Excited? I wouldn't say I'm excited, no,' I laugh. And I'm not. But I'm definitely interested.

'I am.' She takes another bite. 'It'll be so cool. Just think, this guy's gonna have so much... So much experience. And knowledge. He'll have been right there, in the action, when someone dies...' I see Callum shoot her a look and she trails off, crunching the rest of her apple. I'm not offended; this is Daisy all over. And I'm not stupid either. People die all the time. I know that. Still. It sends a shiver down my spine to picture a man in a white coat watching an old lady float out of her body.

'I can't believe your mum managed to squeeze in a meeting for us with this guy,' Daisy continues, gnawing her apple down to the core. 'He must be so busy.'

'Stop calling her a he!' Callum growls. 'It's a woman doctor, idiot, I've told you that.'

'A woman doctor,' Daisy echoes in wonder. 'Far-out.'

It is pretty cool that Callum's mum has arranged this meeting; she cleans at the hospital and has become quite friendly with a couple of the doctors and nurses. Callum didn't even tell me he'd told his mum about what we were doing, just waltzed in yesterday and said at 4 pm we're off to visit the doc. He knew I'd be pleased. All these religious ideas and theories are interesting and all, but I want to look at the scientific side, too.

'I'm glad you didn't arrange it for tomorrow, anyway.' Daisy breaks my trail of thought. She aims her apple core for the bin but misses by a mile. 'Damn it.'

'Why?'

'I'm not in school tomorrow.' She gestures for a younger kid walking past the bin to pick the apple up for her. He rolls his eyes but does as he's told. Everyone does what Daisy tells them.

'Why not?' Callum asks.

'Just not,' she answers, tossing her hair. Callum and I frown at each other.

'Why not?' he repeats.

'Just not.'

'Why not?'

'Jeez, I'm just not, okay! Nothing interesting. I've just... I have to spend time with my mum and her...' Daisy shudders, 'new boyfriend.'

I think Callum's expression mirrors mine. Daisy's mum has a boyfriend?

'You kept that quiet,' I say, struggling to keep the shock out of my voice. And annoyance. I thought she would've mentioned that. Daisy glares at me.

'I don't have to tell you dweebs everything.'

There's silence for a moment. This is one of those times I can't really tell if she's joking or not.

'Well,' Callum breaks it with a cough, 'you definitely don't tell me anything!'

'What? Yes I do,' Daisy says, poking her straw into her orange juice.

'No you don't!'

'I do!'

Callum's getting red. Angry. I can feel myself grow hot, too. I can see what's about to happen, what's about to be announced. I try to catch Callum's eye frantically, shaking my head. He ignores me.

'So why was I the last one to know about the whole...' He gestures to his eye.

'Whole what?' Daisy snaps. She shoots me a look; a warning look. A look that says, 'If you dared tell him Alex, I swear to God...'

Callum's looking at me, too. I don't know what to say. I don't know what to do. I'm frozen.

'The whole what?' Daisy repeats, her voice louder now. She turns to Callum. 'What, huh? Say it.'

Callum swallows and looks away from us both. He knows he's gone too far. I open my mouth to speak but I can't. The words just aren't forming. What should I say, anyway? Sorry? He's joking? Daisy leaps off the bench.

'If you're talking about what I think you're talking about,' she says in a low voice, 'then you're a horrible, pathetic human being from bringing that up in the school playground.'

Callum's staring down at his lap.

'And you,' she says, leaning forward and looking at me with absolute hatred, 'are a snaky, lying... death-obsessed... ugly... WEIRDO!' She yells the last word, her face turning redder than her hair. I've never seen such a look in her eye. I've never heard this anger in her voice. The kids on the other benches are staring at us.

'Daisy,' I say finally. My voice sounds like Julie Matthews'. 'I didn't mean to tell him... I...'

She leaves before I can string together a proper sentence. Grabs her bag, tosses her hair, and marches off the playground and into the library.

'That was dramatic!' Christine Gibbs on the bench opposite laughs, and everyone carries on chatting. Just like that, as if nothing happened. Callum stands up.

'Don't you dare leave!' I hiss. 'Sit back down. I can't believe you did that!'

'I'm sorry.' He won't look me in the eye. 'I need some air.'

'But we're outside!'

He shrugs and slings his bag across his shoulder.

'Wait!' My heart's thudding, palms sweating, but I ask the one logical question playing on my mind. 'Will you still come with me later?'

*

We walk to the hospital in silence, Callum and I. There's nothing either one of us wants to say about what happened at lunch.

I was furious at the time, of course I was. Though as the afternoon went on, I've realised I can't direct my anger at him. Only myself. I'm the idiot who told someone something I shouldn't. That's all it comes down to. And being drunk is hardly an excuse: I'm sure some tiny conscious part of my brain was still aware that I shouldn't say what I did. But I did it anyway. I know what kind of friend that makes me to Daisy, but that doesn't mean I have to be the same sort of friend to Callum. I can be better. I can stand by his side at this time, like he's done for me.

'Hi,' Callum greets the receptionist and pulls a crumpled note from his pocket. 'We're here to see... Doctor Knowles?'

The receptionist taps on her keyboard. 'Appointment?'

'Yes. No. Well, sort of...'

'Yes,' I interrupt him. 'For four o'clock. Alex and Callum.'

She peers down her glasses at me for a moment, then picks up the phone and tells whoever's on the other end something I don't understand.

'Take a seat.' She points to the row of plastic chairs behind us. Callum and I sit down, leaving a seat free between us. Callum gets his phone out. It's up to me to talk first, I know it. I'm the one that got us into this mess.

'Do you...' I clear my throat. My voice sounds squeaky again. 'Do you wanna come for dinner after this?'

Callum looks up from his phone. 'What you having?'

'Pretty sure Mum's doing sausages.'

He doesn't answer; his phone pings and his attention goes back to it. I try again.

'It would be… good. You haven't been over in a while.'

He looks at me again; I can't read his expression. I wonder if he's angry with me. It's me, after all, that caused all of this. If I had just kept my stupid mouth shut…

'Callum McKay?'

Doctor Knowles (I'm guessing) has appeared in the doorway. She looks young for a doctor: dark skin, dark hair, and very pretty. Callum flicks his hair and stands up.

'Hi, nice to meet you both. I'm Doctor Knowles.' She shakes our hands when we reach her. I bet mine feels sweaty. 'Just call me Nina.'

We follow her down a corridor to a room at the end.

'Take a seat.' Nina sits herself behind the desk. 'How can I be of help?'

Callum looks at me. I take a deep breath. It feels weird not doing this with Daisy. She's usually the confident one, the one that asks all the questions, thrusting her voice recorder in people's faces, dictating when I should make notes. It's quiet without her.

'My sister Jenna has ovarian cancer.' I hate saying it out loud. 'And—'

'I'm sorry to hear that,' Nina says.

'Thanks. And—'

'What stage is she? If you don't mind me asking?'

I have to refrain from rolling my eyes. This isn't what we're here to discuss.

'Have you had many people die in front of you?' I ask instead.

Nina's eyes widen. Callum shoots me a look. I know it was straight-to-the-point but I need to get the ball rolling. I don't want to be sat here for hours discussing the fact that my sister is withering away and cancer is eating her up and she'll never be the same again.

'Well,' Nina clears her throat, 'that's not a question I get asked a lot. I've witnessed four people die.'

Now it's our turn to be surprised. For some reason, I didn't think she'd tell us. It's quite a private thing, I suppose, discussing how many people you couldn't save.

'One was a stroke. Two were in comas and the families opted to turn the life support off. And one was from injuries sustained in a car accident.' She says this so matter-of-factly that she could have been reading headlines from a newspaper. 'I suspect we're not here to speak specifically about those people,' Nina says, more softly this time. She leans closer over the desk slightly. 'Your mum told me what you boys are doing, Callum. For Jenna.'

I can see Callum reddening slightly out of the corner of my eye. I think I'm blushing, too. I thought Mrs Moss was the only adult who knew about this. I mean, I'd gathered Callum had told his mum something, obviously, but not the whole story. It feels weird that she knows.

'I think it's very brave.' Nina leans back again in her seat and folds her arms across her chest. 'A very brave thing to do for your sister.'

Silence falls over us; we sit here, two boys and one doctor, just thinking for a moment. Is she right? Am I really being brave? I don't feel as though I'm being brave. If anything, right now, I feel like I'm failing.

'What happened?' Callum asks. 'What happened when those people... died?'

'Do you mean, did anything happen out of the ordinary? No. I didn't see souls leave bodies, or ghosts, or the heavens open, or anything like that.' She smiles at us sadly. 'I'm not going to lie to you, boys, it's a difficult mission you're on. From the medical side of things, I've never come across any reports or cases or visual signs of a person... moving on, shall we say. But that's not to say it doesn't happen.' I feel myself slump in my seat slightly. So she knows nothing. She's seen nothing. What a waste of time.

'You think we have souls?' Callum asks. 'Even though you can't see them in our bodies?'

Nina shrugs slightly, still smiling. 'I'm an atheist, boys. And that means I don't, in theory, believe in a God or a Heaven or anything of the sort. My mind works in a very methodical, logical way, as many medical professionals' minds do. But...' she lowers her voice, as if she's telling us a secret, 'a little part of me knows that there's more to us than meets the eye. I don't think we're just organs and bones, left to waddle around on the planet finding means to an end. I think there's more.'

I consider this. Nina, a qualified medical professional, who probably believes in evolution and things like that, believes we have souls. Believes there's more to us than body parts. I should be writing this down.

'Do you believe the souls go somewhere?' Callum asks. 'When we die, I mean?' I glance at him; his face is back to his usual colour. And he's being a lot more vocal than when we spoke to the priest. Maybe that's because someone isn't here. Someone who's loud and fun and seems to take over everything. It hits me that Callum and I haven't hung out, just the two of us, in what feels like forever. Of course he's asking questions, being confident, taking the reins. He's Callum. That's who he is.

'I'd like to think so,' Nina smiles. 'I really would. I don't think there's an afterlife per se. As I said, I'm an atheist. A realist.' She laughs. 'But yes, like I said, there's something within us that I think... moves on from this life when our body gives up.'

'And...' I flick back through my notebook for the questions I drafted earlier, 'have you revived anyone who died? Like, their heart actually stopped for a few minutes?'

'I have indeed,' Nina answers. 'A few people, actually.'

'And...' My heart's thudding a little now. Here comes the big question. The question which needs actual evidence. 'Have those people ever said they... they left their bodies and came back? Or anything like that?'

Nina smiles again, differently this time. A sympathetic smile. Her eyes are the same as when she apologised when I told her Jenna had cancer.

'No. No one's said anything like that.'

My heart sinks.

'But,' Nina continues, 'maybe they subconsciously knew they would wake back up. Maybe that's why they didn't go. They weren't ready to leave.'

Yeah, she's probably right. She is a doctor, after all.

Chapter Twenty

Callum didn't come for dinner. It's Sunday now, and I haven't heard from either him or Daisy since the bust up on Thursday. I saw him at school quickly, but we don't have many lessons together and he wasn't in the canteen at lunch. Daisy didn't knock for me Friday morning, but she did say she wasn't coming in, so that wasn't a surprise. I texted Callum to see if he wants to go for a kickabout, but he was busy. I haven't texted Daisy. I think she needs some space.

So on a day when it actually isn't freezing or raining, I'm lying inside, on my bed, alone. I tried to put a film on earlier, but Peter Pan was lying on top of the DVD player and I got side-tracked thinking about when I watched it with Daisy. It feels like forever ago. Looking back on it, I wish I'd kissed her that day. I wish I could kiss her every day.

'Knock, knock.' Jenna pushes open the bedroom door.

'Hey.' I prop myself up on the pillows and pick up a Chemistry textbook, so I don't look as sad as I feel. The last thing I need is to bother Jenna with my stupid friendship problems. She looks tired today; she has all weekend. I don't think she's worn anything but pyjamas for the last week.

'How you feeling?' She sits at the end of the bed.

'How am I feeling? I should be asking you that.' I put the textbook down.

She shrugs. 'I have cancer. We all know how I am.' She smiles wryly. 'Oh, don't look at me like that. I'm joking.'

'It's not a joke though, is it?' I sigh. 'I wish it was. All just a big, stupid prank. It's not, though, is it? If it is, tell me now. I've suffered enough.'

Jenna laughs. 'I would rival Ashton Kutcher if this was all a prank. And it would be a very mean one.'

'True. Are you okay, though?'

Jenna shrugs. 'I'm tired. I feel sick if I take my meds, I feel sick if I don't take my meds. Sometimes I feel so weak I can barely open the fridge. And to top it off, I'm at home all day every day with a cleaning maniac and the smelliest dog in the world.'

'He smells better than you,' I smile.

She pulls her knees into her chest and smiles back. 'Really, though, I'm fine. How are you?'

I take the sight of her in again. The paleness of her skin, the bags under her eyes. She really doesn't need the extra hassle.

'I'm good. Just studying. Got some mock exams coming up.' I gesture at the book.

'Ah, yes. The big GCSE year.' She nods wisely. 'I remember mine like they were yesterday. All the pressure, all the revision, all the stress, coming down to an hour in an exam hall. For what? Pieces of paper just to get a job, or into university. Mine didn't work out how I wanted anyway—I tried my best, but I couldn't get English no matter how hard I tried. That's why I had to start college, remember? To do the whole thing over again, just so I could go off and spend even more time studying somewhere else. Seems silly now.'

I don't know what to say so I just nod.

'Oh God, sorry, not silly for you Al! That's not what I meant at all! I know they're very important…' She trails off and chews her lip. 'It's just that there's more important things in life, you know? Some things are more important than exams.'

'I know.'

'Things like family. Speaking of…' she shuffles a little closer towards me, 'isn't everyone getting along fab these days? It's crazy.'

'It is weird,' I agree. And it is. Since the day I walked home to everyone snuggled on sofas watching TV, pretty much every afternoon has been the same. Dad's not drinking as much. Mum's still cooking and cleaning like a maniac in the day, but morphs back to her usual self in the evening. Kent's here literally all the time, waiting hand-and-foot on Jenna. And where am I? What am I doing? It's like even when I sit with them and watch their stupid game shows, I'm not really present. My mind's elsewhere, thinking of who to talk to, what to google, where to go next for answers. Answers that I'm not finding bloody anywhere.

'You're not liking it though, are you?' Jenna asks. 'The new set-up. It's weird for you, right?'

I'm not sure how truthful to be. 'I guess. It's just... a lot to get used to.'

'I know.' She pats my knee with her bony hand. 'And I'm sorry.'

'Don't be!' I cry. 'I didn't mean... it's not your fault at all! And it is weird, but it's a nice weird, I suppose. Everyone getting on. I'm just not used to it.'

Jenna doesn't answer but I know we're both thinking the same thing: sure, everyone's getting on now, but how long will it last?

*

'Are you going to finish that, love?' Mum gestures at my cereal.

'No thanks.' I push it towards her. 'Not hungry.'

She empties the Weetabix into Roscoe's bowl, who slurps it up loudly. On another day, I'd be annoyed that she didn't care why her son wasn't eating. But it's not another day. It's Monday morning and I'm too busy worrying if Daisy will show up. I glance at my watch: 8:02. She's usually here by 8:15. I got up early this morning. I don't know why; there were no bad dreams or restless sleeps for once. Just a sudden alertness, a need to get up and get ready. But now I wish I'd had the extra half-hour in bed.

'More juice?' Mum hovers by the fridge, looking at my full glass. 'No?'

'No,' I confirm, dreading downing the cup of lumps I already have in front of me. 'Thanks though.' I check my phone. Scroll though Twitter. Scroll through Sky Sports. Check the news. Check my watch: 8:09. I should have texted her. What was I thinking, letting her storm out of the canteen like that? All alone, probably on the verge of tears. I know what she's like when she's angry. She needed a friend. I clench my fists so hard my nails dig into my skin.

'Got time for a cup of tea?' Mum asks, boiling the kettle for probably the third time since I've been up.

'No thanks.'

That's all our conversation consists of these days. Do you want this, Alex? No. Do you want that, Alex? No. We're having this for dinner, Alex. Okay.

'No Daisy this morning?' she asks, spooning some coffee into her 'Best Mum' mug.

I check my watch. 8:15. I don't answer. Instead, I jig my leg. I scroll though Twitter. Scroll through Sky Sports. Check the news. 8:19. She's late. Twitter. Sky Sports. News. 8:22. She'll be here soon.

'Darling?' Mum sits next to me and places a hand on my twitchy leg. 'What's wrong?'

I take a deep breath. She's not coming, that's what's wrong. I love her and she hates me and she's not coming. 'I don't feel well.'

'Oh.' She leans forward and checks my forehead with the back of her hand. 'You do feel a little hot, I suppose. Have some water. Do you want some toast?'

No, I don't want any bloody toast.

'No, thanks. I'm just gonna stay home today. I feel sick.' I stroke my stomach and paint a pained expression on my face.

Mum frowns. 'Well, if you're sure. I'll call the school.'

I climb upstairs and open the door on the left to mine: Jenna's room. She's sleeping peacefully, her face soft and white against her blue bedsheets. I sit on the edge of her bed carefully, making sure not to disturb her. I can't spend another day in my room alone. But I don't think I can go to school without Daisy. I can't see her, smell her, hear her, without being her friend. It would be too painful.

'Morning, Al,' Jenna yawns.

'Oh, sorry. I didn't mean to wake you,' I whisper.

'Don't be silly. Aren't you meant to be in school?'

She looks at me with genuine interest, like she's actually

concerned. She cares. And I sort of need someone who cares right now. I take a deep breath and tell her everything.

Chapter Twenty-One

I can't believe what Jenna's persuaded me to do. After a day of rom-coms, ice cream and wine, she's come up with what she refers to as 'The best plan ever'. Which basically involves her waiting in the car playing The Breakfast Club soundtrack and me ringing Daisy's doorbell with a bunch of flowers.

So here I am, slightly wobbly after two glasses of my sister's Pinot Grigio, armed with the supermarket's finest white roses, waiting for Daisy to answer the door. We had to carefully time it; we didn't want her mum—or, worse, her mum's mysterious new boyfriend—to answer the door. It had to be Daisy. This involved twenty minutes of slowly driving up and down the road, peeking through the living room window and making sure the family car was nowhere to be seen.

'Did you knock?' Jenna calls over the music.

I mime pushing the doorbell.

'It might not work. Knock.'

I shake my head.

'Knock on the door, Alex!'

Fine. I wrap my knuckles against the wood, regret flooding through me already. What am I doing? It seemed like such a good idea. It was in all the movies. Of course, if my life was a movie it would be one of those dramas about a family member dying of a terminal illness rather than a romantic teen comedy.

The door swings open.

It's Daisy.

She's beautiful.

Jenna cranks the music up. Don't You Forget About Me blares

through the air so loud I have to raise my voice a little.

'Daisy. Hi.'

Smooth start, Alex.

She closes the door behind her, frowning. She looks prettier than ever, with ink smudged on her nose, her hair falling out of plaits. So effortless. So her.

'What the hell are you doing?' she hisses, ushering me down the steps. 'Is that your music?'

I turn and mime lowering the music to Jenna frantically.

'Daisy.' I take a deep breath and hand her the flowers. I can still taste the wine on my breath. 'These are for you. I can't begin to explain how sorry...'

'Cut the crap, Alex.' She drops the roses to the floor. 'You're an absolute idiot. I can't believe you told Callum, I really can't. After I specifically told you not to tell anyone! That was private. You weren't even meant to see me yourself.' She folds her arms and raises her chin.

'I just... I was drunk,' I say desperately, scooping the flowers off the floor. 'I know it's not an excuse but look how different you were acting yourself at the party.'

'What do you mean, how I was acting?' she snaps.

'I mean...' I trail off. I don't want to make things worse but I do think this is a valid point. It might even support my cause. 'I mean how you were flirting with all the boys. You never normally do that, it was just the vodka of course, but it made you act different, right?'

Daisy flushes red. 'I was not flirting!'

I'm not sure whether to argue back. I just feel my mouth hanging open and no words coming out. She mumbles something I can't hear.

'What?'

'I said you shouldn't care anyway,' she mutters, looking at the floor, 'if I flirt with anyone or not. It's not like... it's not like you're my boyfriend.'

This is it. This is my chance. My chance to take her by the hand and say, 'Actually, Daisy, nothing would make me happier than being your boyfriend. Would you like to go on a date?' But before I can summon the courage, we hear a huge crash from inside the house. It's so loud I think even Jenna hears it; she turns down the music even more and cranes her neck out of the window.

'Crap.' Daisy's eyes widen. 'I've got to go.'

'But…' I try to hand her the flowers again, but she's already turned away and is running back into the house. 'Is everything okay?' I call.

She falters at the doorway and for a moment I think she's going to run back and kiss me and I'll swoop her up in my arms and we'll be boyfriend and girlfriend and she'll forgive me. Instead she shouts, 'Go home Alex!' and slams the door behind her.

*

Callum's next.

'You can't try with one and not the other,' Jenna insists as she pulls into Callum's road. 'It's not fair. You love them both equally, right?' She raises her eyebrow and I smile in spite of myself. She's right, as always. I can't bear the thought of having absolutely no friends at all.

'I take it I'm not giving him these?' I nod at the slightly squished roses on my lap.

'No, no,' Jenna laughs, slowing the car to a stop. 'You don't need a grand gesture with Callum. You're best friends! Just use your words.'

'I'm no good with words.'

Jenna rolls her eyes. 'Stop feeling sorry for yourself, Al. So things didn't go perfectly with Daisy. But God, she pretty much asked you out! She likes you. She'll just take a couple days to fully come around.'

'I just need them both to forgive me.' I look at the floor.

Jenna sighs. 'I know. And they will! They wouldn't be proper friends if you didn't argue once in a while. It means you're being honest with each other. The things I'd give to have my friends at fourteen back!'

'Really? Why?' I don't get to hear much about Jenna's friends: they're mostly just laughing and drinking wine in her bedroom when they come over. Well, they used to be anyway. And I definitely have no clue who she hung out with when she was my age.

She smiles sadly. 'Because I can tell you for sure that you'll never have better friends than you do now, Al. You have to cherish them. 'Cos soon you'll all grow up and that's when you drift apart. That's just one of the many crappy side effects of growing up.' She leans over me and opens the car door. 'Now off you go.'

I take a deep breath. Why do I feel so nervous? I've been at this house a thousand times, but I freeze on the doorstep. I don't think I can take another person saying they don't want to be my friend today. No, come on, Alex. Remember what Jenna said: Callum and I are best friends. If that's not worth saying sorry for, I dunno what is. I raise my hand to knock, but before I even get a chance the door swings open.

'Oh! Hello, Alex.' Callum's mum towers above me, cigarette in one hand, shopping bag in the other.

'Hi, Ms McKay,' I swallow. 'Is Callum in?'

She takes a drag of her cigarette. 'He's at the park, I think. Footie.'

I know this is my cue to go but my mind's whirring. What do I do? Go to the park? Make a big scene in front of all the lads? Go home and forget about it for another day? Be friendless for another twenty-four hours?

'Well, I'm just off to the shops now.' She looks at me expectantly.

'Right, sorry.' I move over as she bustles out of the house, locking the door behind her.

'Haven't seen you around here for a while, Alex.' Callum's mum flicks her cigarette stub onto the pavement. 'Not since the news about Jenna. I sent a card.' She flattens the stub with her white trainer.

'Yes.' I seem to have lost the ability to speak properly today.

She looks at me sadly. 'She's a lovely girl. Such a shame. Anyway, you should pop over to the park.' She unlocks her car and opens the driver's door.

'Yes. Thank you.'

I watch her reverse her Renault off the driveway before turning back to where Jenna's parked. Was parked. She's gone. Which leaves me no choice. I'm going to the park.

I spot Callum right away. They're doing five-a-side, so he's not hard to see. Sweating, shouting, in the same battered England shirt he always wears. I stare down at my own clothes. T-shirt, hoodie, trainers, jeans. Skinny-fit but not too stiff. I can run. I can play. Before I can talk myself out of it I run over, pulling my hoodie off as I go.

'Alex!' Eric calls from the goal. 'Sick! We need another player.'

'You've got five already!' Joe calls to Eric, stopping the ball mid-play.

'Yeah, but we've got Oscar.'

All eyes go to Eric's younger brother, Oscar. He's a couple of years younger than us and, though always a nice lad, very weedy. Not great on the pitch.

'Fair play,' Joe nods. I risk a glance across to Callum, who's watching the conversation with a mild expression. Here goes nothing.

'All right?'

He looks at me a minute, as if considering what to say. My heart's thudding. Please, Callum. Say something.

'All right?' he grins finally. A genuine, happy grin. A grin that says 'Forget it, mate. Forget all about it.'

I mirror his smile, relieved. In fact, my good mood continues for the rest of the game; I even manage two assists and one pretty good goal of my own, left-foot and all. Callum boos with the rest of his team when it smashes into the net, but he puts his thumb up at me while Joe isn't looking. It's the best afternoon I've had in ages. Just the boys and I with a football, stopping only for a quick trip to the shop for orange juice and snacks. Yes, Daisy and I aren't a hundred percent back to normal, but the conversation we did have leaves me hopeful. Hopeful that maybe we can even be more than friends. I just feel so light, so carefree. I feel, for once, like a normal kid with a healthy sister.

Chapter Twenty-Two

'So,' Mrs Moss clicks her pen and looks at me expectantly. 'How was your weekend? And your week so far?'

I consider. My weekend was inevitably awful due to my lack of friends. Monday was a different story; a whirlwind of wine and The Breakfast Club and sort-of-making-up with said friends. Yesterday Daisy didn't turn up in the morning. I waited and waited but she was a no-show. Mum made me go to school anyway, which turned out to be fine thanks to Callum.

And then, completely unexpectedly, Daisy knocked for me this morning. Smiles and blushes and freckles and frizz: as though nothing had ever happened. She never mentioned the argument or the conversation outside her house, and neither did I. I'd like to keep it that way, to be honest. There's been far too much confrontation for me already.

I realise suddenly Mrs Moss is still waiting for an answer. 'Fine,' I say. 'On Friday, Callum and I interviewed a doctor about her experiences. With death.'

'Ah.' Mrs Moss makes a note on her pad. 'Very interesting. How did that go?'

'Well, it wasn't massively helpful,' I tell her, 'because she hasn't actually been there when many people have died.'

'What sort of doctor is she?'

I shrug and Mrs Moss laughs.

'She was nice, and she told us the truth,' I say. 'Not all adults do that, so that was nice of her.' Mrs Moss resumes a serious expression.

'Of course. And what truth did she have to say?'

'Just about how she's never physically seen a soul leave a body.'

'Okay. Well, don't feel disheartened, Alex. I'm sure that's still a crucial piece of information to add to the scrapbook.' She makes another little note and tilts her head to the side slightly. 'And if your issue with the doctor was that they hadn't seen enough death, perhaps your next step should be to visit someone who does have a lot of contact with the dying?'

She's right. Why haven't I thought of this before? Someone who sees loads of people on their deathbeds will have surely seen something, know something.

'Who?' I ask, rummaging around in my bag for my own notebook. I'm not risking this idea being forgotten. Mrs Moss is on to something, and I need to get onto it too.

She shrugs. 'Have a think. Have a search.'

Her turn to be vague, huh? I want to press her further, but excitement is taking over; I need to find this mysterious, all-knowing person.

'Okay.' I scribble down what she's said and stand up. 'Thank you. I'm gonna go.'

She stands up as well. 'Are you sure? You don't want to discuss…?'

'No thanks.' I shove my book back into my bag. 'But I'll see you next week?'

Mrs Moss smiles. 'Yes, Alex. See you next week. Good luck with your researching.'

*

A simple search tells me exactly where to go: the nearest hospice to my house is Elm Cottage Hospice, Wing Road. A hospice. Why didn't I think of this before? It's a literal place for the dying, where they can drift off peacefully and happily, comfy beds and books and all that. Much nicer than a hospital bed, in my opinion. And my Maps app says it's only a twenty-eight-minute walk. Easy-peasy.

'Twenty-eight minutes?' Callum groans as I break the news. 'That's, like, half-an-hour!'

'It's only double your walk to school,' I tell him. 'Stop

exaggerating.'

'I'm happy with a little adventure,' Daisy pipes up. My eyes go to her, then Callum, then back to her. Even though Daisy and Callum seem to have forgiven me, I'm not sure they've forgiven each other. They're not shouting or anything but there's an air of tension, of unresolved arguments.

'Great,' I say quickly. 'Let's meet at the hill after school?'

'Sure.' Daisy snaps open her can of cola and looks at Callum coolly. 'I'm in.'

Callum glares back at her. 'Me too.'

I know I should try and sort this mess out, but now doesn't feel like the time. Plus I'm way too excited to be that bothered about their little squabble. This could be it; this place could have all the answers we're looking for.

*

I'm the first one out of school. I make my way to the very top of the hill so I can see Daisy and Callum easier. I don't want to be faffing around any longer than needed.

But—oh, brilliant, here he comes up the hill. Not Callum. Duce, accompanied by two massive, acne-ridden Apes and Patty. All staring right at me. Crap.

Okay think Alex, think. I fumble around for my phone in my pocket and bring Callum up in my contacts.

'Look, it's the Invisible Man!' Duce and his friends jeer. They're getting closer. I turn away from them, the dial tone ringing painfully slowly in my ear. Pick up, Cal. Pick up.

'I hear you went for a little run the other day.' Ape One cracks his knuckles behind me. I turn slowly to face them. 'Where'd you go?'

'Home.' I try and shrug casually, as if it's pretty normal for me to sprint back to my house.

'Why'd you run away, hmm?' Duce leans in closer towards me. 'You scared?' I move back automatically; he smells dreadful. Jokes about deodorant ping around my brain, ready to be fired at any moment. No. Keep your cool, Alex. You don't have time for this.

'Look, I've got somewhere to be, so…' I slide my phone back in my pocket and take a few steps backwards. Callum always picks up his phone. This is the one bloody time I need him to answer and he's probably chatting up some girl somewhere.

'Ooh, he's got somewhere to be,' Duce mimics. 'You think you're something special? If I say stay here, you gotta stay here.'

'Not sure about that logic,' I mutter, growing hot now. I crane my neck past him to the school gates. Where the hell are Daisy and Callum? I can't take Duce and his Apes on my own, not physically. I mean I'm not scrawny, but there's more of them, and it's like they have ugly powers or something. My eyes meet Patty's, my last hope, but she looks away quickly, pretending to get something out of her bag. Damn it. So, my options are pretty much: 1) run or 2) run. And I ran last time. So he'll be expecting that.

'It's my logic. And my logic goes.' Duce puffs his chest out as if his man-breasts will intimidate me further.

'Hey!'

Oh, thank God: Daisy. She's tearing up the hill, school bag bouncing on her hip, her hair a red stream behind her. She looks furious. Beautifully furious.

'What the hell do you want?' She stops between Duce and I, panting slightly. I peer past her hair to see Duce's slightly shocked expression change to a sneer.

'Nothing. Just chatting. Don't worry, I won't let Patty steal your boyfriend,' he jeers. Patty laughs exaggeratedly, throwing her arms around him. Yuck. You couldn't pay me to touch Bruce Cleeve with a bargepole. Who knows what sort of disease you'd contract.

'Oh good. I was really worried you'd let your skank loose on him,' Daisy retorts sarcastically. Despite the situation, I feel myself smile slightly; she didn't deny I was her boyfriend. Maybe I am her boyfriend!

Patty stops laughing and narrows her eyes. 'I'd shut it if I were you, ginge.'

'Or what?' Daisy takes a step towards Patty, folding her arms. My happiness fades. The last thing Daisy needs right now is to get into a hair-pulling match, and the last thing I need is to try and prise an angry red-head off a bigger, taller and scarier Patty. I tug on Daisy's jumper slightly, wanting to shout, 'We don't have time!' but she pulls away.

'Just go home, little girl.' Patty matches Daisy's stance.

I'm considering literally picking Daisy up and carrying her away at this point when, to pretty much everyone's surprise, Duce mutters to Patty under his breath, 'Leave it, yeah.'

I feel my mouth fall open, mimicking the Apes' expressions behind Duce. He would never normally pass up an opportunity to cause a fight, even if it was between two girls. And to not back up his so-called girlfriend? What the hell is going on?

Patty looks livid. 'What? Did you hear what she just said to me?'

Duce looks at his feet. His chest is officially unpuffed. If anything, it looks like it's shrunk inwards.

'He said leave it, sweetie,' Daisy smirks. 'Okay? And I would if I were you. You don't want to get your little Ducey in trouble now, do you?'

'What? What does she mean?' Patty shakes Duce on the shoulder. 'Bruce?'

Duce looks like he wants to melt into the ground and never return.

'What I mean is if big bad Bruce or one of his friends comes at me or my friends ever again, your boyfriend's going to be in a lot of trouble.' Daisy uncrosses her arms and flicks a loose strand of hair out of her face. 'Got that?'

Something in my brain clicks suddenly. All along we've been wondering what Daisy can possibly have hanging over Duce's head, what she can possibly be threatening him with that makes him squirm so much. And now I'm completely certain that somehow, in some way, it all links in to the black eye. It has to.

Did Duce do that to her?

I can't really explain what's happening. I've grown hot all over. My veins feel like they're pulsing. I can literally feel anger surging through me, shooting through my bloodstream and circulating around my body. It wasn't Daisy's mum that hit her.

It was Duce.

He hit Daisy, and he gave her a black eye.

Maybe he's hit her more than once.

I can't think of anything else. In my head I can see him lunging towards her, his fists flying, that stupid, ugly face twisted in rage. Daisy's cowering on the floor, arms above her head, trying to defend herself. He's looming over, grabbing her hair with one hand, the other stretched back, ready to...

'Alex?'

Daisy's voice brings me back to the hill. I didn't realise I was moving, but I must've been. I'm now right in front of Duce, face-to-face, an inch away. It's my turn for my chest to puff out. Oh man, am I gonna enjoy this. Should I say anything? Or should I let my actions speak louder than words?

I think the second option. I drink in Duce's expression of shame and embarrassment and I know, deep down, that he knows what's coming. He'll never hear the end of it, being punched by a younger kid. A younger kid whose sister has cancer. A younger kid who leaves him alone, who goes about trying to get on with his life, keeps his head down, but still gets sought out and picked on. I can't help but smile as I raise my fist. This has been a long time coming.

'Oi!' Ape Number Two squares up to me, nudging Duce to the side. 'Leave it, yeah?'

If I'm not mistaken, there's a hint of worry in his voice. As if he almost wants to say 'please'. Pathetic. Why is he still defending him? Why is he stood there, fists clenched but face sweaty, as if he'd take Duce's punch for him? As if he'd take a beating for his big, ugly King Ape who hits girls. Who hit Daisy.

'Stop!'

It's too late. I don't know who cried out, but I can't stop. Ignoring the other Ape, I've twisted round to face Duce and swung, my fist reaching his face with a satisfying crunch. Duce recoils, snarling like an angry dog. My knuckles hurt, but it's a pain I want more of. My hand throbs with shock and anticipation, ready for the next hit. He's not getting off that easy.

'Stop!' The voice calls again. It's not Daisy. She's just staring at me in absolute shock, arms hanging limply by her side. It's not Patty; she's watching the scene with wide eyes, and a slight smile on her face. I think she's actually pretty pleased with what just happened. But it's a female voice, loud and clear.

Ah. There she is, running up the hill. Mrs Moss.

Chapter Twenty-Three

'I just don't know what to say to either of you.' Mrs Moss exhales deeply. 'I'm so… so…'

'Disappointed?' Daisy offers. Mrs Moss looks at her for a minute as if she doesn't know whether to shout or not.

'Yes,' she says eventually. 'Disappointed. Alex,' she sighs deeply, 'I never expected this from you.'

I'm too full of exhilaration to care much for Mrs Moss' sorry expression. It's the sort of thing I get from people all the time when they find out my sister's dying. And this isn't a moment to feel sorry for myself, anyway. This is a moment to be proud. I got him. I punched Duce Cleeve square in the face. And it felt amazing.

'How long do we have to wait here, Mrs Moss?' Daisy asks. 'Look, Callum's waiting for us.' He's lingering in the doorway behind the desk. Occasionally he peers through the glass and mouths 'sorry' at Daisy and I. Daisy's fuming at him for bringing Mrs Moss out, but to be honest I don't care.

Apparently, when I called Callum I'd forgotten to hang up and had left him a voicemail of the whole conversation between me and Duce. When Callum heard it, he panicked and then did what any good friend would do. Unfortunately, the one time a teacher actually appeared to see Duce's bullying in action, the victim was standing up for himself. And his girlfriend. Girlfriend. Am I getting ahead of myself? Just because Daisy didn't deny I was her boyfriend, that doesn't automatically make me her boyfriend. Does it?

'Another half-hour,' Mrs Moss breaks my trail of thought. 'Then that'll be the hour detention up. Your parents have been informed.'

'We had stuff to do, Mrs Moss!' Daisy pleads. 'It's not our fault that idiot got in our way!'

Mrs Moss shakes her head. 'I don't want to hear any more of it, Daisy. Keep reading your book. There'll be plenty of time tomorrow to sit down with the Head and have your say.'

Daisy rolls her eyes and slumps back in her chair before catching my eye. I wish we were sat closer. She smiles slightly before returning to her book, legs crossed under her desk, face still red. I think I've run out of words to describe her. She's just... everything to me. I don't know if it's still the adrenaline from what happened, or my triumph in giving Duce a taste of his own medicine, or just me finally realising I've got to man-up and do it, but it's decided. If it's not official, I'm gonna make it official. I'm going to ask Daisy to be my girlfriend.

'If we're gonna be half-an-hour,' Daisy pipes up, 'can you tell Callum to go home, Miss? He'll be waiting for ages otherwise.' Mrs Moss sighs but gets up from her desk and goes to the door. Daisy turns to me as soon as she's left.

'I can't believe it,' she whispers, leaning across the desk next to her towards me. 'You punched Duce Cleeve!'

'I know!' I can't help but grin with her. It doesn't feel real.

'I can't believe he ran off. What a wuss.'

'I know! At least he'll be in the dog-house tom—' I stop abruptly as Mrs Moss walks back in.

She eyes us beadily. 'You're not talking, are you?'

Ugh, I wish she'd just shut up for a second. I dunno if it's still the rush from what happened, but I have a sudden urge to shout at her. Like, really shout. She's ruining everything! I just need another minute alone with Daisy, just one more. She was about to tell me how proud she was of me, I bet. Or maybe something even better...

'Do you have something to say, Alex?' Mrs Moss puts a hand on her hip. Oh, so you want a challenge, do you?

'No he doesn't, Mrs Moss,' Daisy butts in. 'And we weren't talking. Just reading.' She catches my eye and winks.

*

The hour is finally up. Daisy and I don't speak as we leave, but we walk together closely. My hand brushes hers and a spark of electricity runs though me: a sign. I take a deep breath. Just do it, Alex. Heart racing, I move my hand closer to hers again and slowly, gently, entwine my fingers in hers. Is this how people hold hands properly? It feels weird. I hope my hand isn't too sweaty. Daisy moves slightly, and it feels as though we fit together now, like a jigsaw. Like our hands are meant to be like this, always. I steal a glance at her face, flushed and happy, beautiful as ever. Now's the time, Alex. Ask her.

'Alex!'

Crap. It's my dad.

*

Silence. The radio isn't even on. It's so uncomfortable. So, so uncomfortable. Well, at least I can say, for the first time in forever, that my dad has picked me up from school. We really should be celebrating this history-making occasion. Obviously his timing couldn't have been worse. That walk home with Daisy could have been life-changing. Life-altering, at least. And now she's sat behind me, probably thinking she'd rather have walked than experience my dad going over speed humps at thirty-five miles-an-hour and swearing at every pedestrian.

'Well, this is me. Thanks George.' Daisy opens the car door as Dad slows to a halt at the top of her street. He grunts in reply as she climbs out, readjusts her bag, and then looks at me. Just for a moment. Then she smiles, shakes her head, and off she goes.

'Right.' Dad revs the engine, swears, then pulls away. 'You and me have some talking to do.'

Talking to do. So official. I don't answer.

'Alex? Did you hit that boy, then?'

Straight-to-the-point. He always has been, my dad. I was a pretty well-behaved child; I only remember him really telling me off a handful of times. One was when we went to an indoor play centre and I laughed at him getting stuck down the tunnel slide. Another was when I jumped into the swimming pool without my armbands or goggles and he had to dive in and get me out. Actually, looking back on it now, I guess we did spend a bit of time together when I was a kid: swimming and play centres and all that. I glance at him, his face shadowy in the dark car, and wonder what changed. When did we stop hanging out, being friends?

'Well?' he asks sharply.

'Sorry. Yeah, I did.' I'm trying to work out if I feel scared or not. When I was little, Dad's shouting was the scariest thing in the world. Now look at him. Balding head, beer belly, and I'm almost as tall as he is. No, the look of him isn't scary anymore. It's more what lies underneath his skin; the way he snaps at Mum. His drinking. The way he doesn't care about me.

'Why?' We pull onto the driveway, but he leaves the car running.

I shrug. 'They're bullies. They're nasty to everyone.' It's not a lie. It's not solely what made me hit Duce Cleeve, but it sure is a big factor. Dad turns the key and the car quietens. Okay, maybe now I'm a little scared.

'Look,' he sighs, not looking at me. 'Your mother wanted me to pick you up and give you a good bollocking. You scared her half to death, you know? When school rang to say you'd been in a fight, she was in absolute tears. You shouldn't worry your mum that way. She's got enough to worry about.' There it is. The little comment that I always get. It comes in different forms, from different people, but it always means the same thing: that Mum and Dad's lives revolve around Jenna now. Not me.

'Right,' I snap before I can stop myself. 'Yes, I know. I get told all the time. Jenna's cancer is enough to deal with. Never mind me and my bloody problems.' I pull the door handle but the car's locked. Crap.

'Don't speak to me like that!' He turns to face me fully. 'Don't you dare, Alex.'

'What are you gonna do about it?' I fold my arms defensively. 'Not like you ever do anything about anything.'

'I look after this family!' he snaps. 'Don't you think that's a hard-enough job on its own?'

I snort. 'You're doing a great job.'

'What was that?'

'I said you're doing a great job!'

He stares at me. I can't read his expression, and I don't want to. I'm done hearing his excuses. I try the door handle again—still locked.

'Look,' he sighs. 'I'm sorry.'

'What?'

'I'm sorry.'

I can't believe my ears. My dad's actually apologising? I know I shouldn't push my luck, but I can't help it.

'What for?'

'You know what for.' He sighs. 'For everything over the past few years. It was all so much easier when you and Jen were smaller, you know?'

I don't know. But I think that's a pretty awful excuse. 'Sorry for growing,' I mutter.

Dad tuts. 'Shut it, you. I just mean… We were friends back then, all of us. Especially me and you.' He turns to face the wheel again. 'We'd hang out every Saturday, remember that?'

'Sort of.'

'Times were easier, then. I'd work Monday to Friday. Me and your mother would go to the pictures Friday night, I'd spend Saturday with you lot and Sunday at the golf club. And that was that. My whole life.' He hangs his head. 'And then, you know, the business closed down. And there was no other work going, not anywhere. We were so desperate at one point, your mum talked about retraining and getting back into an office.'

'Mum, working?'

'Yeah.' Dad gives a single, hollow laugh. 'Out of the question, right? Her place was at home with you and Jen, we both knew that. So, I had to take any old thing going. Driving, shop-work, you name it…' He trailed off. 'My hours changed. My life changed. No more Friday nights out, no more Saturdays at home with you.'

I've never thought of it like that. I mean, I knew Dad had a weird few years with jobs and stopped being around so much, but I never blamed his work for that.

'And I know what you're thinking,' he goes on heavily, 'that things never got better. Even when work straightened out, I was home, but I was never really home. My mind was elsewhere.'

'On the next drink, probably.' I clamp my hand over my mouth. 'Sorry.' Come on, Al. Listen to him. This is the most he's spoken to you in months. Maybe years.

'It's true.' Dad turns away from me to face the window, but I can hear the feeling in his voice. 'I always vowed to be different than my dad. Always. Because I know what it's like, Al, to feel like an afterthought, shoved aside like no one really cares. But I guess I failed. Because that's exactly how you feel, isn't it?'

'I dunno... I guess.' If this conversation was happening an hour or a day or a week ago, I think I'd have a lot more to say. But somehow those things seem stupid now. I've been angry at my dad for a long time, and that anger has gotten worse since the announcement. I used to think he's not handling things: he just hides away with his beer and his TV and pretends everything's fine. But I'd forgotten how sad he must be, deep inside. His daughter is dying, and his son has barely said two words to him since summer. And now I realise: he doesn't drink because he's happy, he drinks because he's lonely. Upset. Angry. He drinks to forget.

'I know I can't rewind time and act differently.' Dad turns to look at me again. I can see a tear has rolled down his cheek. 'I know that. But I can make things right now, Al. And I will. Your mother and I love you so much, you and Jenna. And we're always here for you. I'm always here for you. I'll do better. Come here.' He reaches his arms around me and pulls me in, hugging me. Hugging me? I slowly put my arms around him.

The feel of my dad takes me back to the pool, to the play centre, the football pitch, the cinema, the bowling alley. All the places we used to go, all the time we spent together, all that stuff I always thought had been thrown away. But maybe it hasn't been. Maybe there's still hope for us yet.

Chapter Twenty-Four

I can't explain what happened to me yesterday. It was like, after the fight on the hill—if you call it a fight: it was more a case of me punching King Ape, the Apes ambling off, and Mrs Moss putting me in detention—I experienced every single emotion a boy could. Pride, for finally getting Duce, for protecting Daisy. Happiness, holding her hand. Fear, in Dad's car. What else in Dad's car? Forgiveness, love, understanding. At home, Mum cried, Jenna cried, and we all talked on the sofa for ages. They told me they loved me, they always have, that Jenna's illness would never take that away. Today, I feel like a whole new person. Well, sort of. Maybe that's because I've had hours sat in the isolation booth all morning to 'Reflect on myself and my actions', as Mr Ball put it.

'Alex.' Mrs Moss appears in the doorway, armed with more textbooks and lined paper. Looks like my afternoon will be just as fun, then.

'Hi. Thanks, Miss.'

She places them on my desk and observes me for a minute, folding her arms and leaning against the wall. 'Are you all right, Alex?'

Am I all right? I don't know. At least I'm not raging at Mrs Moss anymore: that'd be awkward. I think I was just emotional yesterday. And then she walked in and ruined my chat with Daisy…

Anyway. In some ways, I don't think I've been this happy in a long time: probably not since way before Jenna's diagnosis. It hasn't officially happened yet, but Daisy's going to be my girlfriend. I finally feel like my home is my home again, that my family care about me. I punched Duce in the face.

I should be feeling on top of the world, right? But I'm not. I can't. Because on top of all that, there's no getting away from the guilt. The ache of sadness, almost regret, that comes with being in a good place. I shouldn't be in a good place, should I? Not when my sister's...

I dunno. I feel drained. My body and my mind are exhausted. And there's still that niggling part at the back of my brain, constantly reminding me over and over time's creeping by, and I still haven't figured out what's going to happen to Jenna. But all this is for a proper session with Mrs Moss. Not an answer to a casual question.

'I'm fine, thanks.'

*

Daisy and Callum are waiting for me by the gates. I'm relieved beyond words that I get to leave school at normal time; my breaktime was before the normal one and I was made to eat lunch at my stupid isolation desk, so I haven't seen anyone apart from teachers all day. I don't think I've ever been happier to fight my way through the sea of blue jumpers to the school gates.

'Alex! We heard what happened yesterday.' Yusuf and Luca appear next to me, grinning.

'What can I say?' I shrug. 'He had it coming.'

'Wow. You're so brave!' Luca exclaims, his eyes shining. They both look so happy, so excited, and a thought suddenly strikes me: though that punch was for Daisy I think it meant a lot to others, too. All the kids like Yusuf and Luca, who've suffered his torment for years, constantly worrying if he's lurking around the next corner, have finally seen Duce get a taste of his own medicine. I feel kinda great that I could make that happen.

'Are you in trouble?' Yusuf asks.

'Not really. Mr Ball spoke to everyone there, and he knows I was provoked. I had detention last night and isolation today, and that's it. All done and dusted.' I clap my hands together.

'And what does Duce get?'

'Not a clue. Don't care.' I tell them, honestly. Whatever punishment he gets will be nothing compared to the backlash he'll suffer from the humiliation of all this anyway. 'I'll see you later, guys.'

''Bye, Alex! Well done!' Yusuf and Luca weave their way out of the gates, laughing and joking, not looking over their shoulders for once, and I can't help but smile to myself.

'What are you grinning at?' Callum tucks my head under his arm and scruffs up my hair.

'Oi!' I break free and give him a shove.

'Why wouldn't he be grinning?' Daisy laughs, linking both of our arms into hers. 'He's the talk of the school! The hero that punched Duce Cleeve. Sounds like a newspaper headline.'

'Oh yeah,' Callum nods. 'You really are all everyone's talking about, mate. I heard your name mentioned at lunch at least a thousand times. And all the girls love it!' I shoot a glance at Daisy who ignores his last comment.

'How was isolation, anyway?' she asks instead, unlinking her arm from Callum's to produce a roll of Hubba Bubba from her bag. 'Want some?'

I break some off and pop it in my mouth. 'Boring. At least it was only one day. Were you in any trouble?'

'Nah.' Daisy hands some gum to Callum. 'Just the detention last night. Lucky Cal brought Mrs Moss when he did, or I may have got off a lot worse.'

'Why?' Callum waves away the gum and unwraps a chocolate bar instead.

'I think I would've started swinging some punches myself!' she laughs, tossing her hair back. The sunlight hits it at a new angle and all these new colours become visible: blonde and strawberry-blonde and red and ginger and brown. I look away before Callum catches me staring.

'No you wouldn't!' Callum says to Daisy.

'I would've!' she insists. 'If you hadn't been such a swot and ran to the teacher!'

'Shut up,' Callum laughs in a way that tells me they've already settled this argument, 'it sounded like Alex was literally about to die!' They both laugh. I try and laugh too, but the last word loops around in my head instead. Die.

'Come on, slow coach.' They've walked off ahead of me slightly. My brain's moving too fast to walk properly. Die, die, die. Death. Dying. Doctors. The cottage!

'Wait!' I call. 'Do you guys have time to go the hospice today?' I check my watch. 'We can make it easy if we go straight there.'

Daisy and Callum glance at each other.

'Come on! We won't be too long. I really want to go, guys.' I try and keep the desperation out of my voice, probably without much success. I can't believe everything that happened made me forget! Yes, well done me for punching Duce. But this is the priority. Jenna is the priority.

'I'm sorry, Al.' Daisy links my arm as I reach them. 'I'm grounded. I can't go.'

Well, we did it without her before. I glance at Callum, but he's looking at the floor. I know what he's going to say before he even opens his mouth.

'Sorry, mate. I've got plans tonight.'

'How about at the weekend?' Daisy asks brightly. 'Saturday? We can all go then. And then we won't have to rush, either.'

'Yeah,' Callum says quickly, 'Saturday's good. Yeah, Alex? Saturday?'

'Saturday,' I nod. I'm not completely happy with waiting another three days, but I suppose it's the best I'm gonna get. And I really don't want to go all the way there on my own.

'Cool. See you guys tomorrow, then!' Callum turns off down his road.

''Bye, Cal!' Daisy calls, waving, before turning back to me. 'What?'

'What?'

'What are you looking at me like that for?' she laughs.

'Like what?' I hope my 'Please be my girlfriend' look isn't too creepy.

'Nothing.' I watch as she blows a bubble and lets it pop,

scraping the leftovers from her lips with her tongue. Okay, here it goes. Come on, Alex, you've had all day to rehearse it. Just ask the damn question!

'I've got something to tell you.' She speaks before I've opened my mouth.

'Me too.'

'Me first.' She blows another bubble, a smaller one this time, which pops neatly. 'Look, I just want to ask: why did you hit Duce?'

'Because he's an idiot,' I shrug. 'He's nasty. He wound me up too much.' I know she knows there's more to it than that, but it's just difficult. Ever since the black eye and then the row about me telling Callum, I've tiptoed around the subject; I know if Daisy wanted to talk about it with me, she would. And she hasn't.

'Why did you really hit him, Alex?' she asks softly. Okay. Maybe she is ready to talk about it.

'I think you know why,' I say carefully. 'I worked it out: why he's so weird around you. It's because... It's because he hit you, isn't it?'

'What? Duce hit me?'

'Yeah.'

Daisy shakes her head. 'No, Alex! Bruce never hit me. He didn't give me...' She gestures to her eye.

'Bruce didn't hit you?'

'No.'

I feel my mouth open and close while I work out what to say. What the hell? If Duce didn't hit her, then who did? Oh God. Her mum? Was I right all along?

'I'll tell you who did,' Daisy says quietly, 'but you can't tell anyone else. You really can't this time. Okay?'

'Okay.' My heart's thudding. I'm finally finding out. And when I do, I'm going to punch them in the face as well.

She sighs and leads me to the kerb. We sit. She spits her gum on the floor and we watch it roll away.

'You know I said my mum has a new boyfriend?' she says eventually.

'Yeah.'

'Well, her new boyfriend is…' She makes a sick face. 'Duce's dad.'

'What!?' I can't help but shout. Duce's dad and Daisy's mum: together?

'Yeah. Gross, right?' She looks at her feet. 'And to make matters worse, he has a wife.'

'A wife?' I echo.

'A wife,' she confirms. 'So yeah, my mum and his dad are having an… affair.' She falters over the word, obviously upset by it. I place my hand on hers. Not to hold it, just to be there for her. Just to let her know it's okay.

'That's awful,' I whisper.

'I know,' she sniffs. 'It's been happening for a while. I found out about it at the same time Duce did. His dad's really high-up in the council or the government or something, so this has to be kept super hush-hush or it could ruin his career. That's why,' she sniffs again, harder this time, 'Duce tiptoes around me. He knows I could tell everyone and ruin everything.' She blinks away tears. I wish I could wipe them for her. I wish I had the right things to say. But what can I say?

'And… And that's who gave me the black eye. Duce's dad.'

'Duce's dad?' I feel my blood growing hot, my heartbeat quickening. Things are worse than I ever could have imagined. A big, ugly bully didn't hit my Daisy. His dad did. 'Who the hell does he think…?'

'Alex, calm down,' Daisy pleads, 'remember, no one can know.'

I want to calm down, I do: for Daisy, more than anything. But how am I supposed to do that? I've just found out that a grown man, a slimy, evil old man has hit Daisy. Bruised her. And is having an affair with her mum! I clench the kerb, tiny bits of gravel piercing my palms.

Daisy rests her head on my shoulder, her messy hair tickling my chin. The feel of it does calm me, slightly. She's here now. She's safe. I swallow hard. I don't know if I want the answer to this, but I want to ask it. 'Has he hit you more than once?'

'No,' Daisy says quickly, sitting up properly. 'Honest. Just that once. I made him really angry. You know I'm good at winding people up. He was sneaking around again while Mum was asleep, making phone calls and all that, probably to his wife. So, I told him to leave. And some other things.' She looks down at her feet. 'Probably shouldn't have.'

'I would have done the same,' I reassure her. 'Anyway, no matter what you said, it doesn't give an old man an excuse to lay a finger on you! If that ever happens again, you have to call me. I'll come and get you. I won't ever let you get hurt again. Okay? I promise.' We link pinkies, the coolness of her finger against the warmth of mine and I look at her face-on, into her beautiful brown eyes. We're so close I can hear her breathing. I want to kiss her. I really want to kiss her.

'Oh crap.' She unlinks her finger suddenly. 'I'm meant to go straight home after school. I'm grounded.'

'Oh, right.' I stand as she does, feeling dazed, overwhelmed. And mainly pissed off. There goes another missed chance.

'Thank you, Alex.' She pulls me in and wraps her arms around me. Two hugs in two days? All this physical contact feels weird. I hug her back, anyway, so hard it feels like her heart's beating in my chest.

'Thank you,' I say, my mouth full of her hair, 'for being brave and telling me. I know it must have been hard.'

She pulls away and smiles, that signature Daisy smile, and walks off. I watch her for a moment, my head full of a thousand questions. Will she be okay? Should I go after her? Will I be in trouble if I hunt down and kill a government man? Do I even feel relieved that she's finally told me what really happened? I don't think I do. Because, if anything, this information has just messed up my life a little bit more. As if it's not messed up enough already.

Chapter Twenty-Five

No sign of Duce Cleeve today.

I didn't see him yesterday obviously, cooped up in that room, so today I'm on the lookout. He could be lurking anywhere, plotting his revenge. Though now I know his little secret I doubt he'll cause me any more trouble. I smile to myself as I get my science books out of my locker; despite this whole messed-up situation with Daisy's mum, things couldn't be better for me in the Duce situation. Not only did I smack him round the face and the whole school knows, I also discovered his dirty dad's secret, which I could reveal to everyone at any moment. Not that I would, as Daisy's asked me not to, and I think that would cause more trouble than it's worth, but still. It's the principle.

Anyway. It's the perfect time. Well, as good a time as ever. Callum's playing football on the field, and Daisy and I are on the bench under the oak tree. There's hardly anyone around: it's pizza day in the café, and most of the lads have organised a big five-a-side tournament over the next few lunch times. So it's me and Daisy.

'Was your mum mad when you got home?' I ask as she finishes her sandwich.

'Nah,' she says through a mouthful.

'Good.'

She takes a final bite and scrunches her rubbish up into a ball.

'A fiver says I can get it in the bin.' She points to the bin; it's at least five feet away.

'You're on.' We shake on it, and I watch her carefully judge the wind, distance and shape of the rubbish before throwing it. It lands a foot to the left.

'Damn! Best of three?' she asks, laughing.

'No way! Cough up,' I joke, not really expecting anything from her.

'It's such a nice day.' She rests her head on my chest again, suddenly soft and slumped against me.

'It is,' I murmur. It is warm for February, but the weather's not what I'm focusing on. It never is when she's around. 'Daisy?'

'Mmm?'

Here goes nothing. I'm sweating again. Do I have some sort of sweating issue? It's just every time I think about doing this, it happens. And my heart goes insane. And I feel like I might be sick. But all in a good way. Sort of.

'Can I… Can I ask you something?'

'Sure.' She doesn't move her head. Does she even want to have this conversation? Does she know what I'm going to ask? Oh God, what if she says no? What if she says no?

'Um… I mean, you don't have to say yes, but I was just thinking… what I wanted to tell you yesterday was…' Come on, Alex. Almost there. 'I really like you. I think you're really pretty and funny and nice and crazy.' I'm aware I'm speaking really quickly. I hope she can understand what I'm saying. 'And I'd like us to be more than friends, a bit. So… would you… will you… be my girlfriend?' There it is. I've done it. She moves her head a little; it stays on my chest but she's looking up at me now, her eyes wide.

'Be your girlfriend?'

Damn it, why is she making me say it again? I swallow. 'Yes.'

She sits up properly now. I can't tell what she's thinking, her face is unreadable. She cocks her head to the side for a moment, as if she's thinking. I don't think my heart can take much more of this.

'Sure.'

Sure.

'Sure?' I echo. Is that a yes?

'Sure,' she repeats with a giggle. 'I'd very much like that.'

Okay, that sounds more like a definite yes. Heart: you can resume normal beating. Body: you can go back to regular temperature. It's a yes! I want to scream it to the empty playground. She said yes!

'Cool.' I hope she can't tell how madly happy I am. I hope she just thinks I'm averagely happy: like anyone would be, like she is. She's smiling a lot, leaning back on the bench, her hand draped over mine. My girlfriend. I have a girlfriend!

*

My heart's still racing as I run home. I can't wait to tell Jenna. After how she helped me with the whole Breakfast Club incident, she needs to be the first to know. Plus, she's been feeling pretty down—more so than usual—the past few days, so hopefully this news will cheer her up. She deserves cheering up. I can picture her now, cracking open a bottle of wine, asking me all the details. She'll want Daisy to come for dinner, to meet everyone as 'The Girlfriend'. She'll want to paint Daisy's nails, to go shopping with her, to watch boring daytime TV with her. I know she will. She'll make her feel really welcome.

But… This is strange. The front door is locked. I try again, just to make sure I'm not being an idiot. Nope, definitely locked. I rap on the door a couple of times, pressing my ear against the letterbox. I can hear Roscoe scrambling around, but no sign of human life. Maybe Jenna has an appointment? I root around for my key, which turns out to be at the bottom of my pencil case, and unlock the door.

'Hey, buddy.' I say, bending down to greet Roscoe as he licks my shoes excitedly. 'Hello?' I call into the house. No answer. Definitely no one here. Roscoe follows me into the kitchen. I make myself a peanut butter sandwich and feed him the crusts, sitting at the empty table. It's quiet. Too quiet. I check my texts from Mum over the last few days, but there's no mention of any appointment. Surely, they would have at least told me I'd need my house key today? What if I'd have left it at home?

'Where are they, hmm?' I ask Roscoe. He swallows the last of his snack and looks at me sadly. 'Where are they?' He wants to tell me, I know he does.

I sit on the floor next to him for a minute, feeling his comforting warmth, hearing his comforting pants, but I can't help but feel worried. A part of me wants to call Mum. A part of me wants to stay safely on the floor with Roscoe until they come home. I mean, they could be anywhere. They could have just popped out to the shops, or to see a movie.

Or they could have gone to the hospital. Something could have happened. Something has happened. I just know it. The dial tone is the slowest it's ever been. Come on, Mum. Pick up. My hand's shaking. Roscoe lies on my feet, breathing slowly, reminding me to do that too. Breathe, Alex. Everything will be fine.

Chapter Twenty-Six

Everything is not fine. After Mum, Dad and Jenna didn't answer their phones, I had to distract myself. I took Roscoe for a long walk, fed him, tidied my room, did some homework and still no news. I made myself some beans on toast, had a shower… still nothing. It's around 7 pm when the front door opens.

'I know, I know, I'm sorry,' are the first words out of Dad's mouth before pouring himself a glass of something that looked and smells gross.

'What the hell's been happening?' I demand. 'I rang you about a thousand times!'

'I know. Sorry.' He takes a sip. 'Not much signal at the hospital.' The hospital. My stomach flips. I knew it. I bloody knew it. 'Your sister's had a funny few days, worse than usual. Not sure if you've noticed?' I feel a surge of guilt run through me as I realise: actually, no. I didn't notice. Where the hell has my brain been? Everywhere but here. At school with Daisy, that's where. For God's sake. What kind of brother am I? I watch Dad down the rest of his drink and pour himself another one, and as he a little voice in the back of my brain pipes up: Of course you wouldn't notice. She's always ill. She's dying.

'Anyway.' Dad slumps into a chair. 'She felt really sick after lunch. So sick, she fainted.'

Lunch? She's been in hospital since lunch?

'Why didn't you call me?'

Dad shakes his head. 'Your mother didn't want to disturb you at school. I know we should've. I'm sorry.' He glugs back some more alcohol. Like he always does. 'We had to wait a long time to be seen. Mum was having a meltdown, screaming at the nurses, making a right scene.' I know he's trying to make light of it all, but there is no light in this. None at all. I just look at him. 'Anyway.' He clears his throat. 'Some tests were done and… Turns out…' His eye flits to the bottle, then back to me. 'She's got a blocked bowel.'

'Blocked bowel? Is that … Is that bad?'

Dad shifts in his seat. 'It's a common… I mean… Well, the doctors have put a little thing through her nose… Nasogastric tube or something it's called. It'll help drain the stomach a little, stop her feeling so sick.' He tosses back the last of the drink, his eyes going back to the bottle.

'I said is that bad?' The tone of my voice makes his eyes widen. I didn't mean to snap, not really. I just want an answer. Although I also sort of don't.

'Yeah, Al. It's bad.' He sounds just as annoyed as I do. 'It means it's advanced. It's spread. It's gotten worse. It means…' He looks at his feet. 'It means time's running out.' He caves in then and reaches for the bottle again. I don't blame him.

*

'Do you want anything?' Mum pops her head into the living room. 'Tea? Toast?'

'No thanks, Mum,' Jenna says. She sounds like she's got a really bad sore throat.

'No thanks.' I haven't been able to stomach anything since last night. Since another announcement. The worst one yet.

'You've Been Framed? Emmerdale? The news?' Kent's flicking through the TV channels, looking at Jenna hopefully. It's like her love for crappy TV has completely fizzled out. Everything's fizzled out.

'How about a nice film?' Mum asks, taking a seat next to me.

'Sure.' Kent flicks on to the movies section and begins reeling them off. Jenna doesn't want any of them, I know she doesn't. I want to scream at them all, Leave her alone! She just wants to lie there for a while. Wouldn't you?

Mum swallows. 'Jenna, your father and I have been thinking, and we're going to cancel our trip.'

'No, Mum…' Jenna starts to protest.

'Jenna, really. We can't. I know it's only one night, but that's one night too many.'

'Cindy, please,' Kent pipes up, 'we've been through this. I know you're worried, but it's all under control. I'm going to be here every minute to look after her.'

'I know, Kent, but I really should be the one to…'

'Cindy, you've had this room booked for months,' Kent says firmly. 'And all your theatre tickets and everything! You need to go. Nothing's going to change here.'

'You really shouldn't miss it, Mum,' Jenna agrees. 'I don't want you to stay. I want you to go.'

Mum sighs deeply. 'Let me go and speak to your father again. I just… I don't know.' She leaves, taking some empty mugs with her, and the room falls into silence once again.

'I don't know what she thinks she's going to miss,' Jenna croaks. 'I'm not gonna fluff it in the next couple of days, am I? They said three months minimum.' My heart sinks, just as it did when Mum told me the news last night. Three months. Maybe more, they can't be sure. Three months.

'Too early for jokes like that,' Kent nudges her and settles on an old Disney film. 'Look, Beauty and the Beast is on.'

'I don't like that film anymore.' Jenna rolls away from the TV, curling herself into a tighter ball. Kent tucks the blanket around her.

'Sure you do.'

'I don't like anything anymore.' She sounds on the verge of tears. I can feel my own eyes growing wet. I don't like anything anymore either. None of this is fair. None of it.

*

The dreams have come back. They never completely went away,

to be honest, just became less scary and more bearable. I think it's because, for a while, I had a focus, a mission; the time frame was unlimited, it felt, though looking back now it never really was. Her days were always numbered, I just never liked to admit it. Well, now those numbers are less than I ever wanted to know. In the thousands, maybe even the hundreds, maybe even less.

The thought of it makes me want to throw up, though there's nothing in my stomach so it'd be pretty much impossible right now. I haven't eaten since around 6 pm on Wednesday; it's now 4 am on Friday. I don't feel hungry, though. I don't feel anything but anger and pain. Like someone's physically hurt me, like I've been hit by a car or something. And just miserable. What's the point? What's the point of all of this? What was the point in putting her on this earth just to take her away so soon, so painfully? Who did this? What did this? Or are scientists right, and it's all just evolution and cold, hard facts? Maybe no one's entitled to a full and happy life, you just get what you're given. Well, what Jenna's been given isn't fair. My sister should be here until she's ninety-something, hobbling around, a bag of wrinkles and laughter, able to leave to venture beyond when she's ready. She's not ready now.

'Please.' I clasp my hands together and squeeze my eyes shut. It's my last hope. 'Dear God, if you are up there—or somewhere—and you can hear me, please listen. My sister is poorly. They've given her months to live. And...' My voice is breaking. 'I know you probably get these requests all the time but I'd like her to stay. Please. Just a little while longer.' I can feel the tears rolling down my cheeks now, but I'm not strong enough to hold them in anymore. 'I promise I'll be a better person. We'll all be better people. We'll start going to church and reading the Bible... I mean, I have read it before, but not in a while. Anyway... please. Please help Jenna. Amen.'

I keep my eyes closed for a moment, feeling the last few tears trickle off my face. I hope He heard that. I hope someone heard that. I really don't know if there's any creators, any Gods for real. But if there is, they need to help me. Help Jenna. Taking a deep breath, I roll over to face the clock again. 4:17 am. Still hours until anyone will be awake.

Mum and Dad go for their stay in London today. I know it's hard for Mum to leave Jenna, but I think it'll be nice for them to go and take their minds off things for a while, if they can. I'm so lucky I've had Daisy and Callum and—in a weird sort of way—even Duce and schoolwork and things to fill my days. And, of course, the project. The Scrapbook of Beyond. Which now we really, really need to finish.

Chapter Twenty-Seven

Friday passed in a blur. I must've fallen asleep again, because I woke up late afternoon to Jenna and Kent taking a nap, and Mum and Dad already gone. Kent ordered pizza for dinner and made me eat some. I went back to bed. And now here I am: 7 am Saturday morning, waking up to a text from Daisy. I'd fallen asleep while we were messaging last night. I'm not ready to talk about things properly with her, but I filled her in a little about why I haven't been at school. She's been sending lots of kisses and well wishes and—though I appreciate it, I really do—my mind just isn't on Daisy right now.

'Alex?' There's a tap on the door.

'Come in.'

'Hi.' It's Kent. At 7 am, in my bedroom. 'Can I come in?'

'Um, sure?' I hide myself under the duvet a bit more and put my phone face-down on the bedside table. 'What's up?'

Kent sort of laughs. 'It's gonna sound crazy.'

'Good-crazy?'

'Is he awake?' Jenna calls from the corridor.

'Yeah,' Kent shouts back.

'Oh good.' She marches in, a completely different person from yesterday. Well, still pale, still skinny, still sick. But she's dressed, make-up done, wig on, smiling. I can't help but smile, too. 'Morning, smelly.'

'Morning.' I sniff my armpits. Yes, I do smell.

'You need a shower before we go,' Jenna laughs at my expression.

'Go where?'

'That's what I was saying,' Kent says. 'So, your sister had a crazy idea…'

'Not crazy!' Jenna jumps on the bed next to Kent. 'Exciting. Fun. A live-for-the-moment idea. I need those, you know?' She looks at me as if expecting an answer. I nod.

'She wants to go to the seaside,' Kent finishes, raising his eyebrows in a sort of 'yes-I-know-it's-mental' way.

'Um…' They're both looking at me—Jenna grinning, Kent apologetic—as if they're waiting for my approval. 'You know it's March, right?'

Jenna bursts into fits of laughter. 'Yes, silly! We know what month it is. The perfect month for the seaside. It'll be nice and quiet. Now hurry up and shower.' She rolls herself off the bed, still giggling, and dances out the door and down the corridor. I look at Kent.

'I know what you're thinking,' he holds his hands up, 'and I know, it's a little crazy. And I know your mum probably wouldn't approve. But,' he leans towards me slightly and lowers his voice, 'this is what your sister needs. A day out, some fresh air, some fun with her two favourite guys. What do you say?'

What do I say? There's a small, sensible part of me that wants to say 'No, idiot! She has medication and stuff, she can't just roam around on the beach!' But the bigger part of me knows it would be wrong to keep her cooped up inside, like a caged animal. We have to face it; we know Jenna's not going to be here for much longer. And I'd way rather have fun with a smiley, happy sister than be sat inside with a sad one.

'I'm in,' I whisper. We bump fists.

'Now go get that shower,' Kent instructs, getting up from the bed. 'Because trust me: you really do stink.'

*

Well, Jenna was right. The beach is very quiet.

'It's beautiful!' she breathes as we pull into the carpark. 'Look, Al! Look at the sea!' It's a murky grey, waves crashing against the rocks by the shore. It does look pretty cool. And it looks even cooler because Jenna's so excited about it.

'Come on, then!' We get our picnic and beach bags out the boot, clip Roscoe onto his lead and run down to the sand. I forgot how nice seaside air is, so fresh and free. And cold. Bloody cold.

'Let's go in the sea!' Jenna exclaims, kicking off her shoes.

'Already?' Kent groans. 'We just got here!'

'We'll have more time to dry after,' Jenna insists. 'Come on. Al?' Okay, so I said the sea looked cool, not that I wanted to jump into it. But what I want or don't want doesn't matter, I suppose. It's Jenna's Seaside Day, after all, so if that means I get hypothermia: well then, that'll add to the memories.

'I'll race you down there!' she exclaims, flinging her wig into the beach bag. 'Ready…' I take off before she says go, laughing at her shouts from behind me. Holy crap it's freezing. Are we mental? I stop directly before the water's edge, sticking my toes in first. The cold shoots through me like pain.

'Come on, loser!' Jenna splashes right in ahead of me. 'Ah! It's bloody freezing!' She's up to her shoulders now, waving at me. 'Come on!' Here goes nothing. I run in as she did; surely, it's better to just do it all in one go, anyway, than to faff around not getting your shoulders under. But jeez. Jeez jeez jeez it's horrible. Jenna splashes water in my direction.

'Missed me!' I splash her back; my aim's better. I get her right in the face.

'Argh! You'll pay for that!' She swims over to me messily, water flying everywhere. I swim in the opposite direction.

'Come catch me then!'

'Be careful, you two!' Kent calls; he's stood where the waves meet the shore with Roscoe, who looks very unimpressed with the beach.

'Do you think there's sharks?' Jenna calls. 'I think I just felt one!'

'There will not be any sharks in English seas in March,' Kent reassures her, laughing. 'Maybe you felt a big fish.'

'Ew!' Jenna propels herself closer to me. 'Get it away, Al!'

'I'm no good at catching fish,' I laugh. 'But I do feel like I'm turning blue. Race you to the beach?'

'You're on.' Jenna dunks my head underwater and swims off; I can hear her cackling and splashing away. I was not ready for that. My eyes feel like they're going to fall out. Great, so I'll be blue and blind by the end of the day. The things you do for family.

*

She's asleep now. Our drive home has been much quieter than our journey there; Jenna drifted off in the first ten minutes, so map duty's down to me now. I'm not surprised she's exhausted—we were literally out all day.

'Take the next exit,' I instruct Kent.

'Cheers.' He indicates then moves into the inside lane. 'Do you think she had fun today then?'

'Yeah,' I say. 'I really do. I haven't seen her smile that much in ages.'

'Me neither,' Kent sighs. 'It was great to see. Just... a shame.' I don't know exactly what he means is a shame. Maybe that Jenna's fallen asleep before we had dinner. Maybe that this could be her last time at a seaside. Maybe that she got cancer in the first place. I feel a lump rise in my throat as I look at him: Jenna's loyal boyfriend, sticking with her through all the good and bad. Okay, there was that glitch a few months back, but I do think Kent's a good person. He was just learning to deal with things, like we all were. Like we still are.

'Thanks, Kent.' My voice is quieter than I thought it'd be. 'For taking us today.' I didn't mean to add that end bit on. I just meant to thank him, for everything.

'No worries, mate. You know I love her.'

'I know.' There's so much more I want to say, but I can't find the words. I think Kent knows, anyway.

Chapter Twenty-Eight

Sundays mean roast dinners. Well, they did before the announcement. A massive chunk of hot chicken or beef, peas and carrots, crunchy potatoes, gravy. Yorkshires from the packet. Mum's done a few roasts since, but they've always been so much fancier. She makes everything from scratch, spends hours 'seasoning' and 'flavouring' with weird herbs and spices. The veg and Yorkshires don't come from the freezer anymore: she makes and prepares them from scratch. Basically, it's another opportunity for her to hide in the kitchen. And today's no different.

'When will it be ready?' I can't help asking. It's almost 6 pm and I'm bloody starving. It makes me ten-times hungrier when I can smell it all cooking for hours.

'Five more minutes!' Mum calls from behind the fridge. 'Go and lay the table for me, Al.'

I do as she says; she's been in a pretty good mood since getting back from London and I wanna keep it that way. I think if she knew about our beach trip she'd feel a little differently.

'Get everyone up at the table!' Mum calls, still clanging around in the kitchen.

'Sure, Mum.' I slope into the living room where I'd left everyone to find it empty. Excellent. Well, Dad's probably gone to the garage or the loo or something, so I'll leave him to it. I climb the stairs instead; Jenna and Kent must've gone up to Jenna's room. I reach her door and go to knock, but something stops me. I can hear noises in there. I think she's crying. I move my face closer to the door.

'Shh. It's all right,' Kent's saying softly. I pull away. I shouldn't be listening to this. I can't listen to this. It's like, just for a while yesterday, I forgot Jenna was ill. I think she managed to forget, too. She just got to splash around and play arcade games and bury Kent in sand like someone without cancer would. But she never gets to keep that feeling for long. It's looming over her now, looming over all of us.

*

'So. You've had quite an eventful few days, Alex.' Mrs Moss crosses and uncrosses her legs. For the first time, she looks uncomfortable. I don't think she knows what to say.

'Yes.' I say. I don't know what to say either. If you call finding out my sister has possibly months to live, a whirlwind trip to the beach and an endless stream of nightmares eventful, then yes, I suppose it was. I'm so mad at Mum for making me come into school today. I put up a good fight, but she insisted, saying I can't stay off forever. I wanted to yell back, 'Well, Jenna's not going to be here forever!' but I didn't. Like Dad and Gran and everyone's said before, she has bigger things to worry about than me.

'And… Is there anything you can think of that school can do to support you during this time?' Mrs Moss looks at me expectantly.

Yes. Let me have some time off. Let me see my sister.

'No.'

'Are you sure, Alex?' She leans in towards me. 'Anything at all? Maybe…' she flicks through her notes. 'More frequent counselling sessions? A time-out pass? A social group therapy, maybe?'

I just look at her. With her stupid fringe and her stupid sad smile and her stupid buttoned-up blouse. I hate her.

I don't hate her.

She's only trying to help. That's all she's ever done. Come on, make an effort, Al. You never know, maybe one of those things will make things slightly easier.

'A time-out pass might help,' I tell her. 'You know, in case I get upset or something.'

'Yes, of course.' Mrs Moss writes it on a post-it note. 'I'll get that sorted as soon as possible for you. Anything else? Do you want to see me or another counsellor more? Or maybe we can speak to your mum about counselling outside of school?'

'That's enough about me,' I say before I can stop myself. 'I don't want to talk about me, what I need. I don't need anything except my sister. And I can't have her for much longer.'

I'm so tired. So damn tired. Tired physically, tired mentally, tired of talking about counselling and this and that and the other. I know I probably sound a bit rude, but I'm past caring. Past caring about anything but what I set out to do in the first place.

'If I can't save Jenna, then I need to find out where she's going. I really do, Miss. It's the only way I can help her, make things better for her. Not properly better, but, you know, a little bit. At least if we know she's going somewhere where she can be safe and happy, somewhere she can look down on us then...'

'Of course.' Mrs Moss takes a deep breath. 'Well, Alex, you know I'm here to help in any way I can. And if the way you'd like help is to carry on with researching the beyond, adding to your scrapbook, then I'll be of any assistance I can. Have you visited the hospice yet?'

I shake my head.

'Okay, so that's on your list of places... I really would try and go there soon, Alex, I think it'll be very informative. Not only for your mission, but to,' she swallows, 'to maybe have a think about if that's somewhere Jenna will go.'

'Somewhere Jenna will go?'

'You know,' she looks uncomfortable again. 'To... pass.'

To pass. To die.

'Right.'

'You know, I go to a hospice every week, to visit my uncle. They're really, well, they're friendly places.' Mrs Moss reaches for a tissue.

'Your uncle's in a hospice?' I try and hide the shock in my voice.

'Yes.' She wipes under her eyes, which have black smudged under them.

'You've never told me that.'

'No.' She smiles slightly. 'I felt this was the right time.'

I don't think she's telling the truth. There's no 'right time' for this sort of thing. I think she didn't tell me before because it's hard to tell people someone you love is dying. That's something no one prepares you for: how damn difficult it is to get the words out. To see the same shocked, sympathetic expression a hundred times, to hear 'I'm sorry to hear that', over and over.

And now, for the first time, I'm that person. 'I'm sorry.'

'Not your fault.' Mrs Moss takes a deep breath and chucks the tissue in the bin behind her. 'And this isn't my counselling session, it's yours. I just thought I'd let you know that when—if—Jenna goes to a hospice, it's nothing to be scared of. They're generally very warm, welcoming places. You'll see, anyway, when you visit.'

'Thanks, Miss.'

'No problem. Right.' She clicks her pen. 'And have you thought of any other avenues you'd like to explore?'

'I dunno,' I say. 'To be honest, a lot's riding on this hospice visit. I've found everything else so... hard to find a proper answer. Religion is so difficult to understand and believe in, you know, with all the scientific evidence and that. I'd like to think it's true but...' Should I tell her? I'll tell her. 'I prayed to God and heard nothing back. If He's there, if someone's there, why are they ignoring me? Ignoring her?'

Mrs Moss puts her notebook down. 'Some things are difficult to explain and understand,' she says softly. 'And what happens when life ends is a prime example of one of those things. It's not called "life's greatest mystery" for nothing, Alex. And in the case of religion,' she picks the notebook up again, 'it's all very speculative. It doesn't matter what everyone else believes in, simply what you think is true.'

'I don't know yet.' My voice is shaky. 'It's hard.'

Mrs Moss nods. 'It's very hard. But if you haven't found what you're looking for yet, Alex, then you need to keep looking.'

Chapter Twenty-Nine

Today's the day: the Hospice Day. Daisy's not grounded anymore, Callum doesn't have any plans, and we're all prepared to go. I've got my notebook, Daisy's got her voice recorder, Callum's got... well, Callum's more moral support. I make my way up the hill outside school and go over the route in my head: left, down to Parsons Green, cross the road, past the dentist...

'Oi!' The voice sounds familiar, but I can't place exactly who it is. I ignore it anyway; everyone's rushing out of school. They're probably speaking to someone else.

'Oi!'

I turn around this time. Oh, brilliant. It's an Ape. Not King Duce himself—I haven't seen him since my fist hit his jaw—but the other, less important one. Still big, spotty and ugly though.

'What do you want?' I don't know what he thinks he's doing, ambling up to me in the exact spot I smacked his leader. Maybe he wants to relive it. Maybe he wants to have a go at hitting me this time.

'You better watch out, mate.' He looks me up and down. 'Don't go givin' it all the big un' now.'

Why does this always happen when we're in a rush to go somewhere? It's like the Apes can smell we have places to be and want to hold us up. Well, I've got no patience for it today.

'Yeah, right. Off you go then.' I wave him away just as I spot Daisy and Callum climbing the hill behind him. At least they're out on time today. We've got a schedule.

The Ape laughs. 'I'll go where I want.'

'Well done. Me too.' I speak as if I'm talking to a baby whose stood up for the first time. He scowls.

'Hey, Al.' Daisy and Callum have reached us. Daisy gives me a peck on the cheek and the Ape recoils.

'Gross. You going out with a ginger, Alex?'

Daisy pretends to jump back in horror. 'Yuck! What the hell is that?' She opens her bottle and starts flicking water at him. 'The power of Christ compels you! The power of Christ compels you!' Callum and I burst into laughter.

'Come on, Dave.' Patty has appeared out of nowhere, tugging at the Ape's sleeve. 'Leave the kids alone.'

We all stare at her. I used to think she was one of the meanest girls in school, strutting around with Duce on her arm. But she saved Yusuf and I before. And now she's scaring another Ape away, helping us again. I don't think a mean girl would do that. I think she must be nice deep down. Patty shoots me a smile before linking arms with the Dave-Ape and pulling him away.

'Let's go.' I grab Daisy's hand and we make our way down the hill.

'Why was he even trying to talk to you?' Callum asks as we make our way towards the hospice.

'Not a clue. Probably had some threatening message from Duce for me.'

'Lucky Patty came when she did.'

Daisy snorts. 'Yeah, right. I saw you smiling at her, Al. You can't be her friend! Don't you remember all the names she called me?'

I stare at her. From what I remember, Daisy called Patty some pretty nasty names right back. And doesn't it count for anything that she just saved us another Ape headache? Surely she just needs to forget about the name-calling and move on? No, something on Daisy's face tells me she's not gonna do that anytime soon. I'd better just keep my mouth shut on this one.

*

'It's a left here, right?'

We turn down towards Parsons Green, Daisy's hand still in

mine, Callum eating sweets as per usual, sun in the sky, and I feel sort of happy. Is that wrong? I don't know. It never feels right to be happy when Jenna's not. But I'm trying to be positive. Like Mrs Moss said, I haven't found what I'm looking for yet, so I have to keep going. No use moping about indoors for days; I'm not going to find any answers in there.

'We're here.'

The building itself doesn't look unfriendly; in fact, it's got some nice flowers outside the front, the bricks are a warm red and, even though I can't see inside, I can just tell it's going to be cosy. I take a deep breath. 'Let's go.'

Inside, the reception is quiet. Some old, crackly music is playing from a radio and the woman behind the desk hums along, tapping away on her computer. Daisy nudges me and smiles encouragingly.

I clear my throat. 'Um, hi.'

The woman carries on tapping. For a few seconds I think she's going to completely ignore me, but she types her final few words with a flourish and looks at me expectantly. 'Yes?'

'Hi.' Am I a broken record today?

'We're here to speak to a member of the care staff,' Daisy steps in. 'If possible.'

The woman frowns. 'Debbie', her name tag reads. 'May I ask what this is regarding?'

We falter. Daisy catches my eye and shakes her head as if to say, 'No. Debbie won't understand.'

Callum joins us at the reception desk. 'We want to talk about admitting his sister here,' he jerks his head at me. I feel my breath catch slightly. No we don't.

'It's okay,' Daisy whispers.

'Ah, right.' Debbie pushes back her chair and stands up. She's a very short woman and actually looks shorter than she did sitting. She must have a very high chair. 'Do you have an appointment at all?'

'Appointment?' Daisy echoes. 'No. It's sort of... We'd just like to have a brief chat with someone today, please.'

'Well.' Debbie leans across the desk slightly. Up close I can see the colour of her face doesn't match her neck. 'What would you like to know? Fees, visiting times, et cetera? I can give you a leaflet if that's the case.' She gestures to the stand next to the reception desk full of brightly coloured booklets.

'Er, no not really,' Daisy says awkwardly. 'We need to discuss some more... in depth ... medical questions. We'd really like to have a quick chat with one of your ward staff.'

Debbie narrows her eyes. She reads the badge on our uniform. 'Are your parents here?'

'No.' I've finally found my voice. 'Just us. They're at home with my sister. Look, Debbie, they don't know we're here. I just... I need to help somehow. You know?' I give her my saddest smile.

Debbie falters a little, then smiles back. 'Okay. I'm sure someone will have a couple of minutes to sit down with you. Let me take you through.' She comes out from behind the desk looking even shorter—she's only shoulder-height on Daisy—and leads us through the double doors behind her to a living-room-looking space. There are a few people in here; an older man and woman sat on the three-seater sofa, holding hands. Four children of different ages on the carpet in front of the TV. Two men at the table playing chess. It's weird.

'Take a seat,' Debbie instructs us, gesturing to the spare sofa. 'I'll just go and have a word with Jack.' She drifts off to speak to one of the men playing chess; I hadn't noticed until then that he was in a blue uniform. They speak with their heads close together, looking over at us as we perch awkwardly on the sofa.

'This is weird,' Callum echoes my thoughts. The whole concept does seem strange; bunging all the dying people together in this weird house-place to see out their days. What are they meant to do all day? Play chess? Watch TV?

'Hello, dears.' The old woman on the sofa opposite leans forward and waves at us.

'Uh, hello!' Daisy gives her a wave.

'What are you all doing here?'

'Oh, Miriam, leave them be,' the man next to her grumbles. 'They don't want to chat to you.'

'How rude!' The woman who must be Miriam slaps him on the leg. 'Of course they do. Don't you, lovelies?'

'Sure,' Daisy nods. Callum shoots me a warning look but, actually, my mind's whirring. Maybe this is a good idea. Maybe we shouldn't have just come here to talk to the staff; surely the residents will have just as interesting things to say?

'Right.' Debbie's come back. 'Jack's just going to finish his game then he'll pop over for a chat, all right?'

'Thanks,' I nod.

'But not too long,' Debbie warns, backing out the door. 'He's got a job to do, remember?'

'Yeah,' Callum says under his breath as she goes, 'so do we.'

'What did you say you're doing here then? Visiting?' Miriam has appeared on the end of the sofa, squished against Daisy, who's trying not to laugh.

'Sort of,' I say. 'We're here to do some research. Could we ask you some questions?'

'Ooh, questions! Are you from the telly?' Miriam asks eagerly. She flattens her hair down. 'Will there be cameras?'

Daisy lets a laugh escape.

'No. No cameras,' I tell her gently, shooting Daisy a 'shut up' look. 'Just questions. How long have you been in here?'

'Well, now, let's see.' Miriam places a wrinkled finger on her chin. 'What day is it today?'

'Tuesday.'

'Since... ah...' her face falls slightly. 'At least two weeks.'

'I see.' I debate getting my notebook and pen out of my bag, but I don't want Miriam to think I'm rude. 'And... do you like it?'

'Like it?' Miriam chuckles. 'This is where I've been left to die.' We stare at her in stunned silence as she chortles to herself for a moment. Well, she's straight-to-the-point, I guess.

'What are you dying from?' Daisy whispers. Her laughter is long gone.

'A brain tumour, my lovely.' Miriam's face falls again. 'A bad one. It won't go. It won't leave me alone.'

'I'm sorry,' Daisy and I say together. I feel for this woman, I really do. I know I said she was old earlier, but up close she doesn't look as old as I thought; maybe fifties or sixties. I have a feeling a lot of those wrinkles and grey hairs are from her illness. She's someone's daughter, someone's mother. Maybe someone's grandmother. And she's being taken away, just like Jenna is. It's not fair.

'Nothing to be sorry about,' Miriam waves her hand dismissively. 'Hardly your fault. But, returning to the question, I suppose it's a good a place as any. My husband gets to visit a lot,' she nods at the man on the other sofa, 'and there's lots of activities and things. I get my room exactly how I like it. It's really very nice.' She stops abruptly and narrows her eyes. 'You're not coming here, are you? Any of you? Please, no. You're far too young.'

'No, no,' I shake my head quickly. 'Not us. But…' I never had the intention of discussing Jenna with anyone here. I mean sure, we kinda had to use her to get in in the first place, but that's all. But, for some reason, I want to tell Miriam. 'My sister has cancer. She's going to die soon.'

Miriam's eyes well up. She reaches across Daisy's lap and clasps my hands. Hers are freezing. 'Goodness. How awful. How truly, truly awful.'

'We came here to ask people some questions,' Daisy butts in. 'About… Well, we want to find out what's going to happen to Alex's sister. After… You know. When she dies.'

Miriam lets go of my hands and dries her eyes. 'I see.'

'What do you think?' Daisy asks, turning awkwardly to look at Miriam. 'What do you think happens?'

Miriam sighs. 'What a big question. What a huge, gigantic, colossal question for such a small person.' She glances at the children in front of us watching the TV. 'I hope for their sakes something beautiful. And for your sister, of course.' She looks back at me, her eyes still pale and watery. 'I think, really, all we can be certain of is that death is just life's next big adventure. We can never be certain what lies beyond that door. Never. But isn't that part of the fun?'

'Fun?' Callum mouths at me, his eyes wide. He thinks she's crazy. Maybe she is. But who isn't? I like that saying. It makes it seem so much less scary; like something to—in a weird way—look forward to. I picture Jenna walking through clouds to a door hanging high in the sky. It's the same as the front door of our house. When she opens it, a beam of light spills out and she walks through. She walks through, smiling.

'What a beautiful way of looking at things,' Daisy breathes. 'Thank you, Miriam.' Miriam nods at her, smiling. She sure is smiley for someone with numbered days. And maybe that's because of how she sees things. She's very close to her next big adventure. Her biggest one yet.

'Aren't you... Aren't you scared, though?'

I'm surprised to hear from Callum. He's looking at her like she's the bravest woman in the world. I think she might be.

Miriam shakes her head. 'My dear boy, what would be the good in that?'

I think back to the conversations I've overheard between Jenna and Kent and my stomach tightens. 'I think my sister's scared.' I catch Daisy's eye. It's brimming with tears.

'I don't think she's scared.' Miriam reaches across for my hand again. 'I think she's just a little sad about leaving such a great brother behind.' My breath catches in my throat. 'And a mother and father and friends: so many loved ones. But what is a life without love? Love is natural; it's with us all, at some point. Much like death.'

'But it's so unfair.' Daisy's voice is a whisper. 'To have to leave everyone you love.'

Miriam smiles at her. 'It would be unfair if it didn't happen to us all, but it does. And I'd like to think that our goodbyes here signify hellos elsewhere, beyond this life.'

I smile with her, despite myself. There's something about her that's so calming, so kind. And clever. Like if anyone was to know the answers, it would be Miriam.

'Er, hi. I was told you wanted to ask me some questions?' The man—Jack—has appeared next to the sofa. The chess game has obviously finished. I look from him to Miriam, almost not wanting to leave her yet. I feel like I have so much more to learn from her.

'Yes. Thank you.' Daisy stands up, Callum does too. I look at

Miriam, still sat on the sofa, gazing up at everyone.

'Thanks, Miriam.'

She smiles at me. 'No problem, Alex.'

Chapter Thirty

'What can I help you with?' Jack sits down across the table from us. We're in the room leading on from the one we were just in; it still has a sort of living-room-vibe, but no TV and more tables and chairs. It's very quiet.

'Well.' I swallow. 'We were just wondering if we could maybe ask you some questions?'

Jack hesitates. He takes in our school jumpers, rucksacks and faces. 'What about?'

We look at each other. 'Your job, I guess,' I say carefully. 'Your experiences with people here. It's for a... project.'

'Right. Okay.' Jack looks a little uncomfortable.

'Do you mind if we record this conversation?' Daisy asks, producing her recorder. Jack raises his eyebrows but nods. 'Cheers.'

I take the lid off my pen and hold it above my notebook. 'How long have you worked here?'

'Coming up for two years now.'

'And do you like your job?'

He raises his eyebrows. 'It's... I mean generally, yeah.'

'What made you choose to do this job?'

Jack exhales deeply, puffing his cheeks out. 'I dunno, really.'

'Well, it's quite a specific career choice,' Daisy chimes in. 'You're literally looking after people that you know will die soon.'

'I suppose so.'

'Do you ever get sad about it?' Daisy asks.

'Sure.'

'You see a lot of people come in and out?'

'Sure.'

I scribble this down.

'And have you ever… Have you ever been there when someone's actually… died?' Daisy's voice has turned to a whisper.

Jack looks at her for a moment. 'What is this all about? If this is for some weird ghost hunt or something, count me out.' He pushes his chair back. 'Debs said you wanted to talk about your sister coming here, not—'

'Sorry, sorry,' I say quickly. 'Please don't go. That is what we're here to talk about. Sort of.' Well, he's given me no choice but to tell him what we're doing outright. I hope he doesn't think we're too mental. 'Look, um, as Debbie said, my sister has cancer. And now it's got worse. So we're on a mission to find out where she's going. You know, once… once the cancer gets her.' I can feel my breath catch again, like it did earlier. 'We've been going around researching, talking to people, trying to find out…'

Jack tucks his chair back in and sighs. 'Look, mate, that's a very admirable thing you're doing. I bet it hasn't been easy, either. But it's an impossible question.'

Daisy rolls her eyes. 'Are you telling me that, after being present when people die and when their souls literally leave their bodies, you don't have a clue what happens to them?'

Jack looks at his hands. 'It's difficult every time someone passes,' he says quietly. 'Earlier, you asked me if I ever felt sad. Sure I do; sometimes it's very clear to tell when someone isn't… ready… to leave.'

'What do you mean?' Callum asks.

Jack sighs. 'Never mind. I probably shouldn't even be entertaining this. Look, kids, it's a question you'll never get the answer to. I'm sorry about your sister but—'

'No, please wait!' My voice cracks as he slides his chair back again. 'Please. I know you don't think we'll find out, but whatever information we can get really is important. Please. I need to piece it all together. I need to know where my sister's going.'

He sighs again, heavily. 'I don't know, though, mate. I really don't. All I know is… Look, you're right, I've been around a lot of dying people. Some people go over a couple of days. Some people go to sleep and don't wake up again. Some people say their goodbyes, tie up everything neatly with a bow and off they go. To where exactly, I don't know. But,' he trails off, looking down. 'This is just my opinion, right? There's no facts to back it up. But I feel like it all depends on the person.'

Depends on the person? I flick through my time with Jenna over the last few weeks; has she done anything to start tying things neatly? What does that even mean, anyway? 'Go on,' I say.

'Well, you know. It just feels as though, like I said, the people with their affairs all neat and tidy, accepting of their fate, go peacefully. They're comfortable, I suppose; done everything they've needed to do. And that doesn't mean just older people feel that way,' he shoots me a look. 'Kids, too. We had a little boy here for a while, Hayden... what a great lad. Always so happy. Only nine.' He pauses and looks down again. 'All his life he had this condition. He always knew he wouldn't have a long life. So did his family, though that didn't make it any easier for them. I think it made it easier for Hayden, though. When it came to the day, he was so brave.' Jack's eyes are glazing over. I'm not writing anymore. I can't. 'And ready. He knew it was happening, and he spent his last moments comforting his friends and family. He even told his mum he was going to be fine.' Jack gives a hollow laugh. 'It's like he knew, wherever he was going, that he would be okay.'

I'm picturing it now: a smiley, cheeky nine-year-old boy playing with a football, drawing, playing in the park. Well, those are the sorts of things I did when I was nine. Did Hayden get a normal childhood? Did he even get to play, or was he always attached to tubes and monitors? I feel sick. It's not fair.

'Wow,' Daisy breathes. 'That's... I mean... poor Hayden.'

'Yeah.' Jack has a faraway look in his eye. 'There are people at peace, people ready to go, happy, even, to go. And I feel they're the people who transition the smoothest.'

'What do you mean?' Daisy asks.

'Well, others aren't so ready,' Jack says heavily. 'People diagnosed late, maybe. People with plans and futures they didn't get. They're not happy about being taken away from everything they love here.

They're angry. Understandable.'

I feel my heart jump. Will Jenna fit into that category? I'm sure she hasn't done everything she wants to do yet. Will she be angry? Is she angry? I know I am.

'What happens to them?' Daisy whispers. 'Why aren't they ready?'

Jack shrugs. 'I guess they haven't accepted their fate yet.'

'Their fate?' I can hardly hide the anger in my voice. 'It's not fate when someone's torn from their family. Cancer isn't fate. It's a monster.' The calmness I felt with Miriam has long gone, replaced by twisted anger. It's misplaced, I know it is: Jack didn't inject my sister with the disease. He didn't mark her date on the calendar with a big, fat red 'X'. No one did. But having no one to blame doesn't make it any easier. It makes it harder. Daisy grips my hand under the table.

'I know it is. One of the worst ones of them all,' Jack sighs. 'Especially, you know, when you don't have time to come to terms with it.'

'I have come to terms with it.'

Jack raises his eyebrows. 'Says the kid running around with a pen and notepad looking for an answer to the biggest question in the universe.'

I squeeze Daisy's hand tighter.

'No offence. I know we all cope in different ways,' Jack says quickly. 'But have you ever thought of... I dunno, something more practical you could be doing? To help your family? To help your sister?'

'Like what?' Callum asks.

Jack sighs. 'Look, like I said, what you're doing is brave. You're a determined bunch, I can tell. But, as well as thinking about what's over the other side, you could be doing something to get your sister ready to get there.'

I turn to Daisy. She shrugs. 'What do you mean?'

'I mean, like I said, Hayden was ready to go through that door. So much so that he wasn't scared and he wasn't sad. Because he got everything he wanted out of his short life and his family could see that. Don't you want that for your sister?'

Of course I do. In fact, if we're going down that route, I don't want Jenna to have to prepare to go through any door. Except the church door, to get married. The University building door, to graduate. The front door of the first house she buys with Kent. The revolving door to that big building she's always wanted to work in. My stomach drops, like every other time I remember: she won't need help opening those doors. She won't be going through them. So yeah, okay, maybe I should help her get ready for the one she is going through. But that doesn't mean I have to stop finding out what lies beyond it. Because that, in my opinion, is still the most important part of all.

Chapter Thirty-One

'Morning, Jenna. You up?' I push on the door cautiously. She's not usually awake before I go to school, but I'm hoping this morning she is. I need to speak to her.

'Come in.' She's in bed, wrapped up in multiple blankets, hot water bottle clutched to her stomach. She looks freezing.

'Jeez. Are you okay? Do you need anything?' I sit on the end of the bed awkwardly. I hate seeing her like this, like she's been for the past few days. Weak, uncomfortable, in pain. I hate it because no matter how many cups of tea she's brought or baths she's run or hugs she's given, they never make a proper difference.

'I'm fine. It looks worse than it is.' She props herself up on her pillows. 'Just a little cold. Any stupid bug feels a hundred-times worse with cancer.'

'Right. Anyway.' I don't know how to ask it. I mean, I've known I've wanted to ask it for ages, and yesterday just gave me the final push. I need to know if there's anything Jenna still wants to do, anything left she wants to see. Anything I can help her with. So that she can prepare, as Jack said. I don't mean take her to America or anything massive, I mean little things. I don't know what. Maybe it's stupid, but time's too short to worry about feeling stupid.

'You okay, short-stuff?' Jenna asks, hugging her knees into her chest. She always used to call me that, until I outgrew her.

'Don't you mean tall-stuff?'

'Shut up,' she laughs. 'I swear this illness is making me smaller on top of everything else. Or maybe more crooked, like an old lady. Just need some more wrinkles now.' She frowns, making lines appear on her forehead. 'I suppose that's one good thing about this. I'll never get those.'

'That's not a good thing,' I snap before I can stop myself. 'None of this is good. There's nothing good about it at all! It's all awful.' I regret it as soon as the words leave my mouth. That's not what you came in here to do, Alex, you idiot.

'Right.' Jenna tilts her head. 'Seriously, what's up? You're a grouch this morning.' Of course I'm a grouch. You're dying, Jenna. Time's running out and I still don't know what's going to happen to you; if you'll be happy, if you'll be at peace, if I'll ever see you again. I think I'm allowed to be a grouch.

'Alex!' Mum calls up the stairs. 'Come down for breakfast. You're going to be late!'

I look at Jenna, a shivering shadow of my real sister, and ignore Mum. I push my anger down: deep breaths, Alex. Yes, maybe you're allowed to be a grouch, but that doesn't mean you should be. I'll put it down to lack of sleep. I genuinely think I only got about two hours last night.

'Sorry. You're right, you won't ever be a bag of wrinkles. Not like me,' I force a laugh, but my joke seems to have the opposite effect; Jenna's eyes glisten over.

'God, you're right. I won't ever see you get any older.' She sniffs hard. Nice one, Al. Good job cheering her up.

'Sorry, Jenna. I didn't mean... Don't get upset.'

She buries her face in her hands and bursts into tears, her whole fragile body shaking.

Why am I so bad at this? I shuffle towards her awkwardly. 'Come here.' She throws her arms around me, breathing heavily through her cries. 'Sorry, Al.'

'It's okay.'

She pulls away after a moment, inhaling and exhaling deeply. 'It's just sad, isn't it?'

'You're telling me.' I give her a minute to fully stop crying. 'Anyway, that's sort of what I came in here to talk to you about.'

'Go on.' She reaches for a tissue from the box next to her bed and blows her nose noisily.

'Well...' Here goes nothing. 'I just wanted to know... So you know how we went to the seaside the other week?'

'Yeah.'

'We went because you really wanted to go, right?'

'Yeah.'

'And I've just been wondering,' I say carefully, 'if there's anywhere else you want to go. Or anything else you want to do. Together.' I stop myself from adding: 'While you still can.'

'Oh.' She breaks into a huge smile. 'Al! That's lovely. What a kind thing to ask!' Jenna throws her arms around me again and I squeeze her back.

'So is there?'

'Sure there is,' she beams. 'Loads of things.' She reaches into her bedside cabinet drawer and pulls out a fluffy notebook. 'I'm not expecting anything on this scale of course,' she says, flicking through the pages, 'but when I was first diagnosed, I made a list of things I wanted to do before, you know, before things got worse.' She hands it to me. Written in her neat handwriting is a double page of bullet-pointed activities and places.

'Wow.' I scan down the page, stomach plummeting at some of them: Berlin. Alton Towers. New York. But others seem doable; she's got laser quasar, a picnic in the woods, watch the sun rise too.

'The ones with ticks by them are the ones I've done,' she explains, gesturing to a few. 'With Kent or Mum or some friends or whatever.' Quite a lot are ticked. I take it all in. Everything my sister wants to do. There's so many things. I wonder if I made a list if it'd have this much on it.

'Here's one we could do today,' Jenna suggests, pointing to a line halfway down the second page. 'If you don't mind skipping school, anyway.'

Feed the ducks.

'Feed the ducks?' I have to ask to make sure it's right. She wants to feed the ducks?

'Don't laugh!' She hits me gently on the arm. 'It's something we haven't done since we were little. Don't you want to walk to the canal and feed the ducks?'

I can't believe how simple it is, how simple loads of her wishes are. So easily done. Hope starts mounting inside of me, though I try and stay level-headed. Maybe we can get all of these done. Maybe Jenna can still have the life she wanted.

'Sure,' I say, closing the book. 'Let's feed the ducks.'

*

Jenna, Roscoe and I head out just before lunchtime. Surprisingly, Mum didn't have a problem with me staying off school. In fact, when I told her what Jenna and I were doing, she looked really happy about it. Daisy was fine too: I dropped her a text explaining what was going on and she just replied with 'No worries. Enjoy xx'. I know Callum will have her back, anyway, if Duce turns up at school.

'Right, I'll wait here with R, you pop in and get a loaf.' Jenna presses a £2 coin into my palm as we reach the store. 'Just the cheap stuff. Ducks aren't fussy.'

'I bet.' I take the money and head inside, realising I don't come in here enough to know where the bread is: I only ever buy energy drinks and chocolate. I weave in and out of the aisles, looking for the signs hanging from the ceiling. I can't see bread for the life of me. Maybe they don't sell it?

'No, Mark, not that one.' I halt at a familiar voice. Not superfamiliar, but vaguely. About halfway down the aisle, I see a short woman with bright red hair. It takes me a second to clock who it is, but my mouth hangs open when I do. Daisy's mum.

'Why not this bloody one?' A tall man next to her thrusts a box into her hand. 'Look just go and pay. This is risky enough as it is. I'll be in the car.' He strides away from her in the opposite direction from me. I didn't really get to see his face, but I'm pretty certain I know who it is. Duce's dad.

Crap. Now Daisy's mum's walking towards me. What should I do? Will she recognise me? I turn to the nearest shelf and pretend to root through the shampoos. She walks past without saying anything, thank God. I watch her as she makes her way to the till, little box still clutched tightly in her hand. Crap. Is that what

I think it is? I wait until she's out of eyesight before I hurtle down the aisle, heart racing. I stop at where she was stood moments ago and survey the shelf. Pink and blue box. Yep: pregnancy test. I've only ever seen them in Sex Ed classes, but there they are, lined up on the shelf. And Daisy's mum had one.

*

'Look at that one!' Jenna lobs a chunk of bread towards a brown duck bobbing further back from the others. 'She's lonely.'

'She's shy,' I agree, throwing some bread for her.

'The others bully her.'

'Ugh, here comes Tiffany. What a know-it-all.' Jenna throws some bread for her anyway.

'She made up that rumour that Bert can't fly. What a know-it-all.' I agree.

'Bert's such a sweetheart. Look, here he is.' One of the smaller males swims right up to the canalside next to us. 'So friendly.'

'Hi, Bert.' I drop some bread down to him. He quacks loudly.

'He even knows his pleases and thankyous!' Jenna exclaims. 'What a gentleman.' Roscoe barks indignantly.

'Sorry, buddy.' I tear off a crust and feed it to him. 'We forgot about the biggest duck of all.'

'King of the ducks,' Jenna nods seriously. 'He doesn't even bother to swim in the canal. He roams along the road like a true ruler.' Roscoe snorts in agreement.

'Last slice. Wanna share?' I tear the final piece in half and give some to Jenna. She looks down at it sadly.

'Last piece already.'

'Well, they are greedy,' I say, tearing my half into smaller pieces.

'True. My last piece is for Prudence.' Jenna throws her whole half to a goose lurking further down from the swarm of hungry ducks. 'Geese are underrated.'

'Well, thanks ducks. It's been a pleasure.' I slot the bread wrapper into the bin and take Roscoe's lead from Jenna. 'Shall we?'

We walk in silence for a few minutes. I know I should probably say something, but I just can't stop thinking about what I saw in the shop. Daisy's mum can't really be pregnant, can she? I wonder if it's Duce's dad's. I wonder if she'll keep it. Should I tell Daisy? That's the toughest question yet. I mean, she is my girlfriend. We shouldn't have secrets, surely. But telling her will only upset her. If I don't want it to be true, Daisy really won't want it to be. It'll make her so upset. And I can't be the one to make her feel that way. I think I'll keep this one to myself.

'Shall we stop and get lunch?' Jenna asks suddenly. 'I've always wanted to go there since they did it all up.' She points at the tiny Greek restaurant across the road.

'I don't have a lot of money,' I say hesitantly, patting my pocket to see if the fiver I grabbed earlier is still in there.

'Shh, silly. It's on me! Well, Mum and Dad.' She waves Dad's credit card in my face.

'Will Roscoe be allowed in?'

'Sure. Look, they have little tables outside anyway. It'll be fun, Al.' She looks at me pleadingly and I'm taken back to the seaside day all over again. I want her to be happy. I need her to be happy. And I don't want this day to be over yet.

Chapter Thirty-Two

'Excuse me, where are your books on "death", please?'
The librarian peers down at Daisy like she's an alien.
'Pardon?'

'The books on life and death,' Daisy says firmly. 'You know. The afterlife and all that. Heaven. Hell.'

'Right, yes,' the librarian blinks rapidly. 'On the left of medical. Top three shelves.'

'Thanks.' Daisy takes my hand and leads the way. We burst into laughter as we round the corner.

'I don't think I've ever seen anyone blink so fast,' Daisy giggles.

'Her eyes looked huge behind those specs!'

'Like a bird!' Daisy uses her fingers to widen her own eyes. Her impression is pretty good. Her idea of coming to the library was pretty good, too. I've googled for the project a thousand times, but never thought of going to read a good old-fashioned book.

'Ah, here we go.' Daisy stops and points to the shelf in front of her. 'Now, what do we fancy? The Underworld... The Myth of the Afterlife... Theories of Death...'

'All sound very positive so far,' I roll my eyes. 'Do none of these authors actually believe in anything, then?'

'What about this one?' Daisy pulls down a huge, thick, black volume with The Mystery of Life After Death written across it in droopy letters. 'And these.' She pulls down a few more and we're soon armed with seven books between us. 'Nothing like a bit of light reading.'

We stagger to the nearest free table and set them down. Daisy sits next to me and hands me an earphone. 'I'm putting it on shuffle, so don't judge my music taste,' she warns.

'I won't.'

We both open our books as the first song comes on: Don't You Forget About Me by Simple Minds. The song I played for her outside her house. I turn to Daisy and she shakes her head.

'I liked this song before you did that,' she insists. But she's smiling; she's so pretty when she smiles. Without even thinking properly, I lean in towards her and our noses touch.

'Excuse me!' We jerk apart to see the big-eyed librarian at our table. 'No kissing in the library!' I know I should be embarrassed but the sight of her, with her ruffled blouse and huge glasses, I can't help but laugh. Daisy's shoulders start to shake next to me, too.

'Her eyes are too big for her own good,' Daisy hisses as the librarian strides off, turning back to glare at us. 'Anyway, stop distracting me, Al. Get reading.'

We weren't allowed to check any library books out; apparently Jenna's got some overdue and I very nearly had to pay a fine. I wouldn't be surprised if that crazy librarian made that up, though.

'We should hang out more often.' Daisy slides her hand into mine.

'We hang out all the time!'

'I mean just the two of us, silly.' We pause to cross the road. 'It's been nice.'

'It's been very nice,' I agree.

'Do you want to come for dinner on Tuesday?'

I stop. 'Dinner. On Tuesday?'

'Yeah.' Daisy pulls my arm. 'Come on, it's getting cold.'

We carry on walking. Dinner at Daisy's? I was never even allowed in her house when we were friends. And now all of a sudden I've been asked over for dinner? Crap. What if Daisy's mum saw me in the shop after all? What if she wants to talk to me?

'Well?' Daisy squeezes my hand. 'Are you free?'

Right, two options.

1) go to dinner. What's the worst that could happen? Well, Daisy's mum could corner me. I could accidentally make a comment about her and Duce's dad. They all hate me.

Or 2) not go to dinner. Put it off, make an excuse, only for Daisy to get annoyed, go home and tell her mum I've been rude. Then they all hate me.

What a great situation to be in.

'Yeah, maybe,' I say vaguely. 'I'll ask Mum when I'm home.'

'Okay.' Daisy seems satisfied with that answer. 'Mum really wants to meet you.'

'She didn't seem bothered about meeting me when we were friends,' I can't help but comment.

Daisy sighs. 'Yeah, well, she's taking a bit of interest now. So that's good, isn't it?'

No.

'Yes.'

'Are you scared of meeting her?' Daisy teases.

'Not her.'

'What? Oh.' Daisy shakes her head. 'He won't be there, don't worry.'

'Cool.' We walk in silence until we come to Daisy's street. I wonder if I should walk her right to her door; that's what boyfriends do, isn't it?

'Well,' Daisy says, stopping by the street sign. 'I'll see you Monday.' Maybe boyfriends drop off at the top of the street, too.

'Yeah. Thanks, Daisy, for coming with me today.'

'No problem.' She looks at me expectantly. Right, okay. We're saying goodbye. What are we supposed to do? Hug? Kiss? I feel so nervous all of a sudden. We've said goodbye as boyfriend and girlfriend before, but not after spending a day together like this, just us two. Did I just have my first date?

'Um...' I want to ask her what she wants. I can't do that, can I? Come on, Alex. Give her a hug. Taking a deep breath, I lean in towards her, arms out. Just as I get to where I'd put my head above hers, she tiptoes slightly, so we're eye-to-eye. She puckers her lips and moves in close. Here it goes. I squeeze my eyes shut. They always shut their eyes in the movies. Our lips touch. This is so weird. A nice weird, though. Should I open my mouth more? She's pulled away before I can decide. We stand for a second, looking at each other. I can't believe we kissed! Maybe I should compliment her on her kissing. Or say something funny.

'See you Monday.' She flashes me a smile and turns to walk away. Oh God. I know she smiled, but I still feel awkward. Like I didn't do enough.

'Wait!' I jog back up to her. She turns and looks at me, sort of hopefully I think. Yes, Alex. You've made the right decision. Kiss her again. Go on. I lean down, gently and carefully, and do it. Softer this time, and slower. This feels better. More natural. I don't know how long we've been kissing for, but when Daisy pulls away I feel like I've grown really hot.

'That was lovely.' She smiles again, shyer this time. I could stay and look at her all night. Except I can't, because that kiss was too nice. And I don't want her—or anyone—to see how nice it felt to me. I try and cover myself awkwardly. I hope she hasn't noticed. Crap. This is so embarrassing.

'See you,' she says eventually, turning to walk away again. I can't stand and watch her go this time; I've got to get home, pronto, before I run into one of Duce's Apes and become the laughing stock of the school. Stupid body.

Chapter Thirty-Three

I can feel my eyes drooping, my body slumping. I'm so tired. I haven't slept properly in weeks. Hardly at all over the last few days. It feels like it's suddenly catching up with me now, all at once.

'Alex?' Mum shakes my shoulder.

'What?' My voice sounds snappier than I meant it to. But why does she have to shake me like that? It's not like I actually did doze off. I didn't even give myself a chance of an early night last night, though. When I got back from the library I lined up a load of documentaries online and watched them one after the other, hunched at my desk with two cans of Coke to keep me going. I can't remember actually falling asleep, but I think I missed the end of the final one, which I started at around 2 am. It's not like any were particularly helpful, either: most were just cheesy replays with actors and rubbish special effects.

'No need for that tone,' Mum mutters, snatching my empty glass from the table. It takes all my effort not to roll my eyes. It feels like every time we all come together—Mum, Dad, Jenna and I—a few days later it's as if we're strangers again. Since Jenna's latest hospital trip, Mum's barely said a word to me, let alone ask if I'm actually okay. And now a selfish part of me wonders if it's not actually Jenna she's scared for, it's herself. That's the way she acts, anyway; like no one's feelings matter apart from hers.

'Are you going to school today?' she asks with her back to me.

'Does it look like I'm going to school?' I ask drily. Is she actually so oblivious to me that she hasn't noticed I'm wearing my uniform?

She whirls round, tea towel in hand. 'Well, you've had a habit of skipping class lately, haven't you? Thought I'd better check in case I wake up to a fine tomorrow morning.' I really don't have the energy for this. Pick your battles, she always used to say. Well, she's picked the wrong one today.

'Oh yeah, I forgot all I do is cause you problems,' I snap. 'Like you haven't got enough already.'

'Yes, I've got enough on my bloody plate without you!' she shrieks suddenly, throwing the tea towel down on the kitchen top. Roscoe stirs on my feet; I know even he thinks she's being unreasonable. More than unreasonable; horrible. She's got enough on her plate without me. Not my attitude, not me skipping school, but just me. Her son. I push my chair back.

'What the hell is wrong with you? Enough on your plate without me, your son?' I stand, which takes a lot more effort than usual. 'Sorry your own child is just an added inconvenience.'

'You know what I mean,' Mum hisses. 'You just never make anything easy, do you? I have one kid with cancer, I've got another that does nothing to help. It's never do you want a cup of tea, Mum? Do you need a hand with the housework, Mum? You're out all the bloody time, and when you're actually home you're moping about in your room!'

'You don't want tea or help with the housework!' I shout. 'You want to run around and do everything yourself because it takes your mind off things! Why shouldn't I be allowed to go out and take my mind off things?'

'I don't get to take my mind off things!' Mum screams. 'My daughter is dying. You think I get to forget that, even for a second?' The room's spinning now. I grab onto the table.

'My sister's dying, too.' My voice comes out a whisper. I need to close my eyes, just for a second.

'Alex! Alex? Oh god.'

I feel weird.

'Wake up! Jenna! Call an ambulance!'

My eyes flicker open. Mum's looming above me, very red in the face. There's something wet on my hand. I turn my head slightly to see Roscoe's tongue licking my palm.

'He's awake! Alex? Can you hear me?' Mum waves three fingers in front of my eyes. 'How many fingers am I holding up?'

'Three.' I swallow. My mouth's very dry. 'Can I have a drink?'

'Yes, yes, of course. Is... Does your head hurt? Does anything hurt?'

I don't think I hurt, but I can't really feel my body. Am I paralysed? Have I had a stroke?

'Here.' Jenna's bent beside me now, holding a cup of water. 'Drink some of this, Al.' Mum props my head up and Jenna tilts the liquid into my mouth, cold and smooth. My throat feels better, but my brain still feels like it's not working.

'Try and sit up, my love.' Mum props me against the table leg, feeling my forehead with the back of her hand. 'He's very hot. Are you sure we shouldn't call 111?'

'Nah,' Jenna shakes her head. 'He was only out for a minute or two, right?'

Out for a minute or two?

'Did I faint?'

Mum and Jenna look at me, Mum on the verge of tears, Jenna on the verge of laughter.

'Yes, idiot,' Jenna hands me the water. 'Have another drink.' I shakily raise the cup to my lips. It feels like my body's forgotten how to move.

'Why can't I move properly?'

'You're moving fine,' Jenna insists. 'You're just confused. You need a nice sugary cup of tea and a nap.'

I glance at Mum, who's staring wide-eyed at Jenna.

'Right. Tea.' She springs into action, boiling the kettle and clanging around the cupboards. Jenna stays on the floor with me, smiling encouragingly every time I sip my water like I'm a baby sipping his bottle. I wish I was a baby again. Then maybe Mum would like me.

'You're such a diva,' Jenna whispers. 'Jealous I'm getting all the limelight, hmm?' I start to protest but she's laughing. 'It's a joke, Al. Seriously, are you okay?'

'I think so.' I feel like my words sound more normal now. Everything's coming into focus a bit more. Jenna looks exhausted.

'Are you okay?'

'Me? I'm fine.' Jenna pats Roscoe, who's lying next to me.

'You not been sleeping well?' I press.

'Could ask you the same.' I wonder if I look like Jenna does.

'Here, love, a nice cup of tea. Do you think you can get up and sit on a chair?' Mum asks anxiously, pulling one back.

'Why don't we sit in the living room?' Jenna suggests. 'Comfier. You go on in, Al, I'll help Mum.' She gives me a hand to my feet. I try and walk as normally as I can, but I feel a bit like a robot, like my joints need oiling. I can't believe I fainted. Jenna's right, I am a diva. It must be exhaustion, has to be. I should've just gone to sleep last night. If only it was that easy. I lie on the sofa and pull Jenna's blanket over me, suddenly feeling just as tired as I did earlier, when I was sat at the table. I should close my eyes. Just for a minute.

'See, he's gone to sleep,' Jenna's voice sounds far-off. 'I told you, he hasn't been sleeping. There was a light coming from his room till like, 4 am this morning.'

'Bless him,' Mum sighs. 'Did you hear our argument? I said some terrible things to him, Jen. I feel awful.'

'I love you, Mum, but I think sometimes you forget,' Jenna says, 'that you're not the only one who's upset.'

Mum says something then, but her voice is too quiet to hear, and I'm too tired, and everything's soft and slow and warm. I let myself go.

Chapter Thirty-Four

Today's the day. The Dinner-at-Daisy's Day. I'd tried to worm out of it, I really did, pretending I still didn't feel well, but Mum insisted that I really couldn't miss another day of school.

'Mum says do you want to eat anything in particular later?' Daisy asked as soon as I stepped out of the house. My heart sank; I was hoping she'd forgotten.

'Well, I don't know if my mum wants me to eat at home tonight,' I said carefully.

'You eat there every night,' Daisy cried. 'One night at mine. Mum's making a real effort. She's getting pudding and everything.'

'I can't stay too long,' I tried again.

Daisy shrugged. 'That's okay. It'll be nice for you to come for a little.' There it was. The final guilt trip into accepting.

So I just nodded and smiled and shrugged all the way to school, underneath thinking: what the hell am I going to do? I even text Mum at lunchtime asking if I could go, mentally begging her to say no. That way I'd have evidence to show Daisy. But an 'Ofc. Have fun x' message pinged back two minutes later. My last escape route gone.

I considered texting her again but didn't bother. Things have been a little awkward since yesterday morning. The argument hasn't been spoken about, but I don't feel as though that's a good thing as I haven't apologised to her and she hasn't apologised to me. I know I normally cave in and just do what I can for the quiet life, but I couldn't bring myself to say sorry this morning without her saying anything to me first.

She's meant to be the adult. She's meant to be the brave one, the more mature one. It's easier for older people to say sorry when they're wrong. And besides, what she said to me was far worse than what I said to her; she basically said all I do is cause her grief, that I don't make anything easier. Well, news flash: nothing makes it easier for me, either, least of all her, but that doesn't mean I scream at her over breakfast.

Anyway, back to dinner. The thought of looking Daisy's mum in the eye, knowing she may or may not be having Duce's dad's baby makes me squirm. Actually, it makes me consider poking my eyes out completely so I don't have to look at her at all. But I think Daisy might not love me anymore if I have holey eyes. She'd have to guide me everywhere as well. Maybe I could train Roscoe to be a guide dog?

Shut up, Alex. You're going to be a good and loyal boyfriend and sit and have dinner with your girlfriend's mother. You're going to smile and laugh and ask questions and be as polite as you can. And you're not going to think about what you saw in the shop.

'Well, here we are.' Daisy shuts the door behind us. I can't believe I'm finally in Daisy's house. Whatever else this evening brings, surely that's an achievement.

The hallway's very small and cramped, with shoes piled everywhere and coats bulging from the coat hooks. I think of my own hallway, tidied and hoovered and wiped down at least once a day. I think Daisy's is nicer. More homely.

'Well, come through.' I think for the first time since I've known her, Daisy sounds a little nervous. 'This is the living room.' A bog-standard room. Again, it looks very lived-in, with magazines and posters and unfinished cups of tea. Similar in the kitchen. 'And back here's my bedroom.'

Her bedroom!

First off, it's pink. The colour I thought least likely to be on Daisy's walls. She's looking at me, waiting for me to say something. What am I meant to say?

'Uh, nice.' Smooth, Alex.

She laughs. 'Yeah. It's been the same décor since we moved in. Couldn't be bothered to repaint. Plus, I like that it clashes with my hair.' She climbs onto the bed. 'Wanna sit?'

My heart leaps a little. Does this mean she wants to kiss? I climb on the bed next to her.

'Very squishy.' Another smooth comment. I'm full of them today.

'Yeah,' she giggles. There's silence for a minute. Come on, Al. Do something. I reach across and place my hand on hers.

'It's nice, isn't it?' she says, holding my hand properly.

'What is?'

'You being here. I never thought you'd be allowed in, let alone for dinner!' Daisy laughs. 'My mum's so strict about boys.'

I want to say, 'Maybe she should be stricter with herself,' but I just nod instead.

'I'm not sure if...' she trails off. 'I mean, you're my boyfriend, right? And girls should tell their boyfriend's everything. Right?'

'Erm...'

'Because I know you're worried about Duce's dad,' she rushes on, 'so I feel like I should tell you...'

My heart drops. 'Has he hurt you again?'

She shakes her head. 'No, no. Not me...'

It takes a minute for the penny to drop. 'He hits someone else?' I feel my eyes widen. 'Your mum?'

Daisy looks away. Crap. So now she's not only possibly pregnant, she's possibly in deep trouble. I didn't know my anger towards Duce's dad could get any worse—turns out it could. I feel like I need to punch something right now. What did Daisy and her mum do to deserve this? Daisy sniffs loudly and wipes her eyes on her sleeve. Okay, we can't just sit here in silence, Alex, pull it together. What the hell do I say? 'I'm... sorry?'

Good one. I should know not to say rubbish like that. I should know first-hand not to say rubbish like that. So why did I!? 'Can I... do anything?'

'No!' She lets go of my hand and faces me properly. 'You can't do anything, Alex! Or tell anyone, please! It's not every day, it's not all the time, and Mum says she's fine. She'd tell me if she wasn't fine. But she said I can't tell anyone, so you have to keep it to yourself! Promise?'

I want to tell her. I want to tell her more than anything what I saw in the shop. Maybe it would change her whole perception, make her realise she and her mum need help. Serious help. But... she's looking at me, those green eyes full of tears, and I know it'll make things worse. So much worse. And what if she gets mad at me for not telling her sooner? What if she breaks up with me?

'I promise.' I take her hand again. 'But you have to promise to tell me if things get worse. If your mum says she's not... fine.'

'I will!' Daisy leans her head on my shoulder. 'I promise.' I rest my chin on her head, her curls tickling my skin. All I want is to protect her, to look after her. Why does her mum have to make that such a damn hard job?

'Anyway, it's cool that you're here,' Daisy changes the subject. 'With everything going on, I mean. It's cool you can make time for me.' That surprises me a bit. Daisy never really says anything about feelings. I mean, I know she's not saying she loves me or anything, but she's saying she appreciates me. It makes my tummy flip. I should probably say something nice.

'I'll always make time for you.' Oh God, that sounds so cheesy. Daisy must have thought it was sweet, though, because she's leaning across me now with her lips puckered. Time for another kiss. Okay Al, don't get too excited. We don't want a repeat of last time.

*

'Looks good, Mum.'

Daisy's mum brings out a French stick and block of butter and places them in the middle of the table. I always used to think, because of the hair, that she was literally an older version of Daisy, but I can tell now that's not the case. She's got a completely different nose—longer and pointier—and her mouth is different. She looks scarier.

It was especially scary when she first came home and slammed the door and shouted, 'Daisy you better not be in your bedroom!'

Luckily, we'd finished kissing by that point and were watching TV in the living room. I dread to think what Daisy's mum would've said if she'd seen us ten minutes earlier. The whole mood changed when she came home, though. Even though she went straight into the kitchen to start dinner, I felt like she had eyes in the back of her head.

'How was work, Mum?' Daisy asks, shovelling some meat into her mouth. I look down at my own plate and try not to let my disappointment show. I love steak, but only well-done. This one looks like it could still moo.

'Fine. The orders for last Friday finally came through, though fat lot of use they were.' Daisy's mum sips her wine. 'Vicky went crazy, you know how she gets. Ron called the manufacturers directly, but they didn't have a clue.' Daisy nods wisely while her mum talks. Meanwhile, I've been eating the more cooked parts of dinner and trying to look like I'm enjoying it. I'm aware there's silence now, though. Maybe I should say something? I should say something.

'What's your job, Ms Miller?'

She looks at me like she's not sure why I spoke and now I sort of wish I didn't. 'I'm in events,' she says eventually. 'Do you have a job yet, Alex?'

I'm not sure whether she's joking. I'm about to force a laugh when I actually look at her face and realise no, she's not joking, and she's probably the sort of person who never makes jokes.

'No,' I say, reaching for some bread for something to do. 'Not yet.'

'He's only fourteen, Mum!' Daisy says, rolling her eyes. 'Remember?'

'Could he not have a paper round or something?' Daisy's mum insists.

'I might look for one after my birthday,' I say quickly. I don't want her to think I'm lazy. Although I am a liar. I've never once thought of doing a paper round.

'I see.' She starts seasoning her steak. 'And what career are you aspiring to get into? You know, when you're old enough.'

'Alex is super-clever,' Daisy says. 'He's really good at everything, mostly science.'

'So… A scientist?' Daisy's mum asks drily.

I can feel myself growing hot. Not hot like I'm about to kiss Daisy hot, hot like angry hot. Yes, I'm fourteen. No, I don't have a job. Sure, I'm pretty smart. And I'm nice, too, and interesting, and I try my best to make your daughter happy. Because I really like her. Maybe I even love her. Can you say the same? You basically put her in danger every time you let Duce's crazy dad in the house! And I wonder if she'd like to know what you bought the other day? I open my mouth before I can stop myself. 'Didn't I see you in the store last week, Ms Miller?'

Her face is a picture. She's sipping her wine, so I can't see her mouth, but her eyes double in size.

'You didn't tell me you saw Al, Mum!' Daisy cries. 'That's cool.' Daisy's mum puts her drink down and looks at me. I know she's placing me now: oh yes, he was the kid with his head in the shelf down the same aisle. Down that aisle.

'Oh yes,' she says eventually. 'I remember. And please, Alex, no more Ms Millers. Call me June.'

She hides away after dinner. Although I felt embarrassed as soon as the words came out of my mouth, now I feel sort of happy. Like I won. Maybe not forever, but for now.

'I think she likes you,' Daisy announces as I put my shoes on to go.

'You're just saying that.'

'Well, she's frosty with everyone,' Daisy says, 'and you were no different, but at least she told you her first name.'

I look past her shoulder to check her mum's still in the kitchen before lowering my voice.

'Is he coming over tonight? Duce's dad?'

She shrugs. 'I dunno. Hopefully not. He doesn't come over that often, not really.'

I can't tell if she's telling the truth. 'Well, if he does, and you want to come back to mine… And even if you want your mum to come with you…'

'Shh!' Daisy checks behind her. 'Remember your promise.'

'I will. You remember yours, too.'

'Anyway, thanks for coming, Al.' Daisy pulls me into a hug. 'It means a lot to me.' I hug her back, trying to let my worries go. Crap as it was, I made an effort, and to know that made Daisy happy makes it all worth it. I just feel so overwhelmingly sad for her, and even her rude mum. They don't deserve to feel scared in their own home, especially from an old, ugly bully. That's all he is: just an older version of his pathetic son.

'See you tomorrow.' Daisy pecks me on the cheek and I feel my skin grow hot again. As she pulls away she's smiling the biggest signature Daisy smile I've seen in ages. And, all the other drama aside, this is what being a boyfriend is about, right? Making your girlfriend happy? If it is, at least that's one thing in my life I'm doing right. So far.

Chapter Thirty-Five

I'm having steak for the second night running, and I'm not complaining. Mum's cooked it to perfection: no blood, no red; no soggy, soft meat. Just a slab of thick, well-done, crispy goodness.

'So good, Mum,' Jenna says through mouthfuls.

'Thanks, love. Do you want any more? Have some of mine.' Mum starts to shift her dinner onto another plate. Unlike the rest of us, she's not eaten much. She only picked at the bruschetta starter, too.

'Don't be silly, Mum. You have it.' Jenna shakes her head.

'Eat your dinner,' Dad nods before burping loudly. 'It's delicious.'

'Manners,' Mum mutters.

'How was last night, Al?' Jenna asks me.

I shrug. I'm not sure how much I want to talk about it at the dinner table. I've told Jenna that Daisy's my girlfriend, but no one else. I knew Jenna would be excited and happy, I knew she would care. I don't feel like Mum and Dad would.

'Ah yes, dinner at Daisy's.' Mum picks at her salad. 'I was surprised when you asked, Alex. I didn't think she liked boys being in the house. Funny woman.' Funny woman is right. Daisy went on all day about how much Ms Miller—June—liked me. I bet she's secretly been throwing darts at a picture of my face.

'It was fine,' I say. I meet Jenna's eye and she nods encouragingly. She wants me to tell them. Well, what do I have to lose? 'And no, Daisy's mum doesn't really let boys round. But she sort of had to, because... I'm Daisy's boyfriend now.' Mum drops her fork on the floor.

'Great news,' Dad thumps his fist on the table. 'Your first bird!'

Mum, meanwhile, looks like I just slapped her round the face with my half-eaten steak.

'Congrats, Al!' Jenna claps. 'What lovely news. Isn't it, Mum?'

'Yes.' I can tell Mum means the opposite. 'And when did this happen?'

I shrug. 'A week or two ago? I dunno.'

'Really lovely,' Jenna says after a moment of no one saying anything. 'I'm so happy for you, Al.'

Mum clears her throat and picks her fork up off the floor. 'Me too. I like Daisy, she's a sweet girl.' I feel like she's not done talking, but she doesn't say anything else and stares at the tablecloth instead.

'Um, thanks.' I don't know what to say either. I didn't exactly expect everyone to be jumping around and applauding and I can tell Dad's cool with it but, I dunno, Mum's being super-weird. Things are still icy anyway from our argument, but I've accepted she's not gonna say sorry so neither am I. Can we at least just act normal?

'We should have her round for dinner,' Jenna suggests. 'How about one day next week? Mum?'

Mum's lips have disappeared. 'Of course.'

'She's more than welcome,' Dad says loudly. 'Anytime. Isn't she, Cindy? Isn't she?' All eyes go to Mum. She sighs and smiles.

'She is. I'm sorry. I'm happy for you, Al, of course I am. It's just… you're growing up so quickly.' She sniffs. 'And, well, I just wish you'd told me.'

'He is telling you, woman!' Dad laughs. 'Don't be so sensitive. He's a fourteen-year-old lad. They don't often share everything with their mothers.' It's a rare occasion when I actually agree with what my dad says, but this is one of those times. I'd never say this to her, but maybe things would be different if she was different. If she asked me about girls, showed an interest in those parts of my life, maybe I'd be excited to tell her things, like I am with Jenna. But she's not, so I'm not, and that's just the way it is.

'I know. Actually, he's almost fifteen!' Mum dries her eyes on her napkin. 'We need to talk about what we're going to do for your birthday, Al.'

'I don't want to do anything,' I say automatically. I really don't. I don't like being under the spotlight. Last year we went to a restaurant and all the family came: cousins and grandparents and people I didn't even really know. I had to stand on a chair while everyone there—even strangers who worked there—sang Happy Birthday to me. I hated every second.

'We have to do something,' Mum presses. 'What about something fun, like laser quasar or bowling? We can make it a family and friends event. Whoever you want.'

'Now hold on a minute! How much money is this costing?' Dad pipes up. 'Glorified kids parties like that are a fortune. Bill at work paid fifteen quid a head for a quasar party last month for his Milly's birthday. Fifteen quid!'

Mum rolls her eyes and starts clearing the plates.

'Here, let me help.' Jenna leaps up to join her.

'No, don't be silly. Sit down,' Mum says firmly. 'Al will give me a hand.'

Of course Al will.

'I didn't mean to be angry,' she says as we load the dishwasher. 'It was just a shock, you know? My little boy all grown-up with his first girlfriend.'

'Mmm.' I nod. I hate it when she calls me her 'little boy'.

'And now, you know, this might be…' She pauses and takes a deep breath. 'Well, one of the last birthdays your sister is here for. I just think it would be nice if we made a big deal of it, you know?'

I swallow my response. It's selfish, it's horrible, but I can't help thinking it. I know everything revolves around Jenna. I know that, and I'm fine with it. But just this one day, the one day a year that's supposed to be about me: can't it just be about me and what I want?

Chapter Thirty-Six

'And does it happen every night?'

'Pretty much, yeah.' I try and remember the last time I had a full night's sleep, or a dream not involving death. I can't.

'How much sleep are you getting a night, would you say?' Mrs Moss asks. She looks concerned. Okay, she always looks concerned, but she looks more concerned than normal today.

'I don't count,' I say. 'I normally go to bed at about ten. Wake up in the early hours of the morning, usually between two and four.'

'And do you go back to sleep?'

'Sometimes.' Not usually. I don't know what's made me want to talk about the dreams today, but something has. I think, deep down, it's because I want to find someone that can help. Someone that actually wants to help.

I thought that, after fainting in front of her, Mum would have tried to sort me some medicine or something to help me. Taken me to the doctors at least. But she literally hasn't said a word about it. Jenna knows I stay up—she has trouble sleeping too, sometimes—but I'd never expect her to fuss over it. She's dealing with enough of her own crap. Then there's Daisy, who's pretty much always known, but we never speak about it. I'm not sure she'd have any good advice, anyway. So that leaves Mrs Moss.

'This is very concerning,' she mutters. 'I know you mentioned it a while back, but I just assumed…You do look very… Well, you look exhausted today.'

'I am.'

'Have you told anyone else about this? Someone in your family, maybe?'

'My mum knows.'

'And what did she say?'

What she always says. 'Nothing.'

'Right, I'm going to give her a call.' Mrs Moss writes that on a post-it note. 'In the meantime, there are lots of helpful techniques I can suggest to help you doze off peacefully and try and prevent these dreams as much as possible.'

'No offence, Mrs Moss, but I don't wanna be faffing around lighting candles and breathing deeply and all that. I just want something that's gonna put me straight into a dreamless sleep. There must be a pill that does that?' I'm not trying to be rude. I'm just trying to get to the point.

Mrs Moss sighs. 'Well, I do think it's best to try natural remedies first, Alex. What I'd like you to try is clearing your mind before bed. No TV, no laptop—nothing with a bright light—for an hour before you go to sleep. Have a nice hot drink, maybe herbal tea…'

She's rambling on, but I've blocked her voice out. If she thinks it's as easy as no TV and a cup of tea, then she's really not worth speaking to any longer. She's like the rest of them. She doesn't think it's very serious. And I know it isn't, not in the bigger picture; I mean, it's nothing compared to my sister's illness.

Actually, maybe Mrs Moss is right in saying I need to calm down about it. My nightmares don't take priority over sorting everything else out. What I really need to focus on is the mountain of a project that Daisy, Callum and I have been working on. We've seriously been slacking over the past couple of weeks.

When I say we, I mean I. Since the hospice, stuff's just been getting in the way. Like Jack suggested, I've been concentrating more on helping Jenna get things done: but that's no excuse, I suppose, for ignoring the real mission. We need to regroup—Daisy, Callum and I—and go over what we've got. Talk about where we're going next.

Anyway. I just let Mrs Moss go on talking until she's done, nodding in the right places, pretending to care about TV and tea. Sometimes it's important to pretend you care about things so that people don't feel upset. I've come to learn that recently.

*

'Hi, Al.' Mum pops her head out the kitchen as I step in the house.

'Hi, Mum.'

'Want a cuppa?'

'I'm going straight to Cal's. Thanks though,' I call as I run up the stairs. No time for cuppas today.

I wonder as I rummage through my stuff if that was one of the moments she wanted me to say, 'No, Mum, let me make you one.' Oh well. Too late now. I spoke to the guys at lunch about getting together after school and going through all our findings so far, and Callum said he has a free house, so we're off to his. My talk with Mrs Moss reminded me that nothing else is important, least of all my stupid sleeping habits, and that gave me the kick that I needed.

I've just shoved my notebooks and scrapbook into a rucksack when I remember something else I should take. I tiptoe to Jenna's door and press my ear against it: no noise. I knock: no answer. I push it open quietly, relieved to see her bed empty. She must be at Kent's or something. I feel weird being in here without her knowing. Sort of creepy. I open her bedside drawer and get out her notebook, flicking through until I find it: the list. I pull out my phone and snap some photos of the open pages before placing it neatly back in the drawer. There. She'll never know.

*

'Finally,' Daisy says as she opens Callum's front door. 'We were starting to think you'd got lost.'

'Not lost.' I'm panting and I have a stitch; I don't think I've run so fast in ages. 'Just getting the essentials.' I follow her into Callum's living room, where he's sat playing on the PlayStation.

'Turn it off now,' Daisy commands. 'We've got work to do. And I'm thirsty.' She looks at him expectantly.

'Fine. What do you want?'

'I'll have an orange juice. Al?'

'Same, please.' I unzip my bag and start piling the books and pieces of paper onto the floor.

Daisy grabs a cushion and plonks herself next to me. 'Wow. There's so much!'

'Not all good,' I tell her. 'And none of it conclusive.'

'Well, that's to be expected. Thanks, Cal.' She takes a glass from him. 'It's a huge mission we're on. I'd be shocked if we had the answer already.'

'Already? We've been at it for months!' I think I sound a bit snappy. I don't mean to be; I just don't want to sit here and talk about how well we've done so far, how huge it is, how we're all trying our best. We need to talk about how we can improve, what we can do next. Not sit and pat each other on the back.

'I know,' Daisy says calmly. 'But we're only three kids. Three kids trying to find out where we'll go when we die. We should be proud of ourselves that we've got this much together.'

'Yeah, mate,' Callum says uncomfortably as he sips his juice. 'Don't get worked up. Let's break it down, have a look at it all.'

I look at them both, my best friend and my girlfriend, and I know they're right. There's no point being angry about it; we haven't found the answer yet. But we will.

'I've got something else, too,' I say. 'Jenna's made a list of things she wants to do. Before... you know.' I show them the phone.

'Like a bucket list,' Daisy says. 'Cool.' Her and Callum sit in silence for a minute.

'I know she won't get all of it done,' I say quickly. 'Going to Berlin and stuff like that; she knows she can't.' I swallow the lump in my throat at the thought of Jenna never being able to travel again.

'Yeah, no, this is good, though,' Callum says quickly. 'Like Jack said, it'll help her get ready and all that.'

'I'm just not sure how I'm gonna do most of them.' My voice cracks a little and I clear my throat. 'You know, with her feeling so unwell.'

'But some of them are more than doable,' Daisy points out.

'And there must be a way around some of the others. Improvisation and all that.' She hands the phone back.

'Yeah.'

Daisy reaches over and pats my hand. 'Honestly, Al. You're doing so well already. Jenna will be over the moon if you guys get even half of this stuff done!'

She's right. I need to stay positive. I need to keep trying. 'Thank you.'

'Anyway. About this list.' She downs the rest of her juice. 'Let's have a look.'

Callum picks it up. 'Okay. So, we've looked into the sciencey side with Dr Nina and the hospice... We've done the religious side with Julie and the church...' He scans down the sheet of paper.

'We read some books on mythology,' Daisy chimes in.

'And I've watched some documentaries.' I add. Useless documentaries, but documentaries nonetheless.

'Right.' Callum's silent for a moment. 'So... what next?'

Daisy snatches the paper off him. 'Isn't there another idea written down?'

'No,' Callum retorts, taking it back.

'Not everything's written down,' I say quickly. 'That was just a rough starting list.'

They both look at me.

'Right...' Daisy starts picking her nail. 'So, now we've done all that. Where now?'

Where now? Good question.

'I know! So, we've done Christianity and reincarnation, right? And Al, you said you looked online at Sikhism and the other popular religions?' Callum asks.

'Yeah.'

'Okay, so what about looking at a lesser-known religion?'

'Like what?' Daisy flicks her nail into the air.

'Well, it's just an idea, you might think it's a bit weird...' He trails off as if he's having second thoughts.

'Go on, Cal,' I smile. 'You're talking to the one that dreams about death: I think it's safe to say I'm the weird one.'

Callum laughs. 'All right, fair point. I was just gonna say, my Aunty Flo's a—you remember Aunty Flo, Al?'

'Sure, sure.'

'Yeah, she's a—damn, what are they called?—oh yeah: spiritualist!'

Daisy and I look at each other. 'What's that?'

Callum shrugs. 'I'm not a hundred percent sure, but I think pretty much they say that life doesn't end with death. There's, like, a whole other life after.'

A whole other life? I consider this. It basically leads on from Miriam's idea that, once you go through the door, there's a whole new adventure there waiting for you. And, sort of like reincarnation, you get a completely new chance at living a life. Maybe staying just who you were before you left. Which has got to be better than scuttling around as a mouse or, as Daisy likes to say, dung beetle!

'So?' Callum's looking at me expectantly and I realise I've been sat silently while all this runs through my head. 'What do you think, Al?'

I think that, to make an informed decision, we need to explore all ideas. I think Callum's an absolute genius for thinking of this in the first place. And I think that, quite probably, I have the best friends in the entire universe.

'Well.' I grab the rest of the papers scattered over the floor. 'That sounds like a plan to me. I think we'd better pay your Aunty a visit.'

Chapter Thirty-Seven

'Wake up.' I can feel a hand on my leg. 'Wake up, Al.' Jenna's voice. I force my eyes open.

'Afternoon, sleepy head.' She's sat next to me on the bed.

'Afternoon?' I echo.

'Yeah. It's almost three! Time to get up.' She shakes me a little again. 3 pm? The clock tells me she's not lying. Well, at least I've got some sleep. Even if it has been in the day instead of night.

'Come on, Al.' She pulls the duvet off me.

'Ah!' I cling onto it. I don't want to get up. I especially don't want to be cold.

'Get showered quick,' Jenna commands, getting up. 'I'll wait in the car.'

'Where are we going?'

'Shopping. I need a new outfit.' She swans out, dressed and ready, wig and all. Shopping? On a Saturday? I want nothing more than to pull the covers back over my head and go to sleep but I know that's not an option. She'd only wake me up again.

*

'So are you excited for Monday?'

We're in the car now, driving to the shopping centre. The traffic is already terrible. I'm too hot, I'm hungry, and now I've just been reminded that my bloody birthday is on Monday. My mood could not get any worse.

'No.'

Jenna laughs. 'You're so weird about birthdays, Al.'

'I'm not weird. Everyone else is,' I insist. 'I don't like all the attention.'

'No, you don't,' she nods. 'You never have, even when you were little. We'd all be sat waiting for you to crawl or stand up or something and you'd go all red and cry, like you were embarrassed.'

'I'm not embarrassed,' I say. Well, maybe I am a little. I'm one of those dorks that blushes every time everyone looks at me. I'm awful at pretending I like gifts. I'm no good at thanking people and telling them I love them. Birthdays just aren't for me.

'Whatever,' Jenna says, finally pulling into the car park. 'You got any change?'

I root around in my pockets. 'Two quid.'

'Lucky it's just a quick visit, then,' she says, pulling into a parking bay. Quick visit? Excellent. I've been dragged around the shopping centre with Jenna before and it was a four-hour experience.

She insisted I wear my new shirt as soon as I bought it. Suddenly, my Foo Fighters T-shirt was old and ugly, and this new H&M button-up was the best thing she'd ever seen. I wasn't sure I liked it at first, but Jenna's very persuasive when she wants to be. After the fifteenth time of her telling me it brought out my eyes, I eventually caved in. Plus, it was in the sale. Meanwhile, Jenna took me to six clothes shops before buying a yellow sundress, saying it was too cold to wear it. She snuck off and put it on anyway while I had a burger.

'The plus side of chemo is my leg hair still hasn't grown back,' she said. We're in the car on the way home now. Jenna keeps swearing and swerving and asking me for the time.

'I wish you'd woken up earlier,' she grumbles as we hit another red light.

'Sorry,' I say. 'I don't sleep very well.'

'Yeah,' she sighs. 'Me neither. That's why I let you have a little lie-in.'

'Could we not have gone shopping tomorrow?' I ask as she screeches to a halt at a roundabout. 'You seem a bit... rushed.'

'Not rushed,' she mutters. The car stalls. 'Damn.' We sit in silence until we get to our road.

'There's a lot of cars down here,' I notice. Maybe next door's having another early BBQ. They always start having them as soon as we get a bit of sun. We've had a nice March so far, but it's still March. Then again, we went to the beach earlier this month, so who are we to talk?

'Here we are.' Jenna pulls onto the drive and switches the engine off. She looks at me. 'Straighten your shirt a bit.' She reaches across and smooths my hair. 'There.'

'What are you doing?'

'Nothing. Shall we go in?'

'Sure.' I grab the bags from the boot and follow her to the front door. Before she opens it, Jenna turns around, a huge smile on her face. And something clicks in my brain; the shopping trip, the rushing home, the parked cars... Something's happening. Something for my birthday.

'Surprise!' The shouts echo through the house as we step inside. Yep. Knew it.

'Happy early birthday, darling!' Mum rushes forward and throws her arms around me. Behind her, I can see the usual: Gran and Grandad, Auntie Elle and Uncle Kai, cousins, neighbours, Mum's friends, Dad's friends... And some faces that don't usually make an appearance. Callum and Daisy are at the front of the crowd, waving. Next to them, Yusuf and Luca. Next to Yusuf and Luca are Joe, Eric and the guys we play football with. Some of Daisy's girl friends: Lola and Gee and Marley. I can't believe it. There must be at least fifteen of them. Who invited all these people? As Mum pulls away, Jenna wraps her arms around me from behind.

'Surprise, Al.' She pecks me on the cheek. 'I know attention isn't your thing, but I thought if I invited enough people they wouldn't be too fussed about sitting and watching you unwrap your pressies.'

I turn and face her. 'You did this?'

'Yeah. Do you like it?'

I glance behind me at the huge crowd of people in my living room talking and laughing and waiting for me to go and talk to them. 'We'll see.'

*

Turns out I did like it. Jenna was right, as usual; the amount of people there meant I didn't have to sit and pretend to be surprised every time I opened another card or gift. And there were no party games, no cake with candles: just a big buffet of food on the dining table and cans of beer in the fridge and music in the background. It had been a warm day, so the backdoor was open, and people spilled into the garden. I was glad someone had picked up Roscoe's poo; that's my job, and I've been slacking recently. And there was no pressure to run around and hug and kiss everyone, either; people made their way to me and I made my way to them when it felt comfortable. I even had a non-Jenna related chat with Dad at one point, which was weird but nice.

I spent most of my time with Daisy and Callum, though Joe and Eric and the other lads and I had a kickabout at the back of the garden for a while, too. They all thought it was cool that Mum had brought beers: I knew that would have been Jenna's idea as well.

'See ya later, squirt.' Kent grabs his jacket and ruffles my hair.

'Finally taking the hint?' I gesture at the empty room behind him.

'Ha-ha. I was saying goodnight to your sister.'

'I'm joking.' He lingers in the doorway a moment, as if waiting for me to say something else. Which I guess I probably should. 'Erm, thanks, Kent.'

'For what?' He slides his trainers on. 'Coming? Don't think I made a huge difference to the ambiance.' He winks.

Come on, Al. Don't be awkward. Just say it. 'No, well, yeah, thanks for coming.' I clear my throat. 'But thanks as well for the whole thing. The party, I mean.'

Kent grins. 'You're not going all soft on me, are you?' He pulls me into a headlock.

'Ow! Get off.' I push him away but I'm laughing. And I mean it, I am thankful. Not just for the party—for everything. But now's not the time to get into that. Daisy lingers behind me in the hallway, stroking Roscoe. I jerk my head in her direction meaningfully.

'Right, right, I'm off.' Kent grabs his keys from the side, then lowers his voice. 'Seriously, though, don't thank me. This was all down to that amazing sister of yours.'

I don't doubt it was. But I also know that she's too tired to have done all of this on her own.

''Bye, Kent!' Daisy calls after him, straightening up as the door slams. 'Right, I'd better go too, Al.'

'Do you have to?'

'I'll see you at school.' She laughs, standing on her tiptoes to give me a kiss. 'Thanks for the party, Cindy!' She shouts.

'You're welcome, love.' Mum pokes her head out from the kitchen. 'Feel free to come over anytime.' She looks at us for a minute, still smiling but also looking like she might cry, before disappearing.

'Ignore her,' I mutter.

Daisy laughs. 'Did you have a nice time though?'

'I did,' I say honestly. 'It's the first birthday I've enjoyed in ages. Thank you for coming.'

'Wouldn't have missed it for the world.' She kisses me on the tip of my nose this time. I wish she'd do it again. I wish she'd kiss me everywhere, right here and now. 'See you on your real birthday.' Daisy winks and opens the front door; Roscoe lets out a little whine and tries to flop on her feet. Even he doesn't want her to go. But she has to, and she does, disappearing into the dark, hair flying out behind her in the wind. She wouldn't let me walk with her. Maybe I should run after her anyway? Or would that look creepy? I step out of the house to see her turn the corner and go out of view completely. Too late.

'Has she gone?' Mum has reappeared.

'Yeah.'

'Excellent.' She holds two mugs of tea up and jerks her head towards the living room. 'Time to open your presents!'

It's not the same opening presents without Jenna. She went to bed after people started leaving and the sun began to set. I knew she was tired, especially for the last hour or two; she was just sat with Kent in the living room, covered in a blanket.

*

'Knock, knock.' I push Jenna's bedroom door open slowly.

'Come in.' Her voice sounds so weak. I hate when she sounds like this. I always remind myself that she's had a long day, that she'll sound like her old self in the morning. But what is her old self now? She's been like this for months. This is Jenna now.

'Hi.'

'How was it, party animal?' She props herself up with some pillows and smiles at me. How different she looked a few hours ago, with her make-up and hair and dress. She's back to her usual pale grey colour now. Not that she's not pretty; she's always pretty. It's just now she's a pretty girl with cancer. Earlier you'd never have known she was this ill.

'It was amazing. Thank you, Jenna.'

She smiles and closes her eyes. 'And now I can go in peace.' She slumps a little further down in bed and sighs.

'Ha-ha.' I wait for her to reopen her eyes a minute. Wait. Is she breathing? Her chest doesn't look like it's moving. 'Jenna?' No. This can't be happening. She can't go now. Not now. I reach out to her, squeezing her shoulder. 'Jenna?' Oh my God. My heart feels like it's about to burst. I need to get Mum. I need to get Dad. I need to get someone.

'Ha!' Her voice makes me jump. 'Got ya.'

'What the hell, Jenna?' I leap back off the bed. 'You idiot! You scared the life out of me!'

She cackles. 'Should have seen the look on your face.'

'How do you know what I looked like? You had your eyes closed,' I mutter, sitting back down. 'That's not funny.'

'I know.' She stops smiling. 'Sorry. Just thought it would lighten the mood. On a serious note, though,' she sits up properly again, 'I'm glad you enjoyed yourself, Al. You should have heard Mum when I first suggested the idea.'

'She hated it?'

'She didn't hate it. It was like she was… jealous. That she didn't come up with it herself.' She pauses and her eyes glaze over slightly. 'She did a good job, though, with the food and all that.'

I nod. My heart rate is finally going back to normal.

'Sorry I couldn't hack the all-nighter,' Jenna goes on. 'It's that little condition I've got going on… What's it called again? Ah, yes. Cancer.'

'I guess I can forgive you,' I joke.

'Thanks, Al. Can you forgive me for something else, though?' Jenna asks seriously.

'What?'

'Well,' she takes a deep breath, 'I hate to put a downer on things, but I do feel like I need to apologise.'

'For what?'

She's smiling, but her eyes are teary. One escapes and rolls down her cheek. 'It's crap. I just wish… I guess I'm just sorry that I won't be around for any more birthdays.' My stomach drops. I feel like I might cry, too.

'Don't say that.' My voice doesn't sound like me. 'Yes you will.' I pull her into a hug and feel her shoulders shake. Mine are wobbling, too. 'The doctors said there's no set time—'

'I know, I know.' She pulls away from me and wipes her face on her sleeve. 'I know that. I'm being silly.' She smiles and takes a deep breath, 'I just mean if. If this was my last time to celebrate you, your life, the day you were born, then I'm sorry. Just know that if I had it my way, I'd be here for loads more. Loads and loads.' She throws her arms around me again and I hug her back tighter than ever, hoping with all the energy I have left that Jenna will be here to plan my party next year.

Chapter Thirty-Eight

'Take this left.'

'This left, here?'

'Yeah, this one.'

'Now?'

'Yes, now!'

Daisy and I slide over to right as Callum's mum screeches the car round the corner.

'Could've given me more notice.'

Callum turns around and rolls his eyes at us. I don't think him and the satnav get on all that well. But I also don't think his mum's driving helps: she's very fast and sharp. Not that I'm an expert. Or that I'm complaining; I'm more than grateful for the lift to Callum's Aunty Flo's.

'It's right in a minute, down Wheeler's Lane.'

'Wheeler's Lane?' Callum's mum checks the mirrors. 'Isn't that on the left?'

'No, the right.'

'Are you sure?'

'Yes, Mum, I'm sure!'

Daisy giggles quietly. We gain a bit of speed as the car heads down a hill. Surrounded by fields and trees, it feels like we're a million miles from home rather than just the next town over. I feel confident today, like we're finally back on track. As we whizz past the green, it's like all this nature's giving me the thumbs up; I'm doing something right. We're doing something right.

'Remember when we used to come to Aunt Flo's for sleepovers, Al?' Callum turns to look at me. 'Back when she lived in her flat?

We played with all her weird crystals and stuff.' Yes, I vaguely remember. And if I remember rightly, his Aunty Flo's a bit, well, different. But what's wrong with different? That's why we're here, isn't it? To look at different opinions, different beliefs.

'You only went the once,' Callum's mum tuts. 'I don't think you've even seen her new place, have you, Cal?'

'Nope. Haven't you?'

'Only been the once.' She shudders. 'I like to meet Flo in open spaces if I can help it.'

'Do you know much about this spiritualism stuff, Ms McKay?' Daisy leans forward eagerly. 'Has your sister always been into it?'

'Has she always been an oddball, you mean?' Callum's mum slows the car. 'This turning, Cal?'

Callum's head bows. 'Erm… No. Turns out it was a left. We missed it—it was back there.'

*

Callum's Aunty Flo's house looks like it belongs in a story book. It's covered in ivy and flowers, winding around the windows and door as if they're protecting it. And the building itself is tiny: really old-fashioned, with a thatched roof and everything. I'm half-expecting a witch to open the door.

'Hello! Come in, come in everyone.' Aunty Flo doesn't look too far from what I pictured: well, she's hardly changed a bit since we were little. Same long, purple hair. Same crooked nose. Same friendly smile.

'Wow! I love your hair,' Daisy gushes as we head into the living room. I'm not surprised at all to see three cats stretched out on the sofa.

'Thank you, lovely! Yours is fab, too.' Aunty Flo heads straight to the kitchen. 'Tea or coffee anyone?'

'I'll have a cuppa,' Callum's mum calls back. 'Kids?'

'No thanks!' We perch on the end of the cat-covered chairs as she clangs about in the kitchen. Adjoining the living room is what looks like a dining room: though not a normal dining room. The table is circular, with a dark cloth thrown over it. And instead of cutlery laid out, there's stones and ornaments. I catch Daisy's eye; she mouths, 'Cool.'

'Here we are.' Aunty Flo's back with a creaky tray which she lays carefully on the little coffee table. 'Now. How have we all been?'

Callum's mum reaches for her tea. 'Not bad thanks. You?'

'Oh, you know. The usual.' Aunty Flo picks up her own cup, which looks like it's full of green water. 'How's school, Callum?'

'Fine.'

'Excellent.'

They fall into silence. I don't know where to look, so I stare at the ginger cat, which has now woken up and is cleaning its paws. I wonder how Roscoe would act in this room right now. He's never been a big fan of cats.

'So,' Daisy clears her throat. 'Is it okay, Flo, if we ask you some questions?'

'Of course, yes, of course.' Aunty Flo perches on the coffee table; there's no room for her on the sofas, what with all the cats.

'Shall we move to the table over there?' Daisy reads my mind. 'We can all sit comfortably then.'

'Yes, let's.' We follow her to the mysterious set-up we'd noticed earlier and take a seat.

'I'm fine here,' Callum's mum calls from the living room. She grabs the newspaper from the coffee table and shakes it open.

'She's a funny one, your mum,' Aunty Flo whispers to Callum. We all try not to laugh. 'Anyway. Questions, questions. Who'd like to start?'

I grab the notebook out of my bag. 'Yeah, sure. Okay… So, you're a spiritualist. Would you mind telling us what that means?'

Aunty Flo clasps her hands together. 'Well, we spiritualists are not unlike many other religions. We believe in, and pray to, a God. We try our utmost to live good and productive lives. And we all do that in our own, individual ways.'

I scribble this down. Daisy sets her recorder on the table. 'So, it's not like Christianity? 'Cos that has the Ten Commandments that everyone follows.'

'Yes, you're right. We don't conform to a specific set of rules; we set our own separate values.' Aunty Flo nods.

'That's cool,' Daisy muses. 'So, you're free.'

'Free,' Aunty Flo echoes. 'Exactly.'

'What are these?' Callum lifts up one of the stones.

'Clairvoyance crystals.'

'What do they…?'

'I think we're getting off-track.' I shoot Callum a look. 'Sorry. Our main question, to get to the point, is, well, what do you think happens after death?'

Aunty Flo tilts her head to the side. 'I'll tell you what I believe, children. But you don't have to agree with me. You don't ever have to agree with anyone, on these matters. You're free to make your own decisions, walk your own path in life. Don't forget that.'

I catch Daisy smirking out of the corner of my eye, but I don't really think Aunty Flo's being funny. I think it's actually pretty cool that she's trying to keep our minds open. And I think she's got some important things to say.

'We spiritualists believe,' she continues, 'that no one really dies. Yes, our bodies may give up and fail, but our souls live on. We are reborn, again and again, for different reasons, into different shells, to fulfil different purposes.'

Callum's mum snorts from the sofa. But something she said has stuck with me.

'So you think all lives have a purpose?'

Aunty Flo looks me dead in the eye. 'I do. We're all here to be who we are, to do what we're doing. There's a reason for every single person's existence.'

So we're all meant to be here; we're all meant to be us. I like this idea. It gives me hope. But also worry. What if Jenna hasn't fulfilled her reason yet? What if she's meant to grow up and win an Olympic medal, or start a new charity, or find a cure for poverty? She has so much more to give, so much more to experience.

It's as if Aunty Flo can hear my thoughts aloud. 'When they leave, everyone leaves for a reason.'

I swallow the rising lump in my throat. 'What reason?' I'm

not expecting an answer. Who could really justify taking my sister from me?

'They have fulfilled their purpose.'

This just makes things even more confusing. How could Jenna have fulfilled her purpose? How could she have done every single thing she's meant to have done already?

'I don't think my sister's done that.' I try and keep my voice light, but she can probably hear the doubt.

Aunty Flo reaches across the table and squeezes my hand. 'When she passes, she will have. And remember, that won't be the end. Jenna's body may die, but her soul will live on. And she will have many, many more beautiful lives. Just as we all will.'

Many more? Maybe this is more like Buddhism than we first thought. I don't know if I like the idea any more than the first time I heard it, of Jenna being reborn as someone else, somewhere else. She's still being torn away from us as who she is now. So that doesn't make it better. I can feel my eyes fill up. Crap. Come on, Al, you haven't cried in an interview yet. Don't make this the first time!

'Oh, Al.' Daisy puts her arm around me. 'I know it's emotional, but this is a good thing, right? Jenna won't really be gone, not truly.' Okay, the tears are really coming now. What is up with me today? I look pathetic, I know I do. But I can't stop. It's as if all the tears I've been holding in have suddenly been let loose: the dam's broken and the river's flowing. And it sucks; I feel stupid, but in a really weird way it feels kinda nice to let it out.

'For Christ's sake, Flo.' Callum's mum approaches the table. 'That's enough. You're scaring them! Come on, kids, let's go.'

I don't want to leave yet, but I really don't have the energy to fight back. I let Daisy lead me to the door, the tears still coming, and I don't look at anyone, just the floor. Looking at someone will only make it worse.

'I'm sorry, Alex.' Aunty Flo calls from behind me. 'I know it's hard. I know it's sad, trust me I do. And I'm not pushing my beliefs on you, I never would! But please, take comfort in what I know. Once Jenna's through that door, her body may sleep but her soul will be awake! It will never fade!'

Callum's mum slams the door behind her.

Chapter Thirty-Nine

'You spoke to a spiritualist?'
'Yes.'

Mrs Moss leans forward eagerly. 'Alex, that's brilliant! What a great idea. Did she have any interesting ideas to share?'

I shrug. She did, sure. But that doesn't mean I wanna share them with you, Mrs Moss.

She presses her lips together. 'I see.' I wait for her to ask something else, but she doesn't. I wait for her to change the topic, lead it on to something else; ask me how I'm doing with my homework or something. But she doesn't.

So now I'm just waiting. And I'm sick of waiting. I feel like that's all I've been doing for months now; waiting for the answer to fall into my lap tied neatly with a bow, all ready for me to take to Jenna. It's like I've been half-heartedly trying, clutching at books and movies and religions, thinking I'll just stumble across the answer to life's biggest question. I'm an idiot.

'Aren't you going to say anything?'

Mrs Moss sighs again. She's clearly in a sighing mood. 'What do you want me to say, Alex?'

'I don't care,' I tell her. And I don't care if I sound stroppy saying that, either. It's true. 'Just something.'

'All right, then.' Mrs Moss leans back in her seat. 'So, I take it that's spiritualism ticked off your list. Do you have many more ideas on there?' I wouldn't say that's it 'ticked off.' But what's the good in explaining that to Mrs Moss? She's hardly the one with all the answers.

'I dunno. Can I go now?'

She raises her eyebrows. 'You've been cutting a lot of our sessions short, lately.'

I feel bad now. 'I don't mean to be rude, Miss. I just don't really have anything to say today.' Some days talking with Mrs Moss helps. Other days it doesn't.

She closes her notebook. 'All right, Alex. If you're sure. You know where my office is, anyway.' She looks like she wants to say something else, but I get my bag and go. The last thing I need is to hear about how my manners are slacking. I know they're slacking. And she shouldn't take it personally: I can be awful to anyone and everyone these days. Teenagers are renowned for being mean, right? Teenagers with dying sisters, especially.

*

I hate walking home on my own. It's the icing on the cake, today. Mum always says that expression, and I never used to get it, but now I do. It's like the final bad thing on top of a pile of crap (the cake is the crap).

First, my session with Mrs Moss was a waste of time. Then I found out I failed my English mock test. Miss Rhys even suggested I take a dyslexia test, it was that bad. And now I find out Daisy's going to Marley's house and Callum's got detention, so here I am. Walking down the street all on my bloody own. I get my phone out for something to do.

'Watch it!' A woman with a buggy swerves around me. Oops. I can never walk in a straight line when I'm on my phone. One of my many talents. I slide it back in my pocket; I had no messages, anyway.

I'm just waiting at the crossing when I see him over the other side of the road, fag in hand, hood pulled over his head. Duce. Crap. The green man flashes up as he looks right at me. I've got no choice but to cross the road and walk towards him. It's the first time I've seen him since the punching incident. I know he's been back at school—he was only suspended for a week—but he's not in any of my classes. Yet here he is.

237

'Alex.' He straightens up as I walk towards him.

'D—Bruce.' Close one. I don't want any trouble.

'Where're you going?'

'Home.' I'm almost past him now, but he steps in my way.

'Not yet.'

I can't see his face under his hood which normally would be a good thing as it's revolting, but I hate not knowing if he's angry or not. Is he? Surely, he is. I know I'd be mad if a kid smacked me round the face and got away with it.

He tosses his cigarette onto the floor and squashes it with his foot. 'You made a big mistake, Duncan.' He pulls his hood down. Yuck. Even uglier than I remember.

'Don't think so.' I step round him.

'I think so.' He gets in my way again. Bloody hell. I'm just wondering how much trouble I'll be in if I hit him again when the crossing noise goes off and a bunch of kids cross to our side of the road.

'All right, mate?' It's Eric, from football.

'Fine, thanks.' I answer, trying not to smile at Duce's face-drop. That's right, my mate's here. What you gonna do now?

'What do you want?' Eric asks him. Eric's tall and has a bit of a beard already and goes to the gym. I think I'd be bricking it if Eric was looking at me the way he's looking at Duce right now.

'Nothing,' Duce mutters. He glares at me. 'Laters.'

'Freak,' Eric mutters as Duce slopes off. 'What was he saying?'

'Nothing really,' I say, watching him leave. 'Just that I'm in trouble, apparently.'

Eric laughs. 'Ooh, bet you're scared!'

'Who isn't? I've heard if you look at his spots too long you turn to stone.'

'Eric!' One of Eric's friends calls him from up the road. 'Come on!'

Eric looks at me. This is awkward. Should I thank him? I mean, it's not like he rescued me from a burning building, and I totally could have got out of that situation myself, but he did come to help. He didn't have to do that.

'We're playing footie at the green. Wanna come?'

'Sure. Thanks.' There. Now he doesn't know if I'm thanking him for the Duce thing, or the football invitation.

Eric starts running off after his friends. 'Meet you there in ten?'

'Sure!' I call back. A kickabout will make my evening ten-times more bearable. Maybe this isn't such a crap cake after all.

Chapter Forty

'Where's Jenna?' Her car's not on the drive. Her car is always on the drive.

'Her and Kent have gone out.' Mum flicks the kettle on. Damn it. I wanted to get her ideas for birthday presents for Daisy. She told me today her birthday's only six weeks away now and I literally don't have a clue what to get her. I lean against the kitchen counter and wonder whether to ask Mum instead.

'Do you want tea?'

'Sure.' I watch her take three mugs from the cupboard. 'Get up to much today?'

She shoots me a weird look. 'Not much. Why?'

'I dunno. Just making conversation.' Nah, I won't bother asking her advice then. She's clearly not in the mood. I get it; I'm not dissing her. We all have days where we don't wanna chat. I had one the other day. Someone in your family having cancer tends to have that effect.

'Go and sit down,' Mum says, turning away from me to stir the tea. 'I'll be in in a minute.' Okay, she's being even stranger than usual. Even when she doesn't want to talk she makes some sort of effort to ask about school or Daisy at least. I sit on the sofa opposite Dad.

'All right?'

I glance at the empty beer cans next to him and decide to go for the short answer. 'Yeah. You?'

'Yeah.' He turns the TV up. Guess that conversation's finished, too.

'Turn it down, George,' Mum snaps, setting the cups down in

various places around the living room. Roscoe trots in after her and plonks himself on my feet. Dad rolls his eyes and presses the minus button once; it goes from forty to thirty-nine. Mum snatches the remote off him and turns it down to twenty-five.

'Can't bloody hear it now,' Dad mutters, taking a swig of beer. I peer over at his collection again: six cans and counting. Oh, and his cup of tea.

'Because you're drunk, probably,' Mum hisses. 'Have your tea now.'

'What are you, my bleeding mother?' Dad snaps.

'Christ.' Mum puts her head in her hands. Dad looks at me. I look down at Roscoe. The only member of the family who's never made me feel awkward.

'Anyway. Shall we tell him?'

'Tell him what?'

Tell me what?

'What we decided today.' Dad says.

'What did you decide?' I ask. I try and stay out of their arguments normally, but this sounds like something I need to know.

Mum sighs deeply. 'We said at dinner, George.'

'Did we? Oh.' Dad crushes the beer can in his hand and puts it with the rest.

'What is it?' I ask again.

Mum and Dad look at each other. 'It's not something... Not a decision we took lightly, Al. I'd just like you to know that,' Mum says slowly. I'm getting a bit freaked out now. What did they not take lightly? And why am I the last one to know something again?

'We went to look around it today,' Dad says. 'And your sister's going there.'

'Where?'

'To the... What's it called, Cindy?'

'Damn it, George!' Mum snaps. 'You're making a right pig's ear of it. You've had too much to drink. Let me do the talking.'

'Where, Mum?' I ask again. My chest feels tight. Where are they taking my sister? Where is Jenna going?

'Well, not right away, love,' Mum says carefully. 'Not right now.

But soon… We'll be admitting Jenna to a hospice.'

My chest feels tight.

'Now, I know what you're thinking.' Dad sips his tea. 'And yes, you'll still be able to see her. We'll be visiting all the time.'

Mum nods. 'Your father's right, Al. We'll be with her whenever we want.' They're both looking at me now, sort of smiling. The fact that they're trying to look happy about this makes me want to throw up. What is there to be happy about? Little do they know I've been to a hospice. I've spoken to people in hospices. Miriam said it's where she was left to die. Is that what we're doing? Shoving Jenna in there to see out her days? I feel sick I feel sick I feel sick.

'It's where she'll be more comfortable,' Mum goes on, picking up her tea. Her voice is wobbling. 'It'll be easier for her to have her medication, pain relief and things.'

Dad puts his hand on her knee. 'It's gonna be hard, Alex. But it's what's best.' His voice is shaky too. They're both looking at me, like—like what? Like I'm gonna jump up and down with excitement? Like I'm gonna say, 'Oh wow, yeah, that's the best idea I've heard for ages!' What do they want? My approval? They're not getting it. My chest feels tight.

Mum pulls a tissue from her pocket. 'Say something, Alex. Please.'

I want to say something, I really do. I want to shout and scream and yell. I want to ask what the hell they think they're doing, who they think they are, carting Jenna off to see out her days in a room all alone—

'I understand it might feel sudden.' Dad sighs, taking a tissue from Mum. 'Or… maybe it doesn't. You know what's up, you always have. Our smart boy.'

Mum makes a sudden noise like a strangled cat and throws herself at Dad. Her body heaves up and down, her sobs echoing through the house. I've never heard such a terrible sound. I try and think, but my thoughts aren't forming. My brain's shut down. All I know is I need to get out. Get out get out get out of this mess. I stand up. I'm walking. Mum's following me. She's still crying, screaming, but I can't hear her. Nothing sounds real. I'm clipping

Roscoe's lead on. I'm putting my shoes on. Mum's still there. I don't want to listen to her. I need to get out. Get out get out get out. My chest feels tight.

*

It's getting dark now. Not dark dark, but the sky's a sort of deep blue colour and some of the stars are coming out. I don't know how long I've been here. I've only just started to feel normal again. I'm lying on the grass by the river, Roscoe snoring next to me. I wonder how long he's been sleeping for; he's probably just as tired out by the whole thing as I am. I really don't know what happened but, after what Mum said about the hospice, everything just went into a blur. I started to walk but my chest felt like it would explode, and I couldn't breathe. I had to sit on the bench and hold Roscoe and rock back and forwards for ages. I probably looked like a loony. Luckily no one saw. And now, somehow, I've ended up lying on the grass. It's a bit damp and my school jumper probably smells. Mum won't be happy.

She's not the only one, though. How does she expect me to see this as a good thing? But then... Is it a bad thing? Really? At least in the hospice she would be cared for and comfortable. It didn't look like that bad a place, did it? I try and picture Jenna in that living room with Miriam and the others, Jack taking care of her. And, like Mum said, we could see her whenever we wanted. It wouldn't be that much different.

Okay, that's a lie. Everything would be different. My own sister wouldn't be in her bedroom at night. She wouldn't be on the sofa watching The Chase when I got home from school. She wouldn't be sneaking in the house past midnight, drunk and being silly with me in the kitchen.

But if she didn't go to the hospice, would those things keep happening anyway? Probably not. There's no going back. There's no more seaside visits or McDonald's drives or shopping trips now; that's what Mum's saying. Jenna can't do those things anymore. She needs to be in bed, looked after, with her medicine. She needs to be in the hospice. This is who my sister is now.

'Are you awake?' I prod Roscoe. He sits up with a start. 'Sorry.' He sniffs my face, asking if I'm all right. 'I'm not okay,' I tell him. 'But there's no more being okay now. This is it. They're putting Jenna in the hospice.' He cocks his head to the side. 'A place where people go when it's close…' I swallow a lump in my throat, 'Close to the end.' Roscoe licks my cheek. He knows what I'm saying. He always does.

Over the other side of the water, two kids are dribbling a football down the path towards the park: a boy and a girl. Jenna and I never used to play football because she hated getting muddy. We'd do other things instead, like read a page of a story each at bedtime. She always used to tell me to hurry up because I'd stutter over the longer words. Maybe I should take that dyslexia test. We'd draw together, too, then take them to Mum and Dad and make them decide which one was better. Dad would always vote for Jenna's and Mum would always vote for mine. It would always be a draw and we'd share the 'prize'—normally a chocolate bar—together afterwards. I wish I could share some of the pain she's feeling now. Or even take it all. I would, if it meant she could stay.

'Stop, Ruby!' The boy across the water yells at his sister. She nutmegs the ball between his legs and he stamps his foot before chasing after her. Maybe if I'd insisted, Jenna would have played football with me. Maybe she would have grown to like it.

Roscoe nudges my hand with his head and whines softly. He's probably starving. I'm pretty hungry, too. But going home means facing everyone, facing Jenna. I don't know if I can do it. Not on my own. Roscoe snorts loudly. Right. I'm not alone. I never am when he's here.

Chapter Forty-One

'Oh, thank God!' Mum hurtles out of the kitchen as I close the front door behind me. 'Where the hell have you been?'

'Just out,' I mutter, unclipping Roscoe's lead. He trots straight into the kitchen for his dinner.

'Without your phone?' She waves it in my face. 'Idiot!'

'Right. Sorry.' I take it from her. I'm not sorry.

'Doesn't matter, doesn't matter, you're home now.' She pulls me in for a hug that feels too forced. 'I've plated your dinner up.' She follows me into the kitchen, fussing around with loading up the dishwasher while I eat homemade chicken pie and chips. It's cold, but it's good. I'm so hungry that I think even Roscoe's dinner would've tasted fine.

'Is Jenna home yet?' I ask after swallowing my last mouthful.

Mum takes my plate and starts scraping the leftovers into the bin. 'She's in the living room.'

I stand up. 'Does she… Does she know?'

Mum doesn't turn around. 'Yes.'

I pour myself some water, take a deep breath and head in there. Jenna's curled on to the sofa next to Dad, who's snoring loudly.

'Hey, Al,' she whispers.

I perch on the arm of the sofa next to her. 'Hi.'

'You went on a little walk, I hear?' She moves the blanket away from her face, so I can see her properly. She looks tired. So tired.

'Yeah.' I feel like I should say more, but she probably already knows what happened. Anyway, I don't want to talk about me. I want to talk about her. 'Did you go and look round the hospice today?'

She nods. 'Sure did. It's called Elm Cottage. It's not far from your school, actually.'

Elm Cottage. The hospice we've already been too. The hospice where Miriam lives. I don't know if that makes things better or worse. 'Did you like it?'

She raises her eyebrows. 'I suppose so.' I think that means no. I look behind me to check Mum's still in the kitchen.

'You don't have to go,' I whisper. 'Not if you don't want to.'

Jenna reaches out and holds my hand. Her skin feels like it's burning. 'I know.'

'Do you need anything? You feel really warm.' I reach across with my other hand and check the temperature of her forehead.

'I'm cold,' she insists, snuggling further under the blanket, 'but fine. Thanks.'

'What do you really think?' I press. I need to know. If she doesn't want to go, then there's no way I'm letting that happen.

'I dunno. I think maybe it is the best option,' she sighs. 'Anyway, are you really okay, Al? It sounds like you had a panic attack earlier. I don't know why the hell Mum let you out of her sight.'

'Why does Mum do a lot of things?' I mumble, not knowing what a 'panic attack' is.

'True. You're all right though? You're feeling okay?'

No.

'Sure. It's you I'm worried about.' I squeeze her hand.

'Honestly, Al, I'm all right,' she says, yawning. 'It was just a lot to take in, you know? But I do think it's a nice place. A comfy, peaceful place. And that's what I need.'

'Are you not comfy here?' I ask.

'It's not the same here,' she says. 'I can get my medicine easier there.'

'Will you still be able to watch The Chase?'

She smiles weakly. 'Yes, Al.'

'What about Roscoe, will he be able to visit? He knows what's going on,' I tell her urgently.

'We'll sneak him in if not,' Jenna says, closing her eyes. 'Say he's a therapy dog.'

'He might as well be,' I say, thinking of all the therapy sessions he's given me. 'I don't want to be pushy. I just want what's best for you, Jenna. I want you to be happy.'

'I know. Love you.' She closes her eyes. I want to say more, but I know she needs to rest.

'Is she dozing off?' Mum appears in the doorway.

'Yep.' I let go of Jenna's hand and get up to go.

'Wait, Al. I just want to say sorry,' Mum says quietly. 'I know your father and I sprung that information on you suddenly. And I know it's not a nice thing to hear.' I don't know what to say. I'm exhausted. And underneath the exhaustion, angry. She can apologise for something that ultimately isn't her fault, but she can't apologise for basically calling me an inconvenience the other week? I don't get it. It's like she picks and chooses when she wants to make up with me.

'We all just feel,' she goes on, 'that it's the best place for your sister. And like I said, it won't happen immediately: there'll be a transitional period. It's a process. We want everyone to feel comfortable.' The word comfortable makes my stomach flip. How am I meant to feel comfortable in this house ever again without my sister here?

'I just don't get how you're so happy about it,' I say finally, concentrating on keeping my voice down so I don't wake Jenna and Dad.

'Happy? We're not happy about it, Al. This isn't a happy situation,' Mum says gently. 'You know that. We just think it's the best environment for your sister.'

Why does she get to decide? She gets to determine what Jenna needs, where she goes. She gets to say I'm a bloody nuisance and not apologise for it. Just because she's the mother of a sick child doesn't mean she can do whatever she wants!

'Do you understand, Alex?'

'No!' I snap. 'I don't bloody understand! And I don't want to talk about it with you. You never listen or care about anything I have to say. You didn't care where I went earlier, or you would've come to look for me! You don't care what you say that upsets me, or you would apologise!'

'Alex!' Mum pulls me by the elbow out of the living room, shutting the door behind her. 'What the hell has gotten into you?'

'What's gotten into me?' I'm trying really hard not to shout too loud. 'Don't you mean you? You've got one kid who you're shoving into a hospice and another that you literally couldn't give a crap about. I'm not just gonna stand here and pretend—'

'Don't you dare speak to me like that!' Mum hisses. 'I'm not just going to stand here and be shouted at like this! Go to your room, Alex Duncan.'

I climb the stairs as fast as I can. 'Gladly.'

Chapter Forty-Two

I don't know how I managed a full day at school, I really don't. The only thing that actually got me out of bed this morning was the thought of my other option: spending the day in the house with Mum. Which is the last thing I need right now.

'You're being so quiet,' Daisy says, pressing a chewing gum into my palm. I put it in my mouth and don't reply. Like I said, sometimes talking about things helps, sometimes it doesn't. I don't even know where I'd start in explaining what happened last night to Daisy. Or anyone.

'Do you want to come round at the weekend?' Daisy asks. 'We're gonna get a Chinese.'

'I'm busy. Thanks, though.' There's no way I'm going back to Daisy's house yet.

'What're you doing?'

Probably sitting in my room crying and having nightmares about death.

'Nothing.'

'Then why can't you come over?'

'Because I can't!' I sound snappier than I meant to. It's not her I'm mad at. It's everything else in the bloody universe.

'Didn't you like coming to mine?' Daisy asks. She sounds hurt. Normal Alex would recognise this and back off and apologise. Normal Alex wouldn't have snapped at his girlfriend in the first place. But this isn't Normal Alex. I'm angry. I'm tired. I'm sick of the constant stream of bad news that is my life. And Daisy isn't helping.

'It was fine.'

'It was fine? There's no point in us being girlfriend and boyfriend if things are just going to be fine, Alex!' Daisy raises her voice. Again, Normal Alex would worm his way out of this mess. Today, I don't care about escaping. If anything, I'll dig the hole deeper, I don't care.

'Well, your Mum was hard work,' I snap back, spitting my gum on the floor. It's lost its taste already.

'Um, excuse me!' Daisy stops dead in the street. 'My mum was trying her best!'

'Yeah, sure, at offending me.' I'm not speaking loudly, like she is. My voice sounds droney, like I can't hide how bored I am at this conversation. I don't mean to sound bored. I'm not bored. I'm just over it.

'Well, not all mums are perfect, Alex; you know that better than anyone,' Daisy hisses, resuming walking again.

The words come out of my mouth before I can even think about them. 'At least my mum's not with a married man.'

Daisy stops again. 'What the hell, Al? You can't bring that up as something to use against me. That's not how this works.'

'Nothing works in your bloody family.' I'm on a roll now. All my horrible thoughts are coming to the surface and I don't have the energy to stop them. 'Your real dad's nowhere to be seen and your new stepdad has a wife. Meanwhile, when your mum's not getting slapped about she's swanning around buying pregnancy tests…'

Crap. I've gone too far now. It's like I've snapped back to reality. Like the whole day I've been swimming underwater and everything's been blurry, but now I'm up at the surface, gasping for air. Everything's clearer, realer now. I've just argued with my girlfriend. My perfect, lovely girlfriend who's done nothing wrong. I've just told her the secret I've been keeping about her own mum. About her possibly getting a sibling.

'What? Are you serious?' Daisy has tears in her eyes.

'No…' Crap. Which direction is best to take with this? Honesty, I suppose. Now I've said it, there's no going back. 'Look, I'm really sorry, Daisy. I had a hard day yesterday with stuff at home, I don't mean to take it out on you—'

'You saw her buying a test?' she interrupts me. The tears are spilling down her face now.

'Yeah. I'm really sorry.' I've had my fair share of arguments with family and friends over the past couple of months, but I have never ever felt as guilty as I do right now. Look what you've done, Alex. You've made your own girlfriend cry. Because you can't control your temper, now she's suffering. Great boyfriend, you are. Ten-out-of-ten.

'Why didn't you tell me?' Daisy asks, sobbing now. She sits down on the kerb, head in hands.

'I'm sorry,' I say again. What more can I say? 'It's a bit of an awkward situation.' I sit next to her and put my hand on her knee. She turns away. 'It's probably nothing, anyway.'

'Yes, her thinking she's pregnant is probably nothing,' Daisy snaps sarcastically. She stands up, wiping her face on her sleeve. 'I'm going home.'

I thought that's what we were doing anyway, walking home, so I start to follow her.

'No! You wait here. Or walk a different way or something. I don't want to speak to you.' She pushes me.

'Daisy,' I say desperately. 'Please. Let's at least walk together. We don't have to talk.'

'I don't want to walk with you!' she shouts. 'You're a liar!'

'I'm not a liar,' I say, following her down the street as she begins to storm off.

'Well, you kept things from me!'

'I'm sorry! I was going to tell you, I was just waiting for the right time!' I don't know if that's entirely true. I'd never made up my mind properly if I was going to tell her or not. And now I wish wish wish I hadn't.

'There's no right time for that!' she cries, speeding up. 'Leave me alone, Al! I need to be by myself.'

I suppose I get that. Like yesterday, when I left the house with Roscoe, I needed some time. Maybe I just need to give Daisy that, too. 'Okay.' I fall back and let her walk without me. 'Text me when you get home safe.' She doesn't answer.

I lean against the wall, heart thudding like I've just been on a rollercoaster. The guilt is still there, but now I'm frustrated more than anything. Frustrated at myself. What is wrong with me? I stay against the wall for a while—I don't know how long. I'm not in a rush to get home. I bet it will only make my day worse when I get through the front door. I'm not in a rush to catch up with Daisy. That'll just upset her even more. The best place for me to be right now is this wall, where I can't hurt anyone. Just myself.

Chapter Forty-Three

Daisy wasn't at school yesterday. I texted her a thousand times, only getting one response at about midday: 'I'm fine. Not coming in. Still need space.' Callum tried to call her too, but she ignored him. I have a feeling another big romantic Jenna-inspired gesture is on the cards. I need to do something at least, even if it isn't as cheesy as that. Do I have time to go and grab a box of chocolates from the shop or something? I glance at the clock. No, she's due here in ten minutes.

'Are you done?' Mum grabs my cereal and juice before I can answer. I stop myself from saying 'No'; she's scraped all my cornflakes into the bin now, anyway, so fat lot of use it would do. Things have been tense between us since the argument. Very tense. Normally by now she's back to acting as if nothing at all has happened.

'Morning.' Jenna's appeared in the doorway.

'Morning, love. You're up early! What do you fancy for breakfast?' Mum asks, flicking on the kettle.

Jenna yawns and sits down next to me. 'Dunno, not that hungry yet. Morning, Al.'

'Hi.'

'No Daisy again this morning?'

I check the time on my phone. 'She's normally gets here in about five minutes.'

'Hmm.' Jenna pours herself some orange juice. I told her everything that happened, of course. She agreed I was an idiot, but she said it was a difficult situation, that Daisy probably needed her space.

'Here you go, Jen.' Mum places a milky coffee in front of Jenna.

'Thanks. Do we have any croissants left?' she asks. 'The chocolate ones?'

Mum checks in the freezer. 'We do. How many?'

'Cook them all,' Jenna says, sipping her coffee. 'Me and Al will have a feast.'

Mum shoots her a look. 'Alex goes to school soon.'

'He's not walking with Daisy today,' Jenna shrugs.

'These still take about ten minutes to cook,' Mum says through gritted teeth. 'He'll be late.'

'We'll take him in the car,' Jenna insists. Mum looks like she wants to kill me but puts all the croissants in the oven anyway. I'm half-expecting Daisy to show up now, just to annoy her even more. Even though what Jenna's done is really nice, I do still want Daisy to knock on the door. We need to sort things out. I need to say sorry a hundred times, that I shouldn't have got angry at her when, really, I'm angry at everything else. I need to tell her I need her by my side, that I always will. I feel like the worst person in the world right now, after those comments about her mum. I'll say I'll try harder with her, that I won't judge her. She's right; all families have their issues. The fact that I mocked hers while I'm sat here in the kitchen with a terminally ill sister and a mum I am constantly arguing with just shows how stupid I was. How stupid I still am.

'You should text her,' Jenna whispers.

I check to see Mum's busy tidying. 'What will I say?'

'Say you're sorry.'

'I've said that! She stopped replying ages ago.'

Jenna shakes her head. 'Just saying the words I'm sorry won't do anything. You need to explain why you're sorry, why you said those things, and that you'll never say them again.'

'I know,' I sigh. 'I have a lot to say to her. I just don't want to do it over the phone.' As I finish talking my phone buzzes. It's from Daisy! I can't open it quick enough. She's finally ready to talk. She's finally ready to forgive me.

'What does it say?' Jenna asks.

I don't want to read it to her. I lock my phone. Daisy's not ready to talk. In fact, she's so not ready that she's not coming to school again. Jenna opens her mouth to say something else, but Mum starts fussing with plates and refilling drinks and checking on the croissants. So I eat and Jenna jokes and I laugh in the right places and act like I don't care until Mum ushers me into the car to drive me to school. And all I can think of, all the while, is Daisy.

*

And I'm still thinking of her.

'You should go see if Callum wants to play football,' Jenna suggests from the opposite sofa. 'Or go to the arcade or something.'

'I'm fine.'

I'm not fine.

'You're not fine,' she insists, pausing the TV. 'Tell him, Kent.'

Kent shifts uncomfortably next to her and looks like he'd rather not 'tell me.' Normally, watching a game show with a cup of tea, Kent and Jenna opposite me, is my favourite way to spend a weekday evening. Today, I think I'd rather be anywhere else. I don't know what's wrong with me. Well, that's a lie. I'm what's wrong with me. Me and my stupid emotions and my horrible words, pushing everyone away, hurting everyone's feelings. First Daisy and, though we didn't argue properly, I wasn't exactly nice to Callum today. And Mum, though I can't help feeling that one isn't entirely down to me. And just everyone, just everything. I ruin it all.

'Do you want us to take you to Daisy's?' Jenna asks.

Yes. No. Maybe.

'No,' I say eventually. If she didn't want to talk to me this morning, she won't want to talk to me now. Maybe not tomorrow. Maybe not ever again.

'Have you texted her again?'

'No,' I snap. I can feel the unreasonable anger rising again. Get down. Go away.

'Maybe you should call her?' Kent suggests. Why are they reeling off ideas as if this is the simplest problem ever to fix? As if a text or a call would magically make it all better?

'What the hell do you know about it?'

Kent raises his eyebrows. 'Chill out, Al. It's just a lovers' tiff. Have them all the time, don't we, Jen?' He nudges her, and she giggles. 'Maybe you should just let us take you round there, and—'

'Maybe you should stop talking about it!'

Jenna and Kent look at each other like they're disappointed but not surprised. No, like I've just said something totally weird. Like I'm an animal. Like I'm a lion that's eaten someone. Well, that's just what lions do: they can't help it. They're lions. Except I'm a boy, I'm Alex, and I'm ruining everything. Well, that's just what Alexes do.

'We just want to help, Al,' Jenna says gently. I sigh. I know they do. Not everyone's out to get me, I need to remember that. Least of all my sister and her boyfriend.

'I just… I just feel like I ruin everything.'

'Al!' Jenna sits up straight. 'Please don't say that. You don't ruin anything. Come here.' She pats the sofa.

'Nah.'

'Come here! Respect the cancer patient's wishes.'

'Jenna!' She's right though, I guess. I go to squidge myself on the end, but at the last-minute Jenna wraps her arms around my waist and pulls me between her and Kent. 'Get off!'

Kent puts me in a headlock. 'Now, we don't wanna hear that nonsense ever again.'

'You're the kindest, sweetest boy a girl could ask for!' Jenna nods. 'And Daisy knows that. She also knows you're a cranky teenager, and you're gonna have off days.'

I pull myself free. 'Don't do that! I'm not a baby.'

Kent and Jenna laugh. 'Yes, you are. My baby brother. Now, go work on your speech. 'Cos tomorrow, you're apologising like you mean it, and everything's gonna go back to normal. Okay?'

A part of me is pretty mad that they're treating me like a six-year-old right now. But the bigger part of me feels better than I did ten minutes ago. They're a bloody annoying pair sometimes, but they are right. Enough of this faffing about—I need to find my girlfriend and fix this. While it's still fixable.

*

'Knock on the door.'

'You knock.'

I sigh and take a step closer to the house. We're outside Daisy's, Callum and I. She didn't come to school again today; I got no text, nothing. Even if I did, it wouldn't have been enough to stop me coming here today. This silent treatment cannot go on any longer.

'Knock,' Callum urges. Okay. Here it goes. We wait a minute, peering in through the swirly glass. I can see a shape with red hair. Please don't be Daisy's mum, please don't be Daisy's mum…

'What the hell are you doing here?' It's Daisy. Thank God. It's Daisy and she looks so beautiful.

'Please don't shut the door. I'm here to apologise.' I stick my foot out in case she tries to shut it anyway.

'And what are you here for?' She glares at Callum.

He shrugs. 'Moral support.'

'Listen, Daisy. I can't begin to explain how sorry I am. I should never ever have acted that way towards you. You're my girlfriend and you deserve to be treated like that, not someone to take my anger out on. I was just in a mood because…' Here goes nothing. 'Because Jenna's being moved to a hospice soon. The one that we visited.' Her eyes widen. 'I know. And I know what this means. It means she's… close.' My voice cracks. Damn it Alex. Come on. 'And I know that gives me no excuse to speak to you the way I did. Or to have… kept secrets from you.'

I shoot Callum a look. Luckily, he's inspecting the tyres on a BMX lying on the driveway and isn't listening. 'I never meant to,' I continue. 'I'm sorry. I'm so sorry.' I feel like I've spoken too quickly, like I've rushed it. This isn't a thing to be rushed. But it also isn't a thing that needs to be dragged out. I need to say sorry, and I need Daisy to forgive me. I need her back in my life. And it's not flowers and music, it's not a scene from an eighties movie, but it's all I have.

'Who's bike is this?' Callum shouts.

'Mine,' Daisy calls back.

'What! How come you never ride it to school?' Callum starts prodding the wheels again. 'It's sick.'

'I walk to school,' Daisy says, not loud enough for Callum to hear. 'With Alex.' She looks at me, arms folded, hair wild, tough as ever, but like she understands. Like she really knows I'm sorry. 'I'm sorry about Jenna.'

'Thanks.'

She unfolds her arms. 'And I'm sorry I've been AWOL. I've had some stuff to deal with at home, too.'

'What's going on?'

She steps outside and pulls the front door closed behind her. 'Mum and Duce's dad have ended things.'

'What!?'

'Shh.' She glances at Callum, who's now riding the bike down the street. 'Yeah. They split after I spoke to her about the... test.'

'Did she do it?' My voice is a whisper. 'The test?'

'Yeah.' Daisy picks at her fingernail. 'Negative. No baby.'

'Thank God!' I breathe a sigh of relief.

'Yeah.'

I'm not sure Daisy seems so happy. 'Are you okay?'

She sniffs. 'I'm fine.'

She doesn't sound fine. An awful thought pops into my head. 'Duce's dad didn't get mad again, did he? He didn't...?'

'No, no,' Daisy says quickly. 'No, nothing like that. My mum's just sad. I guess she really liked him.' She turns and looks back at the front door. 'I should go back in.'

'Okay. But Daisy?' She stops, her hand on the handle. 'We're cool, right? You accept my apology?'

She turns to face me properly. 'I accept your apology.'

'And we're still... you're still my girlfriend?' I can feel myself going red.

She laughs. 'I'm still your girlfriend.' She turns and looks behind her again quickly before reaching up and kissing me on the cheek. 'See you tomorrow.'

'See you tomorrow.' Well, I don't think that could've gone any better.

'Look at this!' Callum shouts as he wheelies past me. The bike's way too small for him, and a bright shade of purple. He looks hilarious riding it, but somehow he suits it the same time. It is a pretty sick bike.

'Do you think Daisy would mind if I borrowed it?'

'Yes.' I shove him off. 'But I don't think she'd mind if I borrowed it.' I jump on.

'Hey!' He calls after me.

'Come on!' I yell. 'Let's go to the green.' I can hear his footsteps behind me all the way. I haven't ridden a bike in years but somehow it feels so natural. And for five minutes I can forget everything else, all the bad stuff that's going on. I can just be a kid who's made up with his girlfriend. I can just be a kid on a bike.

Chapter Forty-Four

Jenna tried to kill herself. Not just once, a few times. And in different ways. First, she tied a long piece of the rope to the stairs and tried to hang herself. I caught her as she fell. Then she filled her pockets with stones and jumped into the canal. I dove in and brought her to the surface. She took too many tablets, I made her throw up. She stopped eating, I forced food on her. She stabbed herself, I fixed her wounds. It went over and over, each time getting worse and worse and she was getting more and more desperate. It replayed on a loop, her finding different ways to end it all. Until I woke up.

'Morning.' Dad takes a seat next to me at the breakfast bar.

'Morning.'

'Is Jen not up yet?'

'Don't think so.' I scoop up the last of my cereal, chasing the final three pieces round the bowl. They don't want to be a part of this day any more than I do. The hospice thing would be a process, Mum said. It wouldn't happen straight away, she promised. Well, it feels pretty straight away to me.

'How'd you sleep?'

'What?' The question surprises me. Since when did Dad have an interest in my sleeping habits?

He reaches across for the coffee pot. 'Mum mentioned you haven't been sleeping well.'

'She did?'

'Don't sound so shocked.' He smiles wryly. 'Your mother and I do talk sometimes, you know.'

'Right.' Doesn't seem like it lately. 'Well, it's better than a few weeks ago, I guess.'

Dad sips his drink. 'I don't think any of us have it sussed, you know. Your mum stays up until gone midnight just staring at the ceiling most nights. Me on the other hand, well I'm out like a light from nine! We're all coping in different ways, I suppose.'

'I suppose.'

'But I'll look into getting you some tablets or something, Al.' He swills the coffee around in his mug. 'Your mum should've done that already but, you know, she's...' He trails off awkwardly. Yeah, I know. She's... 'Where is your mother, anyway?'

'Dunno.'

'CINDY!' He bellows.

'What?' Mum's suddenly in the doorway. 'You don't have to shout like that. Jenna's still asleep.'

'Stick some eggs on,' Dad says, opening the newspaper. 'She needs to get up, anyway. We're meant to be there at ten.'

'She needs her rest,' Mum mutters, flicking the kettle and getting some mugs out of the dishwasher. 'Tea, Al? Eggs?'

'No thanks.' I don't think I can stomach anything else; I barely managed my cornflakes. I've felt sick ever since that dream.

'Juice?' Mum asks, opening the fridge.

'No thanks.'

'Have something to drink, please,' Mum sighs, putting her hand on her hip and looking at me as if I'm being deliberately difficult.

'Listen to your mother,' Dad mumbles behind the paper.

'Orange juice then, please. Thanks.' She pours me a tall glass and slides it across to me.

'Go and wake your sister up,' Dad says to me, turning the page of his paper.

I stand up.

'No, Alex. Your sister needs to sleep,' Mum glares at Dad. I sit back down.

'We have to leave in,' Dad checks his watch, 'less than an hour, Cindy.'

'I know that,' Mum snaps, folding her arms. 'I'm not an idiot.'

'No one said you were.'

Mum sighs. 'I know. Sorry. I'm just—' Her face crumples.

'Hey, hey, it's all right.' Dad puts the paper down and puts his arm around her.

'All right?' she echoes, her face squished into Dad's shoulder. 'It's not all right.'

I know more than anyone that it's not. But I can't just sit and watch my mum work herself up. Not when, for once, I'm in the right mindset to help. Well, maybe not help. But comfort, at least.

'It's gonna be okay, Mum.' She pulls away from Dad. 'Remember what you said? This is where Jenna can be looked after the best.'

'He's right.' Dad shoots me a grateful smile. 'This is a good thing, Cindy.'

Mum takes a deep breath. 'Yes. A good thing. Thank you, George. Thank you, Al. My two boys.' I don't know why, but I take her hand and squeeze it. I can tell she feels a little better. And that makes me feel a little better, too.

*

'This will be your room.' The nurse opens the door. It's bigger than I expected. For some reason I'd pictured a squished little one, smaller than Jenna's room at home, but it's way bigger. It's got a big bed in the middle and a desk by the window. The walls are light and there's a full-length mirror on the wardrobe. It's very girly. It's very Jenna.

'Amazing, thank you,' she gushes, stepping inside. 'Look how big is is!' We follow her inside, dropping the boxes of stuff on the floor by the wall. Surprisingly, Jenna didn't have as much stuff as it looked. Or maybe she just didn't want to take it all. Anyway, we all managed a box each—well, Dad had a box-and-a-half—without much bother. I suppose she doesn't need her dresses and her heels and her wigs and her make-up now.

'It's lovely,' Mum nods. 'Thank you, Katherine.'

'No problem,' the nurse smiles. 'I'll give you some time to pack away your things. Let me know if you need anything.'

Jenna flops onto the bed. 'Ahh, comfy.'

Mum flops on next to her. 'Oh, it is! Feels like memory foam.'

Dad flops down next to Mum. 'Think I'll just have a nap.'

'Dad!' Jenna laughs. I watch them, my family, all lying on the last bed Jenna will ever have, and I want to scream. I want to rip the mattress off the frame and stab at it, pull the springs out and throw them away. But I won't. Mum was right earlier; this needs to be seen as a good thing. And it isn't a time to kick-off and ruin everything. It's a time to be here for Jenna.

'It is comfy.' I flop down next to Dad.

'Told you.' Jenna sits up. 'And look at the walls. Loads of room for my photos.'

'Loads,' Mum nods. 'Shall we make a start on those? The boys can make the bed.' She follows Jenna to the boxes and starts pulling out all the photos Jenna had in her bedroom. And somehow that makes things a bit better, too. Jenna won't just be sleeping in this big white room with nothing in it; she'll have all her friends and family watching over her.

*

It's all set up as best as it can be. Mum's staying here with Jenna for a while longer, but Dad and I are going home; Roscoe needs feeding and walking, and we could do with some dinner ourselves. It's been a long day. We're just leaving when I catch sight of her, sat on the bench to the side of the building. Just sat there while the rain drizzles down, without a care in the world.

'I'll meet you by the car, Dad. I'll just be a minute.'

He grunts and continues on to the car park; I wait until he's out of sight until I approach her. I almost don't want to get too close: I feel like she's in her own world, not wanting to be disturbed. But her face breaks into a huge smile when she sees me.

'Alex! How are you, my dear? Come, take a seat.' She pats the damp bench.

'I'm fine thanks, Miriam. How're you?'

'Oh, I'm grand. As grand as grand can be.' She catches sight of me hovering above the wet wood and laughs. 'Oh, sit properly, silly! There's worse things in life than a wet bottom.'

Well, that's true. 'Do you want me to go get you an umbrella?'

Miriam raises her eyebrows. 'Whatever for?' She holds her hands out and lets the rain bounce off her palms. 'Ahh, like nature's massage. Try it.' I watch her; she looks so happy, so content. But sicker than last time I saw her. Her skin's ashy and pale and even though she's wrapped up in what looks like three coats, I can tell she's really thin. Almost like a skeleton.

'I'm not sure you should be out here,' I say awkwardly. 'You don't wanna catch a cold.'

Miriam laughs. 'I'm on my way out anyway, dear. I don't think a stuffy nose would be too much bother.' I don't really know what to say to this, so I don't say anything. I just sit and stare at the ground, with the rain bouncing off it, thinking. So this is Jenna's home now. I can't just wander into her room in the morning and chat about life. She won't be on the sofa watching The Chase when I get home from school. She'll be here, all alone. Except she won't be, not really. Not when Miriam's here.

'My sister lives here now.'

Miriam smiles sadly. 'I wondered when the time would come.'

'I didn't want… It's happened so quickly.' I keep my eyes on the steadily falling rain.

'It always does,' Miriam nods. 'No matter if it's days or weeks or months. The time travels faster, it feels, when there's a deadline.'

Deadline. I don't like that word. 'I think you'll like her. My sister, I mean.'

'I'm sure I will, if you're anything to go by.' Miriam places her hand over mine. 'Though I can't promise we'll have the time to become proper friends.'

My heart sinks. 'You don't think… You think she's…'

'Not her, my dear. Me.' She squeezes my hand. 'My time is near.'

I've known her days are numbered since I met this woman. She's sick, really sick; I knew that. I know that. So I have no idea why my stomach's sinking to my feet right now, as if this is the first time I've heard this news. It's just somehow, hearing her say it like this, while we're sat in the rain… It's just hard. It's been a hard day.

'Alex!' I hadn't realised Dad had moved the car to the front of the hospice. 'Come on!' He winds the window back up. He really picks his moments sometimes.

'Sorry. I've gotta go.' I stand awkwardly; getting up makes me realise how bloody uncomfortable wet jeans are.

'Of course you do.' Miriam squeezes my hand once more before letting go. 'We all do, at some point. That's what you need to remember, Alex. A soul leaving this earth is as natural as the rain that falls from the sky.'

I want to say something, ask something, but there's too many words jumbled up in my head right now. I can't make sense of them. I can't make sense of anything. Dad beeps the horn, making Miriam jump. She laughs.

'Sorry. I'll see you soon, Miriam.' I run to the car, hating the feel of my soaking clothes, hating my dad's impatience, hating myself more than anything for missing that opportunity to speak to Miriam properly. She's got more to say, more to teach me, I know she has. I just need more time with her. A lump forms in my throat as I slam the car door behind me, remembering what she'd said about that. Time goes so fast. And she's got a deadline. I just hope it's not before I get to talk to her again.

Chapter Forty-Five

'Daisy, do you have any sevens?'

'Go fish.'

Kent scowls and picks up a card from the pile.

'Cal, do you have any fours?'

'Damn it.' Callum tosses Daisy three cards.

'Yes!' She lays down her set of fours. 'I'm a Go Fish pro.'

'You only learnt how to play it twenty minutes ago,' Kent mumbles. He's not doing very well. And, like me, I don't think his head's in the game. It's elsewhere, thinking of other things. Thinking of Jenna.

'Doesn't matter,' Daisy beams. 'It's obviously a natural talent of mine. Your turn, Al.'

I look down at my cards. My set's crap. And I couldn't care less. 'Daisy, do you have any twos?'

'Go fish!' Daisy laughs loudly.

'Shh,' hisses Kent, glancing behind him at the bed. 'You'll wake her up.'

We all look over. Jenna's still deep asleep. She has been pretty much since she came to the hospice. It's hard to believe it's been ten whole days that she's been here. I still can't get used to it. I hated the first week especially, when I'd come home to a quiet house: no TV on, no empty mugs in the living room. Just Mum cleaning and Dad in the man cave and Roscoe sleeping by the door waiting for me to come home. So, after a while, I decided to come straight to the hospice after school. It makes things easier. Mum and Dad come sometimes, but mostly they're here during the day so it's just me, Kent, and sometimes Daisy and Callum. Which is nice. I get more time with Jenna that way. She's normally asleep, but I think she knows I'm here.

'Kent, do you have any fives?'

'For God's sake,' Kent scowls, tossing two cards at Callum, who grins and places his full set down on the floor in front of him. 'You kids are all cheating.'

'If I was cheating I'd be doing a lot better,' I insist, pointing to my only set.

'Yeah, yeah,' Kent grumbles. 'I give up.' He tosses his cards down.

'Kent!' Daisy exclaims. 'Spoilsport.'

'Whatever.' He gets up and sits gently on the end of Jenna's bed.

'We'll carry on without him,' Daisy says, dividing up Kent's cards.

'Nah, I'm out too.' I toss mine down. 'Let's say you're the winner.'

Callum shrugs. 'Okay, deal.'

'Hey! He meant me,' Daisy argues.

'I was only one set down!'

'Want a rematch, then?' Daisy asks.

Callum rolls his eyes. 'Bit of a hard game to play with two people.' He pulls his phone out of his pocket. 'And I'd better go. I'm meeting Eric and that.'

'Fine. I'll go too, Al.' Daisy hands me the card packet. 'Don't fancy walking home on my own.'

'Okay.'

She leans over and pecks me on the cheek. 'Text me later?'

'Okay.'

''Bye, Kent.' Daisy stops by the bed and smiles down at my sister. ''Bye, Jenna.'

I put the full packet on Jenna's desk and sit on the chair next to it. 'How long are you staying?'

Kent checks his watch. 'Probably another hour or so. You want a lift home later?'

'Sure. Thanks.' I watch him stroke Jenna's cheek gently. When they used to do lovey-dovey stuff like that it made me feel gross.

Now it makes me sad. He's not doing it in a way like he wants to grab her and snog her, he's doing it in a way that shows he loves her. And he does, I mean. Love her.

'How much do you know about what's going on, Alex?' he asks suddenly.

'What do you mean?'

'How much have your parents told you? About Jenna moving in here?' His face is scrunched up like he's trying not to cry.

'I dunno. I'm not stupid.' I feel like he thinks I am. They all do. 'I know people come here to... when it's near the end. They said she's here so she has better access to medicine and stuff.'

'Right.' Kent takes a deep breath. 'Yeah, that's true I suppose. It just seems like you don't know the full extent of it.'

'Full extent?' I echo. I think that means more bad news.

'Yeah. And you deserve to know. You want to know, right? You're her brother.'

'I'm her brother.' I feel like a parrot.

Kent turns to face me properly. 'Did you know that people are only admitted to hospices if they have under six months to live?'

I didn't know that. But like I told him earlier, I'm not an idiot. I knew from when the idea was suggested that Jenna's days were numbered now. Still, Kent saying it aloud doesn't make it any easier to hear.

'And,' he goes on, lowering his voice, 'that, on average, people are only in hospices for something like twenty-two days?' I try and swallow the huge lump that's formed in my throat, but it won't go down. It's stuck. Twenty-two days?

'But that's not even a month.' My voice sounds weird.

Kent nods slowly. 'Three weeks.'

Three weeks? Jenna's already been in here for ten days. Does this mean she only has twelve more?

'It's the average,' Kent says. 'It doesn't mean it will be exactly the same for Jen. But,' he sniffs loudly, 'you can tell, can't you? You can tell she's getting worse.'

'She's tired,' I say.

Kent looks at me like I have one brain cell. 'And you think that's

268

a good thing? That's because she's on a higher dose of morphine. A higher dose of everything, now. They'd rather she be drowsy than in pain.'

'But she can't have twelve days.' I try and push the lump down again. 'I'm not ready. I don't have—'

'I know,' Kent says heavily. 'I know.'

'No, you don't!' I can feel a tear rolling down my face. 'I've been trying to find out where she's going, Kent, when she... when she leaves.' Here comes another. And another. I can't keep them in. 'And I haven't got an answer yet! I won't have an answer in twelve days!' My voice breaks fully now. I'm crying. Like, properly, shoulders shaking, snotty nose crying.

'Mate,' Kent says softly. 'There is no answer to that. You wouldn't find it in twelve years, let alone twelve days.'

I wipe my face on my sleeve and take a breath. Pull it together, Al. 'I need to find out. I need to know she's going to be safe.'

Kent puts his head in his hands. 'Alex, listen. I know you're just trying to put Jenna's mind at rest. But you can't, mate. Not with this.'

'I can!' I snap. 'You don't understand. No one does. This isn't just some stupid idea that I came up with last night. I've been researching for months. We've been to churches, hospitals, we've spoken to loads of people. We've got loads of ideas.'

'Sod your ideas!' Kent hisses. He doesn't look like he's gonna cry anymore. He looks like he wants to punch me in the face. 'What the hell do you think you're gonna achieve, running around interviewing people when you should be spending time with your sister?'

I'm not crying anymore either. The sadness has gone. It's been replaced by shock. Shock and anger. I've never ever heard Kent talk like this, not to anyone. Especially not to me. 'I am spending time with her! What do you think I'm doing right now?'

'Jack-all, to be honest.' He folds his arms. 'You need to stop worrying about what's ahead, Alex, and worry about now. Jenna is dying and you need to be there for her.'

'What, like you're there for her? Like when you were shouting at her on the phone that time?' I know as soon as I've said it that I took it too far. Kent faces away from me, towards the window. I can see a tear roll down the side of his face.

'Look, I didn't mean...' Crap. Okay. Deep breath. This escalated so quickly. I don't want to fight with Kent. He doesn't want to fight with me either, I know he doesn't. He's just emotional. We all are. And we all want something, someone to blame. But the sad truth is, there's nothing, no one. Nothing but cancer.

'I know you love her.' I try and keep my voice steady. 'And if you love someone, you want them to be safe. You want them to be happy. So you're telling me there's no part of you that wants to know what lies beyond this life? To know where she's going? To make sure she'll be okay?'

He doesn't look away from the window. 'Sure there is. But there's a bigger part of me that knows Jenna needs me here. All my energy, all my thoughts, on her, now.'

I know he's not agreeing with me. But in a weird sort of way I think him admitting it shows that he kinda understands. And I think he needs to be alone right now. Maybe I do, too. I sling my rucksack on my shoulder and make my way to the door.

'Sorry. I didn't mean to shout.' He's still not looking at me.

'Me neither. But I didn't tell you this because I needed your approval. I was telling you because I was upset. And I still am. But that doesn't mean I'm gonna stop looking for an answer now.'

I think he says something, but I'm gone. I need to go home and think about all this properly, get an actual plan in place. I have to be there for my sister but I need to be elsewhere, researching for her too. I can do both, I know I can. I just need to figure out how.

Chapter Forty-Six

'Why are we hiding round here?' Daisy peers behind her. 'I feel like a spy.'

'We're not hiding,' I insist. We're not, not really. It just so happened that, when I opened my locker this morning, a note saying 'It's not over' fell out. That had nothing to do with my choice of meeting Daisy and Callum behind the bike shed.

'Are we gonna go to the canteen soon? I'm hungry,' Daisy complains.

'In a minute.' I glance behind her. Thank God, there's Callum. I'm in two minds whether to tell them about the note or not. I know who it's from, obviously; there's only one person it could be. I guess I thought because I haven't been seeing him around school lately that he's laying low, that he's leaving me alone. Obviously not.

'Hey.' Callum leans against the shed next to me. 'What's up?'

What's up. Right. Push Duce to the back of your mind, Alex. Remember why you called this meeting. I take a deep breath. 'I spoke to Kent last night when you guys left the hospital. He pretty much told me he reckons Jenna has a couple of weeks left.'

Daisy gasps. 'Crap.'

'Crap,' I nod. 'I wasn't prepared for this. We weren't prepared for this. I mean, I knew her going into the hospice meant the time was coming, but...' I swallow. The big lump has come back.

'I'm sorry, mate.' Callum pats me on the back.

'Yeah. I mean, it could be longer. Twenty-two days is just the average.'

'What can we do?' Daisy whispers.

'We've got to get to work.' I pull my notebook out of my bag. 'We haven't got much time. I still feel like we're no closer to the real answer.'

Daisy and Callum look at each other.

'I thought we did everything on the list,' Callum says.

'Right. We did.' I flick back through the book. 'But there's some things we haven't looked at in enough detail, I don't think. We need more hard evidence. More witness accounts, more photos, more dates and names and facts.'

'What do we need to look at?' Daisy asks, taking the notebook from me. 'I suppose we haven't really looked into the ghost thing you mentioned the other day, but, ugh,' she shudders, 'I don't really wanna go traipsing around a haunted house.'

'Me neither,' I say honestly. 'But there's other ways we can do it. Different people we can talk to, places we can go; I've been researching and there's a woman who thinks she's a medium that only works across the green—'

Callum holds his hand up. 'Mate, stop. No offence, but I think we need to stop.'

What does he mean, stop?

'I think what Callum's trying to say,' Daisy shoots him a look, 'is that maybe we've found out all we can.'

'We're not even close.' I take the notebook back from her, the lump in my throat getting even bigger.

Callum sighs. 'I think that's the point. We can't get any closer, Al.'

'Yes we can.' I can hear the anger in my own voice. Where the hell has this come from? 'We have to. Didn't you hear what I said? Twelve days, Callum. Twelve days is all we have.'

Callum opens his mouth, but Daisy puts her hand on his arm. 'I know what you're trying to say, Cal. But we need to remember, we agreed to help Alex. And our work isn't done.' She looks at him, trying to tell him something else with her eyes. 'Our best friend needs us.'

'I do.' I try to swallow the lump again. 'I do need you.'

Daisy grabs my hand. 'And we're both here for you, Al.

Whatever you need.'

The lump is going. Slowly. 'I need your support.' I look at her, then Callum, then back to Daisy. 'I need both of you to help me find an answer.'

Callum looks at me. He nods. 'Then that's what we'll do.'

Relief is flooding through me. I really thought, for a minute, that I'd have to do it all on my own. I don't know if I could do that.

'In fact,' Daisy says, squeezing my hand. 'We'll take over from here, Cal and I. I think you need to spend your time with Jenna now, not sat at a computer or chatting to weirdos who speak to ghosts. Leave that up to us.'

'No, no,' I shake my head. 'I mean, yeah, I need to be with Jenna, but I can't just—'

'You can,' Daisy says softly. 'Twelve days. Twelve days, Al.'

She's got a point.

'You shouldn't be at school,' Callum says. 'You should be at the hospice. Talk to your mum later about having some time off. That's what I'd be doing.'

He's got a point, too. I suddenly feel ridiculous for even spending more than a second thinking about that stupid note in my locker this morning, for ever wasting time worrying about Duce Cleeve. He's not important. My sister is.

'Thanks, guys,' I tell them. 'Thanks. I'll speak to Mum. And in the meantime, Daisy, I'll send you the address of that medium.' I get out my phone and copy and paste the address that I found earlier. Looking up quickly, I see Daisy and Callum looking at each other. I can't tell what they're thinking. I suppose it doesn't matter, anyway. They've agreed to help me. They can't break their promise now.

*

I'm really dreading speaking to Mum about staying off school. I know she'll fight it. I know she'll mention GCSEs next year and fines for absences and missing valuable experiences. And we've been speaking even less since Jenna moved to the hospice, so it'll be weird to have a proper conversation at all.

'Chicken Kiev for tea.' She sticks her head into the living room. 'Ready in ten.'

'Okay.' She's gone before I answer. I find it kinda weird that she's still cooking fancy stuff. I thought she'd be spending every minute of every day at the hospice. But I guess since the beginning this is the way she's been coping, the way she takes her mind off things for a while.

I feel myself growing angry remembering Kent suggesting my research is a waste of time. Is he that stupid that he thinks the nightmares, the obsessions, the need to find an answer are all choices I made? They're bloody not. It's in the back of my mind all the time, it's the last thing I think of before I sleep. Does he not think I'd rather spend my time thinking about Daisy, or school work, or literally anything else? I'd give anything to stop the fear of what's going to happen to my sister hanging over me. But it won't stop. It might never stop.

'What if I don't find out in time?' I pull Roscoe up onto the sofa next to me. He licks my face. 'No, seriously, Roscoe. What will happen?' He tilts his head to the side like he doesn't know. Yeah, buddy. Me neither.

'Dinner!' Mum calls. Great. Another meal without my sister. As she got sicker she didn't join us every night for dinner anyway, but at least she was in the house somewhere; at least I knew she was here. It's like without her we're all just mismatched people shoved round a table and forced to talk to each other. At least tonight I have something I need to say. Well, here goes nothing. I bring Roscoe into the dining room with me.

'Stop carrying that dog like a bloody baby,' Dad mutters, cracking open a beer.

'How many of those have you had?' Mum asks, placing plates down on the table.

Dad burps. 'Dunno.'

'Well, aren't you driving?'

'Nah, you drive tonight.'

Mum sighs and sits down.

Come on, Al. Say something. 'Looks nice, Mum.'

She looks up in surprise. 'Thank you, love.'

I take a mouthful and try not to spit it back out. It literally tastes like garlic.

'So, how was school?' she asks me.

Here it goes. 'Fine. Speaking of school... I was gonna ask you something.'

'Oh?' She sips her water.

'I was wondering if I could not go for a while. So I can be at the hospice, with Jenna.' I start picking at the rice. Hopefully that won't have any garlic.

Mum looks at Dad. 'George?'

'Mmm?' Dad's mouth is full of chicken.

Mum tuts. 'Answer your son's question.'

'What question?'

'If he can stay off school to go to the hospice tomorrow.'

'Not just tomorrow,' I say quickly. 'For a... while.'

'A while?' Mum repeats blankly. 'Well, how long's a while?'

'I dunno.'

She glances at Dad. 'Well, what about your studies? Your friends?'

'I just want to spend more time with Jenna.'

Dad burps again. 'I don't have a problem with it, Cindy.'

'Of course you wouldn't,' Mum mutters.

At least Dad's on my side. 'Please, Mum. I can maybe get some work sent home for English, Maths and Science?'

Mum sighs. 'You're putting me in a difficult situation here, Al.' Again, it's me being difficult. 'You really do need to go to school.'

'He needs to be with his sister.' Dad downs the last of his beer and crushes the can in his hand. 'And that's that. I'll call the school tomorrow.' He catches my eye and smiles. Thank God. It sounds pretty final.

Mum mutters something, but Dad just rolls his eyes and doesn't answer. Meanwhile, I've discovered the rice is safe to eat. The rice is safe, I'm allowed off school, and Daisy and Callum are gonna carry on with the research. I think things are as good as they can be right now.

Chapter Forty-Seven

The last couple of days have been weird. It's been crowded at the hospice. Now I'm here in the days too, that means it's me, Mum, Dad and Kent at the very least. Sometimes some of Jenna's college or work friends pop in, sometimes Gran and Grandad, sometimes Kent's mum. Today's a lot nicer, though; Mum's got some errands to do, Dad's gone to work, Kent's at Alton Towers with some friends, so it's just me. Me and my sister.

'Do you need anything?'

'I'm fine. In fact, I'm more than fine. I'm so glad you're here, Al.'

I feel happy and sad at the same time. 'Me too.'

Jenna's phone starts ringing. 'Sorry,' she says. 'Gotta take this. Hi, Kent!'

'Hey babe!'

'Is it busy there?'

'Not too bad!'

I realise Jenna's on FaceTime. She catches my eye. 'Come here, Al. You'll love this.' I clamber onto the bed next to her. Kent's being strapped into a ride. I feel sort of awkward watching him; we haven't spoken since he annoyed me last week.

'Right, ready Jen?'

'Ready.'

Kent flips the camera round so we can see the front of the rollercoaster and the tracks.

'Ready, Al? Hold on.' She holds the phone out.

'What?'

'We're at Alton Towers!' she beams. I suddenly clock what's

going on: visiting Alton Towers was on Jenna's list. And because she can't really be there, Kent's sort of taking her. I suddenly don't feel mad at him anymore.

'Wheeee!' Jenna cries as the rollercoaster speeds off. She waves her free arm in the air, like she really is riding. 'Put your hands up, Al!'

I do as she says, even swaying side-to-side with the way the tracks move. I know it sounds stupid, but if you act like something is real hard enough, it sort of does feel true; we really could have been on that rollercoaster. As the ride slows down and stops, it gets me thinking: there are still loads of things left on Jenna's list. I wonder what else I could help her see.

*

I'm pretty pleased with what I came up with. I ended up texting Mum a list of stuff to bring when she'd finished her errands, expecting to be asked what the hell's going on. But she seemed to know what I was doing. When she arrived at the hospice an hour later, Jenna's face was a picture.

'So I thought we'd cross a few more things off your list!' I handed her my virtual reality goggles and she hugged me tighter than she ever had before. I didn't ask her all the places she was going; I wanted to let her explore on her own. And she definitely did. She wore them for at least an hour while Mum and I set up the picnic in the little hospice garden. From looking back at the photo of Jenna's list on my phone, I remembered it was picnic in the woods, but the garden has loads of trees and plants so it's not too far from proper woods. Mum brought enough food to feed about fifty people, so a few patients came out and joined us.

Jenna was pretty tired by that point, so she only managed half-an-hour outside. She also feels sick a lot, so she didn't eat much, but she was smiling and laughing and thanked me about a hundred times before she went back to bed. Seeing her like that is the best feeling in the world. And it made me realise, while Daisy and Callum are doing what they're doing, maybe I can focus my efforts on helping Jenna complete everything on her list. Maybe I can help her enjoy her days a bit more.

'Knock, knock.' Mum pushes my bedroom door open.

'Hi.'

'Hi.' She sits on the edge of my bed, Roscoe trotting in after her. 'Jenna said she had a nice day today.'

'I had a nice day too.' I bend down and pat Roscoe for something to do.

'Good. Alex.' She takes a deep breath. 'I was speaking to the nurses while you were playing with the VR.' She's not looking at me.

'Yeah?'

'Yeah. And… Oh, Al.' She pulls a tissue from her pocket. Crap. Not more bad news. Please. Surely there can't be any worse news than my sister having weeks to live. Surely.

I pull Roscoe onto the bed next to me. He snuggles under my arm and I can feel his little heart beating. Normally Mum tells me off when I put him on the bed. Right now, she reaches across and strokes him gently with one hand, drying her eyes with the other. 'Things aren't looking good. You know Jenna doesn't have long left now, don't you?'

I can't speak. I just nod.

'There's nothing we can do now. She's in more and more pain so they're giving her more and more medicine, and it's making her very sleepy. Katherine said today—' She breaks off and blows her nose loudly. 'Today might have been the last day she was able to get up and do things.'

My heart drops. 'Do things? But I had more plans… more stuff…'

Mum shuffles closer to me. 'I know, love. I know. We all did.' She wraps her arms awkwardly around Roscoe and I, letting her tears out properly now. I hug her back. There's not much else I can do, not much else I can say. There's nothing that will make her feel better. There's nothing that will make me feel better, either. Just a couple of hours ago I told myself I'd do everything I could to help Jenna finish her list. How am I meant to do that when she can't get out of bed? When she can't stay awake longer than an hour or two? And how can I let this happen, let her start to slip away, when I still don't know where she's going?

Chapter Forty-Eight

'All right, Alex?'

I don't know how long I've been sat here. And no, I don't think I'm all right. My sister is inside sleeping, dying. My friends are on their way here now school has finished, but they don't have good news. I knew it from the tone of Daisy's text. I want nothing more than to be hugging Roscoe, but for some stupid reason he's not allowed in here. What the hell do hospices and hospitals have against dogs?

'It's me, Jack. Remember?' He sits next to me and I drag my eyes away from the ground.

'Hi.'

'It's starting to rain.'

I don't care.

'Okay.'

Jack puts an umbrella over our heads. 'How you holding up?'

I think you can tell, Jack. I'm not holding anything up. I probably don't even have the energy to hold that umbrella. 'Fine.'

'And how's your, erm, voyage of discovery going?'

I look at him properly, surprised he remembered. Then again, I guess it's not every day he gets a group of kids ask him about death and the afterlife and all that. 'Not well.'

'No.' He doesn't sound shocked. 'Anyway, I didn't mean to disturb you. I just wanted to say... I haven't worked with your sister much, but I've been in and out her room the past few days, doing her meds while Katherine's been away. Do you remember what I said before, about people feeling ready to go?'

I cast my mind back to the conversation. It feels like such a long time ago now. A time when I said Jenna was going to a hospice for an excuse, for a way in. And now she's really here. It doesn't feel real. 'Yeah.'

'Well, I feel like your sister is. Ready to go, I mean.' Jack moves the umbrella slightly and I can feel the rain on my shoulder. 'She's aware of it.' I think back all the way to the start of this, to when Jenna told me she was ill. I think she's always been 'aware'. She's always been accepting. Apart from a couple of times when she's cried or shouted, she's always been calm. Like she was all right with whatever happened.

'She's always been ready,' I tell Jack. 'Ready for anything.'

Jack nods. 'She's a strong woman. I'm sure you're very proud of her.'

I always will be.

'I think,' he goes on slowly, 'that this is what you need to remember in this moment. I know you're finding things hard, Alex; any kid would be. But putting all this extra pressure on yourself to find answers to impossible questions isn't helping.' I open my mouth to say something, but he carries on. 'I know how this is all affecting you. But you need to think about Jenna. If she's ready, she's calm, and she's accepting, then why shouldn't you be?'

'Because she might be okay with going,' I say, struggling to keep my voice steady, 'but I'm not. I'm not ready for her to go.'

'I know,' Jack says gently, moving the umbrella again. I can feel the raindrops on my back now. 'I know you might not be, but she is. And this isn't about you, Alex; this is about your sister.'

I don't answer. I can't answer. Because as annoyed as I'm feeling at him, at her, at cancer, at the whole bloody thing, my whole bloody life, I know he's right. I know I started this journey, this mission, to find out what's going to happen to Jenna. But I also started it for myself. It wasn't Jenna that had a fear of death, it was me. As far as I know, she hasn't had nightmares. It hasn't been on her mind every second. That's just me. That's how I've been dealing with it. Jack's right, though; this isn't about my issues. This is about Jenna.

'I wish it was that simple,' I say aloud. Because it's not. Just because Jenna doesn't have a need to know, doesn't mean mine instantly goes away.

'Me too, buddy,' Jack sighs. 'But, if this is any consolation, a wise woman once told me that death should be treated as life's next big adventure. I think that's how your sister sees it, too.'

Miriam.

'Where is she?' I ask. 'Miriam, I mean.' I need to talk to her. I need someone who speaks sense.

Jack sighs. 'You haven't heard the news?'

'News?' No no no. I don't want any more news. I can't take any more news.

He looks up at the sky. 'She passed away a couple of days ago. Moved on.'

Moved on?

Miriam died?

She can't have!

I have so much more to ask her, so much more to tell her! There's so much more she needs to tell me. She's been the only helpful person on this mission, the only one to give me a straight forward answer. The only one not to laugh or look at me like I'm an idiot or pity me, the death-obsessed weirdo with the ill sister. She gave me more in two conversations than I've got from all of the books I've read and the documentaries I've watched put together. She can't have gone. She can't have.

'But...' But what? I know what I want to say: 'But it's not fair'. But none of it's fair. None of it at all. It never has been. So why should I ever expect anything to be different?

Jack shakes his head. 'I'm sorry. But Miriam passed peacefully and happily, Alex. She's onto her next chapter now.' The rain starts to ease up a bit and Jack stands up, taking the umbrella with him. I think back to last week, when Miriam and I had sat on the bench. Death is as natural as the rain, she'd said. But just because it's natural doesn't mean it's easier. 'I'd better go back in. Take care of yourself.'

'How?' I stand up too. 'How am I meant to take care of myself if I can't take care of my own sister?'

'You are taking care of her, Alex,' Jack says softly. 'Taking care of her doesn't mean knowing with certainty where she's going next. Taking care of her means making her laugh, keeping her safe, being her shoulder to cry on. And from what she's told me, you've been all of those things and more. You've been a brilliant brother. You always will be.'

He leaves me in the hospice garden while the last spits of rain hit my head and shoulders, and I feel weird. Torn in half. One half of me knows he's right. It shouldn't matter how I feel about things as long as Jenna's okay with them. And I've done my best in every way; she must know that if she's told Jack. But I can't pretend my fear is going to disappear overnight now some guy's told me not to worry; I don't really know him, after all. I need to hear it from the one voice that matters. I need to speak to Jenna.

Chapter Forty-Nine

She's asleep. And she won't wake up. Not for hours, the nurse said. No point waiting. I wait anyway. I need to tell her things. I wanted to hear things from her, too, but if that's not possible I at least need to tell her how I feel.

'Hi, Jenna.' She's sleeping so peacefully. I know it's probably the drugs. Maybe I can nab some and use them? I could really do with a proper sleep. I still haven't got those tablets Dad promised to get me. 'Anyway. I needed to speak to you. I was just speaking to Jack outside, and he says you're ready now. Ready to go.'

Oh God. Here comes the horrible lump. Get down. Let me finish.

'I'm happy that you're okay with it, Jenna. I really am. But I can't lie, I don't think I am.' I can feel a tear escape and run down my face. I wipe it with my sleeve. Deep breath, Al. You can do this. You're only speaking to a sleeping person. 'I don't know how I can be. Not when I don't know where you're going, what you're doing. It's too much, Jenna. I'm scared for you. What if...' There goes another tear. 'What if this is it? What if you leave your body here, but go nowhere else? Nowhere but the ground?' Another tear. 'I hate thinking about it. I always thought there must be something. But there's so many stories, so many ideas. I can't help feeling...' I take a tissue from the packet on the side. My sleeve's getting soggy. 'Can't help feeling it's all made up. They're all just to make people feel better.' There. My worst fear said out loud. And as crap as it is, it does feel kinda good to say it to someone. Even if it is to the one person I probably shouldn't be saying it to. 'But that could just be another opinion. Miriam told me death is life's biggest adventure.'

I think back to Miriam's kind face, full of lines and wisdom, and how nice she was to me. How nice she must have been to everyone. And how nice Jenna is, too. Surely, when a good person has finished their life, they must be off to something better. 'I think that's how you've always seen it, haven't you? You haven't been scared. I'm the only one who's scared.' I take Jenna's hand. 'But I don't want to be scared for you anymore.' I feel like I have a million other things to say, but I don't want to say them. I don't want to make this too weird, like I'm saying goodbye. She's not going yet. Soon, maybe, but not right now. Jenna rolls away from me with a deep sigh, like the sort of sigh Roscoe does when he's napping in the sun. 'Roscoe will miss you.' We'll all miss you, Jenna.

'Alex?'

Crap. I quickly rub my face with the wet tissue. I really hope they can't tell I've been crying. 'Hi.'

Daisy and Callum hover awkwardly in the doorway.

'You okay?' Daisy asks.

'I'm fine.' I stand up, feeling a sudden urge to leave the room. The tight feeling's back in my chest, like when Mum and Dad told me about the hospice. I need some air. 'Can we... Let's go outside.'

'Sure.'

As I get off the bed, I feel her stirring; just slightly, so slightly you could hardly tell. Her eyelids flutter.

'Al?'

'Jenna.' My heart feels like it's stopped. I wait, but her eyes don't open. Is she even awake? Is she sleep talking? I pat her arm gently. 'Jen?'

She sighs deeply and rolls over.

'Okay... Well, we're just gonna... I'll be back later.' I know the others probably think I'm an idiot talking her like this, but I can't just leave it open-ended. She needs to know I'm not leaving properly. I just need a moment.

'I love you.' She says it so quietly into the pillow that it takes me a moment to realise what the words were. But she's said it. And even in this awful moment, it makes me smile. Maybe she heard what I said. Even if she didn't, she knows I'm here. And she loves me.

'I love you too.'

*

We sit on the wet bench, where Miriam and I sat. I don't tell them that, though. That's a memory I'm not ready to share yet. That's a memory that I just want to keep for myself.

Callum sighs deeply. 'So, we stopped in to see the medium lady. She didn't really want to speak without us paying for a full session. Which is bloody expensive, considering you just sit there and play cards basically.'

'They're not playing cards, idiot,' Daisy says, rolling her eyes. 'They're tarot cards.'

'Whatever.' Callum unwraps a Twix and starts eating it. 'We didn't have twenty quid between us.'

'Oh.' I try not to sound disappointed. Am I disappointed? I don't know. I feel jumbled up.

'Are you sure you're all right?' Daisy narrows her eyes.

'Yeah. Well, kinda. I was speaking to Jack about that woman we spoke to in the hospice before. Miriam? You remember her?'

'She was lovely.' Daisy nods.

'She was. She's dead now.'

Daisy sticks out her bottom lip. 'That's a shame.'

'It is. But then again, it's not. She was ready to go. Ready for her next adventure. She knows the answers now. She knows what's beyond.' We sit in silence for a moment as the rain begins to fall. 'Do you remember what Jack said, too? About people feeling ready to go?'

Callum nods. 'Yeah.'

'Well, he thinks, and I think, Jenna is. Ready.'

Daisy takes my hand. 'I think you're right.'

'I was speaking to her earlier. I was saying I'm not ready for her to go.' I watch the kids in the park over the road, rolling around in the wet grass. It takes me back to speaking to Julie Matthews on the field at school. That feels so long ago. Everything does: the hospital, the church, Callum's aunty. Like weird, fuzzy memories.

'That's okay,' Daisy says, squeezing my hand. 'It's something you can never really be ready for. Not properly.'

'I feel like I need to at least try and be more accepting, though. Like, if Jenna's okay, then I should be as well.'

'It doesn't work like that though, mate,' Callum says. 'You can't just switch off your feelings. But look at what we've learnt in all this. Okay, we don't have a straight answer, but I think we've pretty much got the gist: to have a good afterlife, you've gotta be good in this life. And Jenna's a great person, Al.'

Daisy nods. 'She really is. I think that's all we can do: be a kind person, try our best then, when the time comes, see it as a positive thing. Like that lady—Miriam—said, going through that door is a whole other adventure.' They're right, I know they are. If we got anything from this crazy quest, it's that everyone of all religions and beliefs we've come across agree that people who've lived good lives will be at peace. Some way or another.

'I just need to take care of her,' I say, watching the clouds move. 'However I can. It scares me that I won't be able to when…' I swallow the rising lump in my throat.

'You've always done that, Al. You take care of everyone. And we're going to take care of you right back.' Daisy rests her head on my shoulder. 'Whatever you need: if you need more help researching, or if you want us to burn the whole scrapbook… Whatever!'

Without thinking, I lean in and kiss her. She tastes of Hubba Bubba.

'Ew.' Callum snorts. 'Do you mind?'

I can't help smiling. 'Sorry, mate.'

'Seriously, though, Al,' Callum goes on. 'Ditto what Daisy said. We're both here for you. You know that, right?'

'Right.' I believe them. They've always been here: Callum since I was little, Daisy since she moved into town. And I don't think they're going anywhere anytime soon.

Jenna is, though. I feel my heart sink a little. If I was in a film, this would be one of those parts where everything just falls into place. No doubt if it was an eighties film, Jenna would appear with a Boombox.

But we're in real life. And everything's messy. I still can't work out what I believe in. I want to be strong for Jenna. I want the nightmares to go. And I still want to know the answer. Maybe it's something I'll eventually get. Maybe if I work really hard at school, and go to university, and get a PDH or whatever they're called, I'll get to find out. But, right now, I have to go without knowing. I have to go with the idea that soon Jenna will be going on life's next big adventure. And she's okay with leaving. But I'll never be okay with letting her go.

'Alex?'

Is that my dad?

'Dad?' I leap off the bench just as he rounds the corner. He's doubled over, clearly out of breath.

'We couldn't find you,' he pants. His expression makes my stomach drop.

I almost don't want to ask the question. 'What is it?'

He straightens up, his face wet. It's not just the rain. Dad looks at me, straight in the eye, and I know. I just know, even before he says the words. But he says them anyway. 'She's gone.'

Chapter Fifty

Roscoe doesn't like fireworks. Even as a puppy, he'd squeal and hide under the sofa as they exploded outside the house. I used to keep him wrapped up beside me in Dad's hoodie, protecting him, keeping him safe. The feel of his little warm body pressed against me used to give me a sense of purpose, of responsibility. Even when he grew too big for the hoodie and would try and scare the fireworks off with his barks, he'd still stay snuggled up beside me.

We left him at home last year, though that didn't go down well; he drove the neighbours crazy because the knock-out meds didn't work. This year, he's gone to Gran and Grandad's. They live on a farm pretty much in the middle of nowhere, so they shouldn't have any trouble with him there. After last Bonfire Night, it was suggested that we make it a tradition to go out and see the fireworks every year instead of staying in. So that's what we're doing.

'Al!' Daisy runs over, her breath hot on the crisp air. 'You're here.'

'I'm here.'

Sometimes it doesn't feel like I'm here, though. My body is, but my mind's not. Mrs Moss says that's normal. Nothing about it feels normal.

'All right?' Callum appears behind me.

'Hi Daisy, Callum.' Mum wraps her arm around me. 'How are you both?'

'Fine thanks, Mrs Duncan,' Daisy beams. She's wearing the new hat I bought her, grey and woolly. She looks beautiful.

'It's taking some getting used to, not having you swing by every morning. How're things at your Aunt's house, Daisy?'

Daisy shrugs. 'Okay, I guess. It's only temporary.' She says that a lot, that it's only temporary. I feel like she believes that if she keeps saying it, it'll be true. She doesn't really like to talk about staying at her Aunt's, or her mum being an inpatient. It turns out she was hiding a lot from me earlier this year: when she said her mum was sad about not being pregnant and breaking up with Duce's dad, she was really sad. Like, suicidal sad. That's why Daisy had time off school, to look after her. And she felt better for a while, but after summer ended, she got bad again. She's getting the help she needs now, and Daisy is too, with weekly visits to a therapist. I felt awful that Daisy thought she couldn't talk to me about it at first, but she assured me it wasn't anything I was doing wrong; she just found it hard to put her feelings into words. And I know completely what she means.

'Hey squirt.' I get pulled into a familiar headlock.

'Ow! Hi, Kent.' I break free and give him a shove. I dunno why he still calls me that, now that we're almost the same height. I wonder when that happened?

'You all right?'

'I'm all right.'

We both know that's not true. But that's what you do: when someone asks how you are, you say all right. You say fine. Because that's a whole lot easier than explaining how you really feel. There's not just happy and sad, black and white. There's a hundred shades of grey between, and I've felt all of them the past three months.

'Right, they're about to start.' Dad claps his hands. 'Shall we get a bit closer to the bonfire?'

We move as a mismatched group, family and friends bundled together, all here for one purpose and one purpose only: to continue the tradition. As we weave through the crowds I spot Mrs Moss, Eric and the footballers, and even Duce and his cronies. The note in my locker was the last I heard from Duce. Apparently he's stopped being so nasty to everyone; Luca and Yusuf say they haven't had their lunch money taken in months. I have a feeling the girl he's holding hands with has got something to do with it.

He doesn't even look up as we walk past, but Patty shoots me a smile. We settle by an Oak tree: Daisy one side of me, arm linked in mine, and Callum the other, making eyes at Gee Davies. Mum and Dad are behind, huddled together, and Kent next to them, though a little way off. We're all here, but we're not complete. We never will be.

'Oooh!' The crowd begins the usual fascinated noises as the fireworks are set off with pops and bangs. I never used to get the point of it all: the light and the noise and the colours. It once all seemed so pointless, to spend all this time and energy to light the sky for a few seconds. But I see things in a different way now. Sometimes, the most beautiful sights are the shortest lived. Look at my sister, bursting her way into the world and brightening it up in a way no one else could, before fading away, spark by spark. Just because they don't last long doesn't mean they don't have an impact. A purpose. In the case of the fireworks, they bring everyone together, give everyone a moment away from reality to gaze in wonder at the sky. I see that now.

'They're beautiful.' Mum wraps her arms around my waist.

'Jenna would've loved them.'

I say it without really thinking. I only realise what I've done when I feel Mum's grip around me tighten. She pulls me in, squeezing hard.

'That's right, Al. You did it.'

I did it. After three months and two days, I did it. I said her name.

Around this time last year, I had a dream about Jenna jumping onto a bonfire. It seemed weird at the time, almost creepy. All the nightmares were. She was everywhere and everyone in my dreams: a ghost on the sofa, a living being in a coffin, a shadow in the dark, an angel in the clouds. And now she's all of those things, and yet none of them at the same time. I can't pinpoint where Jenna's soul is now, whether it's with God, or in another body, or next to me, right at this moment. And that quest still isn't finished. It might never be done, but I'm not in a rush for an answer anymore. That's not because life is perfect: it's far from it. My sister was taken from me, and I'll never forgive the universe for that.

But just because I can't see her, doesn't mean she's not here. She's in my mind, my heart. She's in the afternoon showing of The Chase, a trip to McDonald's, the beach in winter, a firework in the sky. All of those things and more. She is beyond.

Did You Enjoy This Book?

If so, you can make a HUGE difference

For us authors, reviews are the most powerful tools in our arsenals when it comes to getting attention for our books. Much as we'd all like to, we don't have the financial muscle of a New York publisher. We can't take out full-page ads in the newspaper or put posters on the subway.

(…not yet, anyway…!)

But we do have something much more powerful and effective than that, and it's something that those big publishers would kill to get their hands on.

A committed and loyal bunch of readers.

Honest reviews of our books help bring them to the attention of other readers.

If you've enjoyed this book I would be so, so grateful if you could spend just a couple of minutes leaving a review (it can be as short as you like) on the book's page at your favourite store and website.

Thank you so much—you're awesome, each and every one of you!

Warm regards
Georgia
x

Acknowledgements

A huge thank you to my beta readers—John Arthur Betts, Andreas Rausch, Alison Belding, Ami Agner, Rebecca Bradley and Elizabeth—and my fantastic publishers for all their support.

Thank you to my friends and family for their love and encouragement.

About the Author

Georgia Springate is an exciting new writer from Bedfordshire. She lives in a crazy house crammed full of eight members of her family, three dogs, a lizard and a tortoise!

When she's not hunched over a laptop writing, Georgia can be found with her nose in a book reading everything from Cecilia Ahern to Voltaire, with a particular fondness for JK Rowling—because, let's be honest, where would any of us be without JK Rowling?

As well as studying, working, reading and generally cramming her schedule with way too many things to list here, Georgia's been putting the finishing touches to her debut novel Beyond, published by Burning Chair.

You can follow her on Twitter: @GeorgiaSpring8

About Burning Chair

Burning Chair is an independent publishing company based in the UK, but covering readers and authors across the globe. We are passionate about both writing and reading books and, at our core, we just want to get great books out to the world.

Our aim is to offer something exciting; something innovative; something that puts the author and their book first. From first class editing to cutting edge marketing and promotion, we provide the care and attention that makes sure that every book fulfils its potential.

We are:
- Different
- Passionate
- Nimble and cutting edge
- Invested in our authors' success

If you're an author and would like to know more, visit www.burningchairpublishing.com for our submissions requirements and our free guide to book publishing.

If you're a reader and are interested in becoming a beta reader for us, helping us to create awesome books (and getting free reads in the process!), please visit www.burningchairpublishing.com/beta-readers

Other Books by Burning Chair Publishing

Burning: An Anthology of Thriller Shorts, edited by Simon Finnie and Peter Oxley

The Infernal Aether Series, by Peter Oxley
- The Infernal Aether
- A Christmas Aether
- The Demon Inside
- Beyond the Aether

The Wedding Speech Manual: The Complete Guide to Preparing, Writing and Performing Your Wedding Speech, by Peter Oxley

www.burningchairpublishing.com

Beyond

Georgia Springate

Beyond